A Decent Home
and Environment:
Housing Urban America

A Decent Home and Environment: Housing Urban America

Edited by:

Donald Phares
University of Missouri-St. Louis

782551

Ballinger Publishing Company ● **Cambridge, Massachusetts**
A Subsidiary of J.B. Lippincott Company

This book is printed on recycled paper.

International Standard Book Number: 0-88410-357-9

Library of Congress Catalog Card Number: 77-2780

Printed in the United States of America

Library of Congress Cataloging in Publication Data
Main entry under title:

A Decent home and environment.

 Includes bibliographies.
 1.   Housing policy—United States—History—Addresses,
essays, lectures.   I.   Phares, Donald.
HD7293.D34   301.5'4'0973   77-2780
ISBN 0-88410-357-9

To my parents, for being there.

Contents

List of Figures

List of Tables

Acknowledgments

Preface

PART I
The Home

Chapter One
The Rise and Fall of Public Housing: Condemnation
Without Trial

Eugene J. Meehan

Conventional Public Housing	5
Changing the Basic Pattern: Subsidies and Privatization	17
Leased Housing	29
Reprise	38
References and Bibliography	40

Chapter Two
A Prescription for Reducing Housing Costs

Joseph M. Davis

Housing's Dilemma   43
The Nature of the Housing Industry   46
Perceived Barriers to Housing Cost Reductions   51
Prescription: A Shopping List of Remedies   54
Summary   58
References   59

PART II
The Environment

Chapter Three
The Dynamics of Neighborhood Change

James T. Little

The Market for Housing Attributes   64
The Arbitrage Model of Neighborhood Succession   67
The Transition Housing Market   71
Long-Run Patterns of Transition   76
References   78

Chapter Four
Redlining in Perspective: An Evaluation of Approaches
   to the Urban Mortgage Dilemma

Michael Agelasto, II and David Listokin

The Urban Mortgage Crunch: Analysis of the Problem   80
Explaining the Mortgage Crunch: Redlining or Disinvestment? 85
The Federal Response: Disclosure   96
State Responses: Disclosure Effected or Considered   111
The Local Response to Disclosure   117
State and Local Responses: Analysis   118
Emerging Approaches to Mortgage-Short Areas   119

Possible Future Responses   123
Conclusion   128
References   129

PART III
Public Policy: Past, Present, and Future

Chapter Five
"A Decent Home": An Assessment of Progress Toward the National Housing Goal and Policies Adopted to Achieve It

John C. Weicher

Changes in Housing Quality   138
Housing Goals: The Relationship Between Means and Ends   145
Filtering As a Means to Achieve the Housing Goal   148
Conservation and Upgrading   151
Implications from the Data for Alternative Policies   152
The Relationship Between Means and Goals   153
References   154

Chapter Six
Emerging Issues in American Housing Policy

Roger Montgomery and Martin Gellen

Forces Affecting Housing Policy   157
The Elements of Housing Policy   162
Strategies to Meet Housing Needs   172
Conclusion   178
References   179

Index   183

About the Editor   189

About the Contributors   191

List of Figures

2–1   Housing Starts in the United States: 1959–76   50
3–1   University City by Census Tract   73

List of Tables

1–1	Units of Public Housing Authorized: 1966–74	4
3–1	Select Indices of Housing Market Behavior in University City by Census Tract: 1961–71	74
4–1	The Evolution of P.L. 94–200: A Comparison of Major Features of Federal Disclosure Bills, 1975	100
4–2	A Comparison of Federal and State Disclosure Requirements	104
5–1	Measures of Housing Inadequacy: 1940–75	139
5–2	Incidence of Selected Housing Deficiencies: 1973–75	143
5–3	Joint Incidence of Housing Deficiencies: 1974	143

Acknowledgments

This volume grew out of a conference, for which I was program chairman, on "A Decent Home and Suitable Living Environment for Every American" held in May of 1976 in Washington, D.C. This conference was jointly sponsored by the American Real Estate and Urban Economics Association (AREUEA) and the Federal Home Loan Bank Board (FHLBB). I am grateful to both organizations for consenting to have five of the six papers presented at this session developed further for inclusion in this volume. I am also grateful to Robert M. Fisher of AREUEA and John P. Floyd of FHLBB for their efforts in organizing the conference.

Acknowledgment is due also to those who helped prepare numerous typescripts of the manuscript: Verdell Allen, Tib Lanham, and Sandy Beard. Finally, many thanks to James H. Laue, Director of the Center for Metropolitan Studies at the University of Missouri-St. Louis, for the time and support necessary to bring this project to fruition.

Preface

The Housing Act of 1949 spoke in terms of a decent home in a suitable living environment for every American family. Certainly these were admirable targets for public policy to postulate. It seems appropriate now, some 27 years later, that we evaluate our progress toward this goal. To this end a conference was organized around the theme of a decent home and suitable living environment. The papers in this volume, with one exception (Chapter 6), were initially prepared for presentation at these meetings. After the conference the papers representing Chapters 1–5 were extensively revised to their present form. Chapter 6 was commissioned specifically for this volume.

The book, as was the conference, is organized around three main themes. The first deals with the "home." It examines the myriad forces at operation to influence both public housing and housing provided through the private sector. Chapter 1 looks in depth at the evolution of public housing policy while Chapter 2 focuses on private housing. The second section turns attention to the "environment" in which housing is located. Chapter 3 examines the process of neighborhood transition and its impact upon this environment while Chapter 4 discusses the availability of institutional financial support for housing in the context of "redlining" versus rational economic disinvestment in urban neighborhoods. The final section looks at "public policy." Chapter 5 makes an evaluation of our progress toward the goal of a decent home and how we got there. Chapter 6 looks forward and outlines some of the major issues to be dealt with in the formulation of future housing policy.

The six papers taken together provide an overview of where we now stand vis-à-vis the objectives spelled out in the 1949 Housing Act. Each paper stands by itself, as each was actually written independent of the others, and yet there is more agreement than disagreement as to our successes, failures, and the emerging issues that will demand attention.

DONALD PHARES

✳ *Part I*

The Home

 *Chapter 1*

The Rise and Fall of Public Housing: Condemnation Without Trial

Eugene J. Meehan

Like so many other social programs in the United States, public housing was a product of the New Deal era. The basic assumptions and procedures that guided its development and operation were hammered out in the 1930s: in the National Recovery Act of 1933, the Housing Act of 1934, and the George-Healey Act of 1936 among others. (R. Fisher, 1959; Ellickson, 1967). The approach that emerged in the Housing Act of 1937 and was reproduced in its essentials in the Housing Act of 1949 dominated the public housing program for the next four decades. Two basic modes of operation were used to supply housing services to low-income families. The original prototype, the "conventional" public housing program, was characterized by the use of a public agency to develop, own, and operate housing facilities. By the end of 1974, more than 860,000 units of housing, 66 percent of the total public housing supply, had been developed by this method. Another 230,000 units, about 18 percent of the total, was produced by a variant known as "turnkey" housing; these units were developed by private interests and then sold to a public agency, usually a local housing authority.

The Housing Act of 1965 authorized an alternative approach to supplying public housing for the poor, the leasing of privately owned facilities. By the end of 1974, leasing accounted for more than 13 percent of the total supply, some 169,000 units altogether (table 1-1). The changes in operating philosophy introduced by the Housing and Urban Development Act of 1974 foreshadowed a major increase in the role played by leased housing in the over-all public housing program. Indeed, if the 1974 act were to be implemented systematically and rigorously and without major alteration it

3

Table 1-1.   Units of Public Housing Authorized: 1966–74

Year	Total All Programs	Leased Housing				Conventional	Turnkey
		Total	New Housing	With Rehabilitation	Existing Stock		
1966	809,884	9,458	n.a.	n.a.	n.a.	n.a.	n.a.
1967	853,398	41,713	n.a.	n.a.	n.a.	n.a.	n.a.
1968	923,675	58,155	n.a.	n.a.	n.a.	n.a.	n.a.
1969	1,034,431	107,964	29,180	23,691	55,093	801,159	96,253
1970	1,119,618	114,372	37,184	27,851	49,336	826,216	150,456
1971	1,175,861	123,944	48,969	22,601	52,374	834,350	183,722
1972	1,260,235	151,467	68,041	25,429	57,997	854,279	214,096
1973	1,293,688	160,726	69,177	25,605	65,944	867,055	222,626
1974	1,316,126	169,038	75,412	23,981	69,645	868,427	230,531

n.a. = not available

Source: HUD, *Statistical Yearbook* (various years).

could put an end to the traditional form of public housing in relatively short order.

CONVENTIONAL PUBLIC HOUSING

The public housing program incorporated into the Housing Act of 1937 was very much a child of the times. The first Roosevelt administration faced a staggering array of problems when it took office in 1933: the economy was stagnant, unemployment was extremely high, wage levels were badly depressed, the monetary and fiscal system was in shambles, and public confidence in government and private enterprise alike had been shaken by the stock market collapse and its aftermath. The housing industry was but one of many sectors of the economy in urgent need of assistance. In the cities, large concentrations of aged and dilapidated buildings lacking in amenities and badly needing repairs posed a hazard to the health of the inhabitants and, so it was believed at least, a danger to the social health of the wider community. Everywhere there was an acute shortage of decent low-income housing, and as indicated by the 1940 *Census of Housing*, overcrowding had been common for years. In the circumstances, it is hardly surprising that the public housing program was construed as a multipurpose activity, a way of simultaneously reducing the level of unemployment, assisting the beleaguered housing industry, eliminating slums and their concomitants, and increasing the supply of cheap and decent housing available to the poor.

Development of a program that could serve a number of masters was very powerfully reinforced by various other circumstances of the times. There were wealthy and powerful interests to be placated—in real estate, banking, construction, and the labor unions—and their aims were not always compatible. The prevailing ideology was characterized by built-in opposition to public ownership or even to extensive governmental intervention into the social and economic life of the nation. The tradition of self-help remained strong, and there was a marked tendency to assume that poverty was deserved and avoidable by hard work. Finally, the superiority of a profit-maximizing economic system, euphemized in school and press as "free enterprise," was taken for granted by rich and poor alike. The corollary assumption that private enterprise is invariably more efficient and productive than any form of governmental activity was accepted as an article of faith by most elements of society. While such propositions may be tautologically true in Adam Smith's economics, the empirical evidence is sparse and inconclusive. In any case, even if the superior efficiency of private enterprise could be demonstrated with respect to the past, there is no reason in principle why it should be expected to continue into the indefinite future regardless of the direction taken by society as a whole. Unfortunately, these beliefs have been much reinforced, quite illegitimately, by uninformed and irresponsible generalizing about "the failure of public housing," even though the evidence suggests quite a different set of conclusions.

Unfortunately for the public housing program, multipurpose activities make for ambiguous policies and uncertain target populations; they in turn become difficult if not impossible to criticize, evaluate, or improve on. In both the 1937 and 1949 Housing Acts, the major concerns were unemployment and slum clearance; low-income housing was only a peripheral goal. Also, primary emphasis was placed on development and construction, not on the provision of housing services. In consequence, progress tended to be measured in terms of dollars spent, units of housing produced, construction wages generated, or number of units of dilapidated housing demolished rather than the amount of quality housing-in-use supplied to the poor. Yet measuring the success of a public housing program in terms of employment provided, slums cleared, or even units built was as much a travesty as measuring the success of a medical operation in terms of amount of time taken, number of persons involved, or the surgeon's fee. Indeed, if the emphasis in the legislation is taken literally, the Pruitt and Igoe developments in St. Louis, commonly ranked among the more prominent disasters in the history of public housing, ought properly be counted among its greatest successes; they were built at great cost, lasted a very short time, and were quite expensive to liquidate. In brief, they contributed more to the local economy in the short run than any other housing development in the city's history.

Ownership and Administration

Given the economic circumstances in which public housing evolved, the locus of ownership and operational control over facilities was of prime importance. Public housing provided a major occasion for breaking the established mode of economic activity. The profit-maximizing production and distribution system then operating responded only to effective demand (desire *plus* capacity to pay); it clearly failed to provide for the housing needs of large segments of the population. That is, it had produced both housing that was too expensive for many, as well as the many for whom the housing was too expensive. How to deal with the situation? Any effort to maintain private ownership and to control the price of housing to the consumer would certainly founder unless production costs were controlled or rents subsidized. Cost control was anathema to owners and unions alike, and direct cash subsidies, much favored by real estate interest, were considered far too expensive over the long run, for they tended to overstimulate demand for an inadequate supply of decent housing and provide unwarranted returns to the owners of poor or marginal quality housing. Public ownership offered a more efficient means of divorcing the cost of housing to the tenant from the cost of development. Its capital could be obtained at preferred rates, taxes avoided, and any return to capital as profit retained in the public coffers. In the long run, ownership is necessarily cheaper than rental or lease. Nevertheless, pressure for public subsidy of privately owned housing rather than public ownership of such facilities finally prevailed, suggesting that in economic matters sheer persistence is more likely to be rewarded by government than is good argument.

Given the strength of the opposition in American society, congressional agreement to public ownership of housing was a tribute to the power of the critique launched against the performance of the economic system. Until 1965, public housing in the United States meant *publicly owned* housing. The program was one of the few large-scale experiments in public ownership in an area traditionally regarded as part of the private sector. In the early days of the New Deal, ownership was vested in the federal government, and operations were controlled by a centralized bureaucracy. An adverse court ruling in 1935 that prevented the use of eminent domain to obtain land for public housing sites coupled with popular distrust of "big government" forced a change in the rules; the Housing Act of 1937 gave title to local housing authorities (LHAs), which were agencies of local government, created within a framework of state enabling legislation. In the circumstances, if public housing has been a dismal failure, as is often charged, the program is strong evidence against further experimentation along the same lines or in parallel areas. In fact, that is a gross misconception. What failed was a particular form of public housing, foreseeably programmed for failure no matter how earnest, willing, or competent the administration. The attack on "public housing" is perhaps the most arrant example of condemnation without trial in the annals of our society.

In principle, public ownership of housing facilities enables the government to supply housing according to need rather than capacity to pay, absorbing the difference between rents charged and actual costs. But public ownership alone is not enough. Had the federal government been able to create enough decent housing to supply all of society's needs and then underwrite the cost of operation to a point where the tenant could readily afford the rent actually charged, program administrators would only need to identify the needy and house them as expeditiously as possible. But if the housing was of poor quality, if the supply was significantly less than the need, or if operating costs were inadequately subsidized and could not be met from tenant rents without imposing serious hardship, the program could not operate properly. If the quality was poor, the supply could not be marketed or the cost to tenant would be excessive; if the supply was inadequate, access would have to be restricted in some manner, probably by income.

Tragically, the necessary conditions for a successful public housing program were neither met consistently nor adequately, primarily because of the program's design. The quality of the construction was often poor and sometimes grossly inadequate. Poor construction and insufficient resources for maintenance, reinforced by a social climate in which vandalism was not impeded but even positively encouraged, produced significantly accelerated deterioration of facilities in the 1960s. The method of financing adopted by the Congress forced local housing authorities to transfer the burden of rapidly increasing maintenance and operating costs, reinforced at times by very serious inflation, to the tenants. By the end of the 1960s, the combination of policies and circumstances had brought most of the larger housing authorities in the nation to their financial knees. Nevertheless, the amount of public housing actually developed—disregarding quality for the moment—was far less than the actual need; the absence of accurate data relating to need rules out any precise estimate of the degree of inadequacy. Fewer than 160,000 dwelling units were authorized and built under the 1937 Housing Act, and the Housing Act of 1949 generated 1,115,000 units up to the end of 1974. But in 1949 it was estimated that 810,000 units of housing, the amount authorized by the 1949 act, supplied only one-tenth of total need. The shortcomings of the public housing program condemned millions to pay an inordinate share of their income for shelter of the poorest quality for years, despite the humaneness of the goals articulated by Congress in 1949. Governmental unwillingness to accept responsibility for satisfying the urgent need for decent shelter produced scarcity that was socially induced and therefore avoidable, though at a cost. In time, government policy tended to exclude from public housing the very people it was designed to serve, though in fairness it must be said that the program was not intended for the permanent poor, and the rhetoric of the times ignored those wholly dependent on public assistance, whether black or white.

Development Policies

The program created by the 1937 Housing Act was built on a local-federal arrangement from which the state was virtually excluded once enabling legislation was passed. Over time, the Congress tended to concentrate on four basic areas of housing policy, leaving most other matters for administrative decision: the amount of housing authorized for addition to the public housing stock; the cost of developing the facilities; the fiscal arrangements that controlled program operations; and the conditions of tenancy. Federal administrators exercised a great deal of control over the program through budgetary oversight, allocation of resources for new developments, auditing, and monitoring of everyday operations. Local governments could influence the program in their areas through the formal cooperative agreement required by statute and less formally through appointment of the governing body that directed the program. In practice, local governments had veto power over certain critical aspects of development, notably size, location, design, and staffing of the facilities. The local housing authority, under the over-all direction of the governing body, had a voice in site selection, choice of architect, design, and so on, plus fundamental control over such aspects of daily operations as tenant selection, maintenance and repairs, legal actions against tenants, staffing, and so on. Until the 1970s, the LHAs were given wide latitude in operations by the federal administration; however, central control over details of policy increased substantially after 1969.

The direct costs of public housing to the local community were spelled out in a required federal-local agreement. The LHA was granted tax-exemption in return for a payment in lieu of taxes amounting to 10 percent of gross rent less utility costs. Whether the payment covered the actual cost to the community—particularly during those periods when rents were high and occupancy virtually complete—is much debated and probably not answerable. However, the collective benefit obtained from public housing certainly outweighed any direct cost to the community beyond what was expended before the developments were built. The 1937 act required local government to eliminate one unit of substandard housing for each unit of public housing built, but the impact of the ''equivalent elimination'' rule was slight, and it was abandoned in 1949. Finally, local governments were to provide such municipal services as police and fire protection, garbage removal, paving, street lighting, and other normal community services. In practice, the obligations proved difficult to enforce. In St. Louis, for example, the local housing authority was forced to employ private security guards by the beginning of the 1960s, and complaints about the quality of garbage collection, street lighting, and so on were common. The net effect of such performance failures was initially a major increase in the managerial burden placed on the LHA and ultimately a large increase in the cost of operating the facilities.

There were two curious gaps in the federal government's development policies. First, little effort was made to control the quality of the housing produced; second, the cost of the site was not limited by any of the statutes. The 1937 Housing Act placed a ceiling on the over-all cost of each dwelling unit and on the cost of each room. These established limits could be adjusted upward by as much as 25 percent in ''high construction cost'' areas, usually the larger cities where powerful construction unions operated. In 1949, limits on over-all cost per unit were eliminated, leaving cost per room as the sole criterion for controlling development cost. Since room limits were included in the legislation, they applied to the country as a whole. In 1970, Congress adopted a "prototype" cost base for dwelling units of various sizes and types of construction, and the Department of Housing and Urban Development (HUD) was charged with establishing these limits and revising them annually. Again, the limits could be exceeded by 10 percent without waiver and another 10 percent with federal approval. Land costs remained uncontrolled, and no qualitative construction controls were specified in the statutes.

The effect of weak control over development costs and housing quality is readily foreseen. Site costs were often unconscionable, particularly in the 1950s when the rate of development was high and projects were deliberately located in cleared slum areas—and forced to absorb the clearing costs. In the long run, the economic inefficiencies generated by land speculation were probably less important than the tendency for LHAs to pay premium prices for apartments so shoddily built that a choir of angels could not abide in them regularly without producing serious disrepair. Poor quality cannot be ascribed to federal miserliness. In St. Louis, the housing authority paid for its projects at rates that equalled or exceeded the cost of luxury housing in the suburbs. It did not receive anything approaching quid pro quo from the housing industry.

The principle underlying the failure is not hard to find. A profit-maximizing economic system is also performance-minimizing. Unless performance criteria for the end product are specified fully (in which case there is likely to be a major increase in cost), the producer is bound by the rules of the game and perhaps by the "facts" of economic life to maximize profits within the limits of the contract price. The most accessible source of additional profit is the quality of the product. The clearest evidence of the pervasiveness of this principle is found in the recent experience of federal agencies whose purposes demand very high levels of performance, as in space exploration or certain aspects of defense. To obtain quality performance, specifications must be developed in much detail and precision, otherwise cost overruns of great magnitude can be anticipated out of the effort to achieve required performance through trial and error. The result in either case is a massive increase in end-product cost. The same trend appears in the general market for consumer goods. In principle, the producer whose goods perform poorly or whose services are less than what they should be is supposed to lose his customers to a better producer. In practice, information flow among consumers is incomplete and the gap between promise and performance is so common that it seems to have little impact on consumer behavior, perhaps because advertising practices reinforce unconcern. Whatever the reason, the producer who can choose between either a significant improvement in product performance at some known cost or artificial demand stimulation for an unimproved product at much greater cost is apparently well advised to choose the latter. The old adage about building a better mousetrap and having the world beat a path to your door no longer holds—if ever it did. Patent medicine is not driven from the marketplace by disclosing that it is only patent medicine or even by development of a genuine cure for the illness the patent medicine purports to treat. Indeed, some experience suggests that a genuine cure may languish unpurchased, while the patent medicine industry continues to thrive; control of hernias and hemorrhoids provides a good example.

Conditions of Tenancy
The more important congressional policies relating to tenancy in public housing dealt with eligibility for admission and continued occupancy, rent levels, definitions of tenant income, and priorities assigned to different classes of applicants. The consistent central concern has been the amount of income that a prospective tenant was allowed to earn and the manner in which excludable income was identified and calculated. Under strong pressure from real estate interests, the prime goal of federal policy was to exclude from public housing anyone with enough income to obtain housing on the private market. Understandably, the real estate interests sought to keep the income level of public housing tenants at a minimum, and since income limits were partly determined by local rent levels based on information supplied by the real estate industry, they were often quite influential. Over the long run, pressure on tenant income levels, taken in conjunction with other fiscal policies, contributed materially to the aggregation in public housing of a highly dependent population whose incomes were very low in relation to the rest of the community and changed much more slowly than general wage and price levels. Between the early 1950s and the mid-1970s, the consumer price index for St. Louis more than doubled, for example, but the median family income for public housing tenants rose from about $2400 per year to just over $3700 per year, far less than was needed even to keep pace with inflation.

The procedure used to determine income limits for those admitted to public housing was fairly complex. The LHA went to the local housing market (newspapers, agents, brokers, etc.) to determine the current price of decent rental accommodations of various sizes. The income needed to ''afford'' such housing was calculated by a five-to-one ratio (six-to-one for families with three or more minor children). That is, if the going price for a three-bedroom apartment was $100 per month, it was assumed that a family with an income of $500 per month could afford it ($600 per month if it included three or more minor children). The maximum allowable income for admission to public housing was 80 percent of that amount or

$400 ($480) per month. Federal policy required a "20 percent gap" between the income sufficient to afford needed housing and the maximum
allowable income for admission to the developments. If other factors
remained constant, the tenant whose income increased by 25 percent over
admission limits was required to leave public housing. He would then be
earning enough to "afford" the housing he needed on the private market.
In principle, the policy was expected to keep everyone with enough
income to purchase housing on the private market out of public housing.
The lack of qualitative controls over estimates of available housing tended
to produce significant overestimates of the amount of "decent" housing
available and significant underestimates of the going price. The relative
value of the facilities afforded by public housing, even in areas where the
stock was badly deteriorated, was attested to by the length of housing
authority waiting lists.

Given the formula used to calculate eligibility for admission to public
housing, the question of what kinds of income should be excluded from
the calculation was of major concern for both tenant and LHA. The 1937
act, which simply counted income from all sources, produced hardships
that clearly contravened the spirit if not the letter of the program. The
1949 act allowed an exemption of $100 per year for each of the first three
children in the family and the first $500 of earnings by a minor. The $100
exemption was later extended to all minors in the family, and over time
exemptions were allowed for child care, tuition costs, medical expenses,
certain kinds of work expenses, and so on. In some cases, special arrangements were allowed because of peculiar local circumstances; the
arrangements that settled the St. Louis rent strike in 1969, for example,
enumerated income exemptions considerably broader than those allowed
by normal regulations. The Housing and Urban Development Act of 1974
consolidated and reduced exclusions, allowing: $300 for each minor,
nonrecurring income, the first $300 of earnings by the spouse, and 5
percent of gross income (10 percent for elderly families). The "20 percent
gap" was then dropped.

Once income limits required for admission were satisfied, the various
priorities established by Congress or administrative action came into play.
Preference was given to war veterans and persons displaced from their
homes by public actions, such as slum clearance, by both the 1937 and
1949 acts. In 1954, a hostile Congress limited admission strictly to persons
displaced by public action, but the policy proved untenable and was
rescinded the following year. The impact of priority assignments probably
varied from city to city but seems not to have been very great. Between
1966 and 1973, for example, fewer than 12 percent of all families entering
public housing had been displaced by public action, and only 1.2 percent
were uprooted by either urban renewal or housing development. In 1956,

the elderly were given priority in admission, and an increase in construction costs of $500 per room was allowed for housing designed specifically for elderly use. That priority was extended to the disabled shortly afterward.

The negative priorities involved in racial segregation were ignored by both the Congress and the administrations. When the program began, developments in many cities were racially segregated and blacks were excluded from white projects, or vice versa, as a matter of course. Formal segregation ended in 1954 when the U.S. Supreme Court refused to overturn a California ruling which held that admission to public housing could not be refused on racial grounds. Within fifteen years, social and economic conditions in many locales combined to resegregate public housing, this time with respect to the rest of the community, by aggregating large numbers of minority group members in the developments.

The rent paid by public housing tenants was linked to family income and not to the amount of space occupied. A large family with little income might pay less for a five-bedroom apartment than was charged a smaller family with a relatively larger income for an apartment with a single bedroom. Technically, the portion of tenant income paid for rent was not limited, though in practice the administrators tried to maintain rents at minimum levels. As housing authority operating costs soared after 1960, minimum and average rents climbed steadily, far more rapidly than tenant income. By 1969, such cost pressures had created very serious problems for most housing authorities. Some of the very poorest tenants were forced to pay as much as three-fourths of their income for rent, and payments equal to one-half of gross income were common. That condition, among others, led to the 1969 rent strike in St. Louis and to significant disturbances elsewhere. The outcry produced one of the so-called Brooke amendments in 1969 which limited the amount that could be charged a tenant in public housing to 25 percent of adjusted income—less for persons of very low income. Unfortunately, that limitation sometimes led to reductions in state welfare payments until this was eventually forbidden by another of the Brooke amendments in 1971. The 25 percent limit was borrowed or copied from the rent supplement provisions of the 1965 Housing Act. Why it was considered proper is uncertain; by European standards, 25 percent of income is a very high rent level. Perhaps the American propensity to relatively expensive single-family housing accounted for the size of the standard.

In 1974, the rental structure was simplified, though the base was retained: rent could vary from 25 percent of income for persons earning 80 percent or more of the median income in the area to 5 percent of income for persons with very large families (six or more minors) or very low incomes (less than 50 percent of the area's median income). The act required LHAs to fill at least 30 percent of their units with families from the very low income group. However, the act also required each LHA to collect at least 20 percent of the total income of its tenants as rent. The confusion engendered by the regulations lasted well into 1976, and the full effect of the requirement on the tenant population remained uncertain at the end of that fiscal year. Median income levels are virtually impossible to determine with any accuracy for a metropolitan area, and the meaning of the median in this context is most uncertain. If the median is calculated from the tax rolls, those who do not file, mainly persons of very low income, are omitted, and that tends to raise the median. If medians are calculated from census data, the results are even more likely to be artificially high. Neither the method used for the calculation nor the reason for using such standards in the first place is very clear either in the legislation or the argument that preceded it.

Fiscal Policies

The public housing program created by the Congress moved toward financial disaster as inexorably and predictably as any Greek tragedy. The quality and cost policies virtually ensured physical structures of minimal quality. Regulations imposed on tenant income guaranteed a very modest rent yield to the LHA. The self-destruct system was completed by adopting fiscal policies that were foreseeably unworkable and sticking to them for more than thirty years in the face of all evidence. To put the matter as starkly as possible, the federal government undertook to pay all capital costs on public housing as they came due; it guaranteed the mortgage, leaving all other expenses the responsibility of the local housing authority. The LHA's sole source of income was rent; no operating subsidy whatever was provided by Congress. Had the matter stopped there, the program could not have survived very long. Economic collapse was rendered more certain by imposing four additional financial burdens on the LHA, to be met out of its rental income alone.

First, utility costs were included in the rent charged the tenant. From the tenant's point of view utilities were a free good; rent was unaffected by the amount used. Predictably, utility costs became a major burden on local housing authorities even before prices began to climb in the energy-scarce climate of the 1970s.

Second, 10 percent of gross income from rent, less utility costs, had to be turned over to local government each year as payment in lieu of taxes. Until 1937, public housing was owned by the federal government and was therefore automatically exempt from state and local taxes. To offset the cost of public services to the developments, 10 percent of gross rent was turned over voluntarily to local governments. When ownership of public housing was vested in local authorities, they became subject to local taxes. However, Congress required local support for the housing program amounting to 20 percent of the federal contribution, a requirement that could be met in full just by waiving local taxes. In return, the LHA was permitted to pay 10 percent of gross rent minus utility costs in lieu of taxes. In 1954, the waiver of taxes was made a program requirement and the payment in lieu of taxes was mandated rather than allowed.

Third, the amount of reserves that any LHA could accumulate was limited by administrative action to 50 percent of one year's rent. That very effectively precluded the LHA from building up the funds needed for capital replacement or even for major maintenance such as roof repairs. As the apartments aged, major maintenance was deferred and handled piecemeal. Unfortunately, an iron law of escalation in damages operates in even the most expensive and luxurious of apartments: the amount of damage to a building or area increases directly and exponentially with the time delay between damage and repair. Maintenance deferral is an open invitation to vandalism, regardless of the age, sex, ethnic background, income level, occupation, or rent level of the tenants.

Fourth, for any year in which an LHA "showed a profit" (that is rental income exceeded gross expenses plus allowable transfers to reserves), the surplus was used to pay capital costs or reduce annual contract contributions. From 1945 until 1953, the federal government actually paid less than 50 percent of the capital costs of public housing, and in the peak years of 1948 and 1949 the LHAs paid nearly 85 percent of their own capital costs. Having salted the wounds inflicted by its actions, Congress added insult to injury in 1954 by requiring the LHAs to repay 55 percent of capital costs from rental income. The requirement had little real significance given the steady deterioration in the financial position of LHAs, but it does provide a good indication of the blindness to long-range impact common among those responsible for policy decisions relating to public housing.

The fiscal arrangements made by the Congress were the most important single factor in the eventual breakdown of the conventional public housing program. Taken in conjunction with inadequate control over housing quality and relatively poor administrative performance (HUD inefficiency has been notorious, even among Washington bureaucrats, and it was very unlikely that LHAs could recruit adequately trained and experienced administrators given their fiscal position), the program was *foreseeably* doomed. The point is vital. It was both humane and reasonable to base the tenant's rent on ability-to-pay rather than the space occupied by the family, and it was altogether appropriate to restrict occupancy to persons of low income. On the other hand, it was also reasonable to expect local housing authorities to operate their developments with the income obtained from rent once capital costs were secured. Imposing *both* requirements without additional subsidy was an act of folly, particularly in the light of the known periodicity of the economic system. The housing program could succeed only if costs, rents, and tenant incomes remained in relatively stable relationship for fairly long time periods. Since economic activity tends to very rapid shifts in costs and prices, and the incomes of the poor do not keep pace with rising costs, the logic of the fiscal arrangements guaranteed a cost-income squeeze in any period of rapidly advancing wages and prices.

Even without inflation, the fiscal apparatus could not succeed. The LHA's income was a function of the price of housing on the local market and the income of its tenants; expenses depended on the size, quality, durability, design, and so on of the developments, the kinds of tenants who occupied the premises, and basic trends in the over-all economy. There was no reason to suppose that the income needed to operate the developments would be generated out of the interplay of this set of pressures. In the private sector, the rental income needed for successful operation of multifamily apartments is calculated by a rule of thumb which states that roughly one-sixth of development costs must be generated each year in rent. In the 1940s and 1950s, about 40 percent of the rent (6.4 percent of development costs) was needed to cover operating expenses; by the 1960s, it was safer to assume that about 50 percent of rental income was required for that purpose. In effect, the private sector estimated that between 6.4 and 8 percent of development costs must be generated each year from rents just to cover operating expenses. An equal amount was needed to pay capital costs, taxes, and return to the investor. Utility costs are normally borne by the tenant and do not figure in the calculation. The gross level of revenues required is approximately the same as the HUD estimate that $754 in annual income is required for each $10,000 of investment in the development.[a]

Public housing authorities rarely succeeded in obtaining as much as 6 percent of their investment in annual rentals; in St. Louis, the return averaged just over 4 percent for more than two decades. Moreover, an adjustment is needed to cover the utility costs and payments in lieu of taxes made by the LHAs; this brings income requirements up to about 10 percent of development costs per annum. Such sums were far beyond the capacity of housing authority tenants to pay, and even if that much rent could be collected, regulations governing reserves would not allow the LHA to set enough aside to meet future replacement costs. Finally, private sector estimates assume good design, sound construction, and proper care by tenant and management alike—conditions not easily met in public housing, particularly after 1960. In the circumstances, the more surprising

[a] The President's Committee on Urban Housing, *Technical Studies*, vol. 1 (Washington, D.C.: G.P.O., 1967), p. 155, n. 5.

thing about the collapse at the end of the 1960s is that anyone would be surprised at the end result. Mere survival was in some cases a major accomplishment.

CHANGING THE BASIC PATTERN: SUBSIDIES AND PRIVATIZATION

The operating pattern for public housing established in 1937 continued with only minor changes until the 1960s. Both opponents and supporters of public housing tended towards what might best be called "mindless incrementalism" in their approach to policy making. Instead of reasoned decisions to increase or decrease resources allocated to specific purposes on the basis of careful study of the effects of operation, mindless incrementalism is marked by increases or decreases in allocations that are unrelated to performance or may even be perverse in the light of performance. Such procedures are a good indication of failure somewhere in the policy-making process, usually in either the supply of information or the manner in which the information is used. In the case of public housing, the failure occurred in both areas: too often, the data needed to correct and improve policy were not available, and in most cases the conventional wisdom that served as a base for decision was mistaken or misdirected. And since the initial conditions to which these policies applied were not determined and the target population was only vaguely identified, there was no way to decide the amount and kind of change produced by specific actions, to locate the major side effects of policy, or to make a reasoned assessment of impact. The program was radically incorrigible until it collapsed; the way it collapsed virtually guaranteed that its performance could not be improved.

In fairness to supporters of public housing, incrementalism was in some degree forced by the opposition; both nationally and locally, hostility to public housing remained widespread, vocal, powerful, and implacable. It was difficult just to obtain a simple increase in the number of units authorized in a given fiscal year. Supporters of the program may well have felt that asking for any policy innovations was too risky; there is considerable evidence to support that point of view.[b] The opposition in Congress and across the country was strong enough to delay enactment of a new housing law from 1945 until 1949, even though the proposed bill had strong Republican support from Senator Taft and others. The public housing provisions of the 1949 Housing Act survived in the House of Representatives by only five votes. And though Congress authorized

[b] See especially Freedman (1969) and various *Congressional Quarterly* summaries of housing legislation.

development of 165,000 units each year for five years in the 1949 act, only 250,000 units were actually funded over the entire decade of the 1950s. As the Eisenhower administration grew increasingly more hostile to governmental intervention in the economic sphere, mere survival of the housing program became increasingly less certain.

On the other hand, the special circumstances in which public housing operations began in the 1940s made the first generation of developments (authorized in 1937) conspicuously successful in the early years, thus masking the fact that they were actually living on borrowed time by special dispensation. World War II brought about a rapid shift in population to war-production urban centers and placed enormous pressure on the existing housing supply. Relatively full employment and higher earnings, coupled with special dispensation that allowed the use of public housing by war workers, created a bonanza for local housing authorities not entailed by federal policies. War workers kept the apartments full, and incomes far in excess of the levels intended by regulations meant premium rents and ample incomes for LHAs operating new developments that required little major maintenance or capital replacement. Even after the war ended occupancy remained high, some of the overincome workers remained, and most of the tenant body was employed; hence, rental income remained relatively high until the end of the 1940s. Difficulties began when overincome tenants were forced from the developments, occupancy began to fall, and maintenance costs and capital replacement needs began to rise rapidly.

Again, the multipurpose character of the public housing program tended to impede any current evaluation of its performance. Additions to the program were usually sold to Congress during periods of moderate to severe economic recession as a way of stimulating the construction industry while simultaneously serving a good social purpose. Even as late as 1974, public housing was linked legislatively to community development and then indirectly to such diverse functions as rational use of land, integration of income groups, and preservation of historic properties. While such mixed purposes may help gain votes in Congress, they also increase the difficulties associated with performance evaluation. In practice, supporters tend to concentrate on areas where success is most easily defended or hardest to attack, and the opposition follows the same strategy while taking the opposite direction. The balance of benefits and costs, which is crucial to reasoned policy improvement, tended to be ignored by both sides.

The Changing Social Environment

While public housing policy remained more or less frozen in its original mold, operating on principles borrowed from the traditional private sector, social change was proceeding rapidly in the housing developments as in the wider community. World War II largely accelerated certain trends established earlier, such as the movement of population from the central city to the suburbs. Persons in the higher income brackets headed for the suburbs early in the century; federal housing and tax policies after 1945 encouraged blue-collar and white-collar workers to follow suit. New and old industries alike moved to the cheaper land on the city's outskirts as they expanded; a burgeoning trucking industry and expanded highway construction program hastened the process by increasing accessibility. The erosion of the city's tax base was hastened by urban renewal, transportation construction, and subsidies to housing and other construction. Despite the countless billions of dollars poured into central cities in an effort to preserve what was mistakenly identified as "the city" as a whole, anticipated investment did not materialize. The inner city became increasingly an isolated clump of older business facilities surrounded by a widening belt of deteriorated housing occupied mainly by the very poor, the black, and the permanently unemployed. Neighborhoods previously characterized by long-term residence and stable social behavior crumbled and fragmented as the elderly died off and the younger workers moved to the suburbs seeking homes they could afford, desirable schools and neighborhoods, and physical separation from the expanding inner city ghetto. The end of the World War II employment boom hardened the differences between inner city and suburb. The recession of 1956–57 had a profound impact on most large cities, and for some the recession of 1961–62 was merely a continuation. Lack of employment, particularly for the young, the black, and the disadvantaged, increased outmigration of the working-age population, leaving behind a body of residents increasingly dependent on public assistance: the permanent poor, the very young and very old, the disabled, and the relatively helpless.

As in other things, public housing developments mirrored the course of events in the wider community. They ceased to be a way station for the working poor enroute to a family-owned dwelling and became a haven for concentrated masses of dependent persons with little possibility of improving their lot through their own efforts. The indicators of their helplessness are classic: real wages that lagged persistently and significantly behind local and national levels; unemployment rates several times the national average; extreme transience in employment; marginal jobs; frequent and often sustained reliance on public assistance; and heavy concentrations of the very young and the very old, usually members of a minority group, often comprising two or three generations of public housing tenants. Tragically, helplessness was actually increasing at the very time when the dependent population was being urged most strongly to entertain rising expectations about the quality of life it lived and the life its children could anticipate. In the past, the liberal rhetoric of national politics had been effectively counterbalanced by the conservative practice of local authorities. After 1945, the federal government became a direct and meaningful participant in local affairs, often bypassing state and local jurisdiction. Unfortunately, the rhetoric of national politics was seldom funded at a level that allowed equal benefits for the entire poor population. Commonly, the rhetoric was implemented by lotteries in which a few cities won but most did not, or by legal changes that could not be enforced without costs the government was rarely prepared to accept—the bussing controversy is a good illustration of the process.

Of course, rhetoric has an impact on attitudes, opinions, and behavior that exceeds the effects of funded programming. To the extent that legalistic liberals supported the pursuit of principle without regard to consequences, they played an important role in the general dissolution of internalized social controls that characterized the 1960s. The subsequent course of events was dramatic evidence of the inability of such institutions as law, police, courts, schools, churches, and families to maintain stability and order when the underlying priorities of society are challenged blindly and persistently. Crimes against person and property increased relentlessly despite enormous expenditures for security and the introduction of highly sophisticated technologies for maintaining social control. Abandoned houses were vandalized systematically rather than allowed to decay unmolested. Public property of all sorts, not public housing alone, was subjected to alarming abuse in every area of society. Both personal and collective behavior was freed of a significant range of prior restrictions. Claims to rights and prerogatives increased exponentially, while obligations long taken for granted were questioned or simply abandoned. The social climate, in brief, became stormy, threatening, and subject to extreme perturbations.

Local housing authorities were caught in a broad flow of events they could not hope to master, bereft of resources, married perforce to inadequate and relatively inflexible federal policies, harassed by a clientele that desperately needed their services yet increasingly could not afford them. The cities were helpless, caught in the same whirlwind; the states, for the most part, looked the other way. Declining productivity in the housing industry worsened the LHA situation by increasing capital and maintenance costs without improving quality or increasing productivity. The real costs of housing began to rise rapidly just as public housing development began expanding. Various contributory factors can be identified: profit-maximizing entrepreneurs used technological improvements to maximize profits, union power forced the inefficient use of expensive labor. It cost more and more simply to maintain the quality of a basic unit of housing; any effort to reduce costs apparently lead to an over-all decrease in construction standards.

A parallel transformation of the population of public housing under-mined the survival capacity of the LHAs in every part of the country. There was a steady decline in the number of employed workers and a steady increase in the number of families wholly or partially dependent on public assistance. Predictably, the amount of income available to each family tended to decline relative to wage and price rates in the wider community. The number of female heads-of-household increased with a concurrent expansion of the number of relatively undisciplined young persons living on the territory. In border cities such as St. Louis, racial segregation based on income became the rule. Public housing became the prime repository for the very poor, the black, the elderly, the female head-of-household and her children, the unemployed and unemployable. Rents declined, expenses soared, and meager reserves were soon ex-pended; the financial position of the LHAs weakened rapidly and se-riously. Declining revenues forced maintenance to be deferred, which led to a deterioration in physical conditions, which stimulated vandalism, which further depressed the quality of the housing supply. The end result was too often a ghastly landscape of mutilated buildings, broken glass, empty apartments, abandoned automobiles, litter and garbage, a waste-land hostage to the criminal, vagrant, truant, and street gang, a hazard to the passer-by and a nightmare to the resident.

Subsidies

Money alone would not solve all of the problems of the LHAs, but without significant additions to their income any efforts to improve de-sign, tenant selection, management, maintenance, or other aspects of performance were futile. Public housing deteriorated in a shocking man-ner predominantly because of the money shortage; so long as funds were available, most developments operated reasonably well. The two St. Louis developments completed in 1942, for example, were exemplars of the kind of public housing intended by the legislators so long as even modest resources were available to maintain them. While the federal government allowed periodic increases in construction costs, modest rent increases, and in rare cases allocated special funds for refurbishing some of the more conspicuous disasters, no regular operating subsidy of any kind was available until 1961, and there was no effective operating sub-sidy before 1972. Yet so long as the LHAs were wholly dependent on rental income, low tenant income meant that they could not derive enough revenue to operate the developments. Under the pressure of rising costs and deteriorating physical plant, the LHAs were literally forced to behave like the slum landlords they had become, increasing rents while services declined until the tenants finally balked and refused to pay. The only possible source of relief was a subsidy; the only realistic source of subsidy was the federal government. The poor were being squeezed dry.

Ironically and—it is tempting but perhaps unfair to say—typically, the first subsidy did little to ease the basic problem when it finally arrived. Instead, Congress subsidized the provision of housing for a whole new class of tenants by offering a bonus for housing the elderly. The Housing Act of 1956 allowed a special bonus of $500 per room for the construction of elderly housing; the Housing Act of 1961 provided the LHAs with an additional $120 per year for each elderly family housed in the developments. In combination, the two subsidies ushered in the era of the elderly poor as favored darlings of the public housing program; in response, their numbers increased spectacularly in the 1960s and 1970s. Since the only special features required for "elderly" housing seems to have been a few feet of handrail in halls and bathrooms and a warning device to be pulled (if time permitted) should cardiac arrest set in, the increased construction allowance was a significant windfall for the builder. The operating subsidy provided the LHA with a parallel bonus, doubly sweetened by the highly desirable characteristics of the elderly as tenants: they usually have no young children; they are not prone to vandalism or violence; they pay their rent regularly; they cause little wear and tear on the premises; and they are almost universally regarded as worthy of assistance, for with some few exceptions, they *are* someone's mother or father and that, in the American scheme of things, guarantees virtue and deserving. And to put icing on the cake, the elderly desired only small apartments and lived readily in high-rise buildings; hence, they were ideally suited to the kind of housing the industry was tooled up to build in the 1960s. The orgy of construction for the elderly that followed was paralleled by a declining rate of construction in "family" housing.

While the move to elderly housing is readily explained, it is somewhat less easy to justify. Granted that the elderly poor required assistance, it is uncertain that their need was any greater than that of poverty-stricken families. In any case, no one bothered to inquire, nationally or locally. The change in clientele was made by substitution and not by addition, by diverting resources from one target population to another, and not by an increase in resources sufficient to handle the additional burden. Since the bulk of the apartments available in the private sector are small in size, it cannot be argued that it was more efficient to deal with the elderly by construction rather than lease; it would have been much more reasonable to try leasing smaller apartments to elderly tenants. The result of the shift, intended or not, was a major reward for one class of prospective tenants (the elderly) and a significant reduction in the effort to service another class of tenants (dependent families). In St. Louis, for example, the percentage of elderly families in public housing rose from perhaps 15 percent in 1955 to about 30 percent in 1970 and then more than 55 percent in 1975, while the total number of units available actually declined.

The next major change in the fiscal structure was made in the Housing Act of 1969; the act limited the rent that could be charged any tenant to 25 percent of adjusted income. The maintenance and operations subsidy needed to compensate the LHAs for lost revenue was not added until 1970, and significant and regular payments were not forthcoming until 1972. When the operating subsidy finally did arrive, it was inadequate! Moreover, the Housing Act of 1968 had already authorized a number of activities that increased the fiscal burden on the LHAs by requiring provision of such tenant services as educational and occupational counseling, additional private security guards, recreational equipment, and development of tenant participation in management through stimulation of tenant organizations. In effect, the "social" dimension of housing operations was substantially expanded while the sources of future revenue and the level of resources to be supplied remained uncertain. The level of support required to operate and maintain the developments proved difficult to estimate; the federal government hedged its commitment and kept the LHAs limping along until HUD, aided by the Urban Institute, generated a formula (HM 7475.12; Urban Institute, 1973). In 1972, a subsidy amounting to 3 percent of development costs was set as a base for operating and maintenance expenses, even though HUD's own earlier estimates suggested that 7.5 percent of investment was an appropriate figure. The amount was later increased to 5.5 percent, still not enough by standard calculations even if the deferred maintenance problem is ignored. The transition to operating subsidies was painful for everyone concerned. Local authorities were caught in the midst of mounting costs, falling income, and increasing tenant pressures; the federal government found itself riding the tiger of escalating subsidy costs. By the end of 1972, the Nixon administration had decided to halt expansion of public housing; a moratorium was announced early in 1973 and remained until autumn. Only leasing was allowed to resume. The pressure for more operating subsidies continued, however, and in 1975 a special utilities payment was made available to adjust the shortfall between LHA income and expenses. Despite all of the subsidies, the LHAs continued to receive the equivalent of a starvation diet, enough to survive upon but not to prosper or return to good health. Moreover, the performance funding system installed by HUD provided a straightjacket for coercing the "expensive" LHAs into cheaper operations.

Beginning in 1970, the federal government tried to improve the physical condition of the developments by providing modernization funds that could be used for capital replacement and major repairs. Some of the larger LHAs also received grants that would help restore reserve balances badly depleted during the previous decade. Again, the resources available to HUD were nowhere near the level of funds actually needed. Moreover, some funds were earmarked and had to be used for specified purposes that were not necessarily the first priorities for the LHA concerned. In St. Louis, for example, nearly $2.5 million was used to remove lead-based paint from about half of the apartments in the two older developments, though funds for such fundamentals as plumbing, heating, and electrical renovation could not be obtained. Given the immense gap between resources and needs, there was probably no alternative to the use of lotteries, though how the wheel was spun remained a mystery. In 1974, for example, a few cities shared in the melon known as the Target Projects Program. St. Louis, one of the lucky winners, received $1.8 million to supplement capital improvements by training staff, developing new administrative procedures, making minor physical improvements, and employing tenants to assist with the work. So important was the last of these functions that TPP was in some quarters identified as the "Tenants Put on the Payroll" program, perhaps with cause. The fact that St. Louis had just begun a tenant management program may have influenced the decision to make the allocation but does not suggest that national spending decisions were based on a careful weighing of the possible benefits of the various available alternatives. Such special subsidy programs indicate the nature of the fundamental unresolved difficulty underlying the entire public housing effort in the United States; so long as Congress cannot or will not underwrite a serious effort to supply decent housing to all those who need help, one set of random efforts may be just as good as any other.

Privatization

The second major change introduced into public housing during the 1960s was increased privatization of various aspects of operations, that is, the transfer of some functions to the private sector usually by authorizing contract relations between LHAs and private organizations for performance of needed services. The cause of the change was the obviously distressed condition of most large housing authorities. The justification was implicit in the received wisdom of the society, primarily the belief that private organization is prima facie more efficient than public. Until 1974, legislation tended to foster privatization rather than force it. The Housing Act of 1974 and the administrative regulations that accompanied it made privatization the central thrust of federal policy for the immediate future.

Three basic elements in the privatization of public housing first appeared in the Housing Act of 1965. First, the act authorized "turnkey" construction, the development of apartments by private entrepreneurs on their own sites for sale to LHAs. The developer contracted with the housing authority to supply facilities; provide a site, architectural and construction services and all other facilities needed; and deliver a finished product ready for use. Ostensibly a response to complaints about the quality of design and construction of conventional housing, the turnkey development proved very popular; most new construction after 1965 was turnkey. How closely the program lived up to expectations is uncertain. Development time was probably reduced, but in St. Louis there was little evidence of significant improvements in design or construction, and while site costs were in some cases lower, construction cost remained at the allowed maximum. There is little reason to suppose that the LHAs could not have achieved the same results with even greater economy had they been given a freer hand in operations.

The second form of privatization authorized by the 1965 act was sale of public housing to tenants. Ordinarily, such sales were limited to detached, semidetached, and row-type housing; high-rise apartments were specifically excluded from the homeownership program. Finally, public housing could be sold to not-for-profit organizations so long as it continued to operate as low-income housing. Neither procedure was widely used; in St. Louis, one small development was set aside as an experiment in homeownership, but none of the housing was actually sold to an alternative organization.

In 1967, the federal government authorized contracts between LHAs and private firms for management services in public housing, with or without the provision of routine maintenance. A standard fee was paid for each unit placed under management. If the contract called for "soft" management, the LHA retained responsibility for maintenance; alternatively, a "hard" contract could be negotiated in which the management firm also supplied routine maintenance. In all such cases, responsibility for capital replacement and major repairs remained with the LHA. Contracts were normally written for one year with more or less automatic renewal, though they could be terminated for cause or by consent.

Both contract development and contract management have been widely used in public housing. Their popularity with LHA management is understandable. Private firms have much more latitude in dealing with their employees than governmental agencies; as legislation against discrimination increased, hard-pressed bureaucrats welcomed the opportunity to escape at least partly from these contradictory pressures. Moreover, private firms do have some genuine operational advantages over public organizations: they can locate and employ needed skills more quickly, purchase with greater facility, experiment more, and cut losses more quickly—there is less inertia effect in private operations, other things being equal.

But the use of contractual services is not without costs. The LHA loses a substantial part of its control over daily operations, and in fact the nature of the relation creates a significant lag time between detecting pending trouble and forcing the contractor to produce a solution. The primary weapon available to the LHA is contract termination and that is not very useful against minor contract infractions such as late reports, modest performance delays, and so on. The development manager who is an employee of a contracting firm is far less accessible to the LHA director than an employee of the LHA. The most serious fault with contractual management, however, lies in its long-range impact on the quality of governmental services. For if it is a fact that governments perform poorly and inefficiently in the managerial arena, purchasing such services on the private market will only guarantee that the inefficiency is prolonged indefinitely and the long-term cost of operations is increased. If governmental operations were for some reason beyond all hope of improvement, there would be no alternative; otherwise, such a policy of despair is unwarranted and short run contracting merely delays the inevitable. In any case, it seems wiser to explore the various means by which governmental performance might be improved before adopting a strategy guaranteed to eliminate future improvements.

Other Changes in Public Housing

Various modifications have been made in the original public housing program over the years, usually in an effort to eliminate observable deficiencies or at least to resond to major complaints. Unfortunately, such changes have all too rarely been grounded in careful study of past experience or parallel operations; most commonly, they have been ad hoc improvisations that rely on the current fad in social science or administration, ignoring appropriateness or performance. In 1968, for example, Congress forbade the use of high-rise buildings as family dwellings except in emergency; a detailed study of St. Louis public housing indicates that the effect of building height on development performance has been grossly overstated. Again, Congress and HUD have urged the scattering of public housing sites, avoiding the large aggregates that characterized building in the 1950s. But a blanket order to scatter all forms of housing is irresponsible and improper, for it ignores the evidence already available about the effects of scattering and concentrating different kinds of populations. Elderly tenants, for example, who formerly lived in scattered (and private) dwellings and now live in relatively small (100–200 unit) developments would fiercely resist scattering since it would end valued social services and close association with others. Again, federal efforts to encourage the development of congregate housing for the elderly without specifying the conditions in which it is most likely to succeed or fail is an invitation to disaster unless efforts are viewed as deliberate experiments—clearly not the intent of the act. A larger-scale error appears in the whole elderly housing program. The federal government encouraged a vast increase in the number of elderly persons housed in public facilities, but the policies to be followed as elderly tenants lost mobility and required increasing amounts of nursing service were left to be worked out between LHAs and state welfare agencies ad hoc and often at great cost to everyone concerned.

An even more striking example of the wayward character of federal policy making is found in the field of housing management. In the late 1960s, HUD apparently discovered that the quality of management available in public housing left much to be desired. Substantial sums were set aside for management improvement, and since some of the horses remained in the barn, the expenditures may have been justified, though there is little to suggest that the experiments and studies sponsored by HUD have contributed much to operating efficiency. Nevertheless, the Housing Act of 1974 contains a rather impressive instruction to the secretary to secure "sound management practices" in housing operations. The specifics that flesh out the meaning of the injunction, however, are less than impressive: LHAs should exercise good judgment in tenant selection, collect rent promptly, and evict those who fail to meet their financial obligations. An unkind critic might note that the LHAs did these things very well indeed for a quarter century before HUD's appearance on the housing scene.

Having stressed the need for good management and sponsored a special institute devoted to the task (and there is probably no more difficult management problem to be found in the field of rental housing), HUD proceeded to make a mockery of its own arguments by committing itself prematurely to a radically new conception of tenant-management relations and then to the principle of tenant management of public housing facilities. The "expanded social services" conception of housing management began with the Housing Act of 1968; the Housing Act of 1969, doubtless stimulated by tenant disturbances in many of the larger housing authorities, reiterated the need for a new approach to tenant-management relations. The initial watchword was "tenant participation" in the operating process: new lease and grievance procedures were established, tenant organizations were encouraged, and managerial control over the conditions of tenancy was significantly reduced by a combination of statutory changes and court decisions. Courts, federal administration, and legislature, aided and abetted by the youthful lawyers in the legal aid societies, combined to erode LHA control over the tenant body in the name of tenant participation in the social process. Tenants were entitled to adequate counseling, recreational facilities, and, most important of all, a voice in the management of development affairs. Moreover, efforts to organize fellow tenants for such purposes were entitled to formal and financial LHA support. Title II, Section 3 (4) of the Housing Act of 1974 is quite explicit:

> The term operation also means the financing of tenant programs and services for families residing in low-income housing projects, particularly where there is maximum feasible participation of the tenants in the development and operation of such tenant programs and services. As used in this paragraph, the term "tenant programs and services" includes the development and maintenance of tenant organizations which participate in the management of low-income housing projects; the training of tenants to manage and operate such projects and the utilization of their services in project management and operation. . . .

The act quite clearly assumes the ultimate transfer of management functions to tenant organizations and directs LHAs to take positive and deliberate action to further that outcome.

The positive HUD commitment to introducing and extending tenant management in public housing is by all odds the most astonishing development in the program's checkered history. Why did it occur? Certainly not by reason of evidence derived from experience. Tenant management was tried on a small scale in Washington, D.C. and Boston in 1971; the first major experiment began in St. Louis in the spring of 1973. The Housing Act of 1974 was signed in August of that year, long before any conclusive or even indicative evidence had been obtained about the operation of the management experiment. At the end of fiscal 1976, the value of the tenant management program in St. Louis was still uncertain. Preliminary experience may have justified further trials, particularly of different forms of manager–housing authority relations, but nothing in the St. Louis experiment justified a full-fledged commitment to the principle. Moreover, normal management practice suggests the contrary. Given the complexity of the task, the notion that managers could be recruited and trained in a few short weeks from any specified substratum of the population bordered on the ludicrous. The decision was ideological, if it was not merely a resort to current fad as a way out of a nasty situation.

Since the reasons why tenant management was promoted in Congress were not included in the official regulations, aside from nominal references to the need for "more participation" by tenants, the point of breakdown in the decision-making apparatus cannot be located and the motives of those involved remain obscure. Cynicism suggests that tenant management is a classic solution to the dilemma posed for the federal administration by potentially unruly tenants: co-opting the enemy and sharing the prize. The procedure operated well in colonial empires as a temporary stopgap but failed eventually, as it did on the American Indian reservations. Unfortunately, the legendary cowardice of bureaucrats and legislators would tend to make even temporary solutions attractive. On that interpretation, the Housing Act of 1974 presages a holding action by the federal government that will make Indian reservations of the conventional housing facilities; handing the reservations over to the Indians is the best cheap strategy available for surviving the transition with fewest casualties. Unfortunately, that approach to the problem does nothing either to provide decent housing for low-income populations or to improve the lot of low-income populations to a point where subsidized housing is no longer needed.

LEASED HOUSING

The long-term future of conventional public housing in the United States dimmed unmistakably in the 1970s. Construction, whether conventional or turnkey, came to a halt, and an ominous provision for closing out badly damaged developments was added to the housing legislation. By mid-1976, Pruitt and Igoe in St. Louis were being torn down and carted away. Despite such notorious examples, it would be a serious mistake in judgment to label all conventional public housing, however developed, an utter failure. Nevertheless, that attitude is common among legislators, tenants, the general public, academics, and even former supporters of the public housing program. The· distinction between failure of a specific effort (public housing as it was practiced in the United States) and failure of a general strategy for supplying low-income housing has been ignored consistently. Some genuine failures, inadequate treatment in the media, and widespread ignorance of the particulars of program operations combined to reinforce the belief that abandoning conventional public housing is the course of wisdom.

Official policy in the 1970s clearly accepted the same premises. When the 1973 moratorium on public housing expansion was lifted, only the leased housing program was permitted to resume operations. Section 8 of the Housing Act of 1974, which gave legal form to the same emphasis, has been the principle focus of federal efforts in the public housing field since the act was passed. The message to the LHAs has been unmistakable: the future lies with leasing and not conventional development or its variants. The 1976 Housing Act included some $85 million for conventional construction, but until further regulations are elaborated its significance is unclear. Concurrently, the channels through which housing assistance was channeled to the population shifted from a federal-city axis to a federal-state axis. A Republican national administration, faced with city governments dominated by members of the opposition party, had no choice but to alter the resource routes so that funds passed through the state governments, where some measure of Republican strength remained. The trend is likely to continue, whatever the short-run outcome of national elections, because of the inertia built into the national administrative machinery and the extent to which the federal-city connections have been dissolved. The over-all effect of the change is likely to be a sharp decline in the role of the LHA, an increase in the authority and influence of the local HUD agency, and transfer of some housing operations from city to state administration. Paradoxically, a federal administration dedicated to decentralization of authority and the principle of local autonomy may create a centralized housing administration with far more power than any of its predecessors managed to exercise and to do so in the name of small government and decentralization of power.

Leasing of privately owned facilities for use as public housing offers a quick and effective device for transferring public housing into the private sector; it has been supported by opponents of public ownership since the mid-1930s. The Section 23 leased housing program was added to the Housing Act of 1965 under cover of the hue and cry raised over the rent supplements provisions of the housing bill. It was supported by the U.S. Chamber of Commerce, the National Association of Real Estate Boards, and various Republicans in Congress known for their hostility to public housing. Leasing began as a very small scale program for using housing stock already in existence as a means of supplementing the more conventional developments; the initial quota was a modest 10,000 units per year for a four-year period. It was justified, in Congress and to the wider public, as a way of reducing costs and making greater use of the existing housing stock which would enable housing authorities to respond more quickly and efficiently to tenant needs. By limiting the number of units that could be leased in any single facility to 10 percent of the total, the sponsors expected to disperse tenants more widely within the general population and thus avoid some of the stigma that had become attached to "the projects." However, since that limit could be waived by the LHA on its own authority, it did not serve as an effective control over concentration or dispersal. Finally, supporters of leasing argued that owners of substandard housing would be encouraged to rehabilitate their holdings in order to qualify for participation in the program; thus, it would contribute to the improvement of neighborhoods and an upgrading of the housing stock.

If the LHA could control the quality, location, and price of housing units leased for use by low-income families, the Section 23 lease program would be a valuable adjunct to conventional housing, assuming that the purpose of an LHA is to supply as much of the need for housing as resources permit. If the private housing market could provide the LHA with a supply of adequate housing of acceptable quality, location, size, availability, and cost, then leasing would be extremely helpful. In general, leasing is likely to be more expensive than building or purchasing, particularly in the long run, because lease costs will include profits, local taxes, and the cost of financing on the private money market. However, a number of factors can interfere in the leasing process. The supply of housing may be inadequate with respect to quality, size, location, or cost, and even if housing is available owners may not be willing to lease their property to public agencies for use as low-income housing. Finally, the tenants themselves may object to certain aspects of the program such as dispersal and separation from neighbors, or distance from home, neighborhood, church, schools, and the like.

As it turned out, the private market did not supply the volume of housing needed by the LHAs (taking the nation as a whole) and that opened the door to a line of development far removed from what Congress had authorized and much more difficult to justify as an alternative to conventional development. As the president of the Section 23 Leased Housing Association pointed out in July of 1971:

> The leased housing program, as originally constituted, did not work because it was premised upon the assumption that there was ample housing available for lease. However, if there was any, very few landlords offered it. Therefore another concept, called ''turnkey leasing'' was developed. This contemplated leasing of new construction rather than existing units (Edson, 1976: 4).

What began as a program for leasing existing housing, for which there is ample economic justification, turned very quickly into a program for constructing new housing to be offered for lease, for which little if any real justification can be offered. The latter required some fundamental changes in the public housing program: the income level of the target population has moved upward, the method of equity funding developed for use with Section 236 housing has been transferred to the public housing arena, and the state has entered the picture as a potential developer and funder. The full effect on the quality and cost of services provided remains uncertain until data on real cases can be obtained.

Lease of Existing Housing

Virtually all of the leasing carried out in public housing made use of the Section 23 program added to the Housing Act of 1937 by the Housing Act of 1965; that program was later superseded by Section 8 of the Housing Act of 1974. An alternative mode of leasing, authorized in Section 10(c) of the Housing Act of 1937, was used briefly in the 1960s and then abandoned. This section required exemption from local taxation, a special agreement between local government and LHA for program operation, and authorized a payment in lieu of taxes. It proved unattractive to both local government and LHA, and only about $500,000 worth of annual contract commitments were made under its provisions, all before 1969.

Section 23 leasing required prior approval by local government; it could not be undertaken by the LHA of its own volition. But since leased property was privately owned and paid full taxes, approval was fairly easy to obtain, other things being equal. Of course, some locales would have nothing to do with public housing in any form whether or not taxes were paid, but these were exceptions. Leasing did not require an LHA, though in most cases established housing authorities administered the programs. Leasing authorizations were allocated through the local HUD agency. The LHA that received an allocation (upon request) advertised its readiness to lease and sought owners willing to supply apartments and prospective tenants wishing to rent them. Leases were negotiated for twelve to thirty-six months in the early days of the program, but in 1966 the time was extended to five years and in 1970 to fifteen years. Some of the "existing housing" being leased after 1970 was quite new, or even built for the occasion.

In most cases, the LHA or other agency leased the units from the owner and then subleased them to the low-income tenant, but the Section 23 program also allowed support for a direct lease between owner and tenant. The owner was paid a "fair market rental" set by HUD, which included the cost of range, refrigerator, utilities, and management services, less any utility costs paid directly by the tenant. Rent levels had to be consonant with general area rents, and the housing had to conform to local standards and building codes. Qualitative criteria were minimal: heating, lighting, and cooking facilities had to be provided; the neighborhood had to be free of "characteristics seriously detrimental to family life"; and reasonable access to schools, transportation, shopping, churches, and so on was required. Usually, the LHA performed simple maintenance, leaving all extraordinary repairs and services to the owner.

Ordinarily, the LHA collected rent from the tenant and paid the owner the rent plus an additional subsidy obtained through an Annual Contributions Contract with HUD. The amount of the subsidy was calculated using a very complex scheme known as the "flexible formula," intended to ensure that no more was paid for leased housing than would be paid if the LHA had constructed the facility (FHA 7430.3). If the leasing program operated at a deficit, the LHA could also receive subsidies normally provided for very large or elderly families ($120 per year per family). There was understandable concern lest the leasing program drive up the price of existing housing in tight markets, and LHAs were cautioned to proceed carefully if the effects of leasing would drive the local vacancy rate below 3 percent.

Tenant eligibility for leased housing depended on income, and the LHA could apply the standards used in conventional public housing if it chose. However, the "20 percent gap" did not have to be maintained; hence, income levels in leased housing could be somewhat higher than in the regular program. Nevertheless, the 25 percent limit on income instituted by the Housing Act of 1969 applied to leased housing as well. Tenant eligibility was decided by the LHA, and in most cases it also selected the tenants, though in principle the owner could make the choice subject to LHA approval or from an LHA-prepared list. Since no rent was paid on vacant units if the owner selected tenants, this method was seldom employed until after 1973, when the rules of selection were changed. Evictions were the prerogative of the LHA alone, though the owner could request eviction of an unruly tenant. Until 1973, the owner could contract with either a private firm or an LHA for maintenance and management services, but after 1973 contracts with private firms were no longer permitted.

In 1971 and again in 1973, some major changes were made in the program that controlled lease of existing housing (Edson, 1976); they were consolidated in the Housing and Urban Development Act of 1974. The over-all effect of the new policies was to place complete responsibility for management in the hands of the owner of the property and significantly to reduce the role of the LHA in the lease arrangement. The lease was now made directly between owner and tenant, omitting the LHA. The owner's duties and responsibilities were extended to include payment of utilities, taxes, and insurance; performance of all maintenance functions; processing tenant applications and selecting tenants; collecting rents; and accepting what was called "the risk of loss from vacancies" (mediated somewhat by HUD's agreement to continue payments if the tenant violated the lease). Though rent adjustments were made annually, increases were subject to limits established in the Annual Contributions Contract; thus, the owner who wished to raise rents actually had to find tenants with higher incomes to occupy his premises. Calculation of subsidies was much simplified: the fair market rent established by HUD was simply added to the estimated administrative expenses, and the estimated family contribution was subtracted from the total.

The changes placed some definite responsibilities on the tenant family for the first time in the history of the public housing program. In the past, the prospective tenant had only to apply, establish eligibility, and wait for an opening. Now, qualified tenants were given a certificate of eligibility, good for forty-five days (renewable indefinitely in the earlier version of the regulations), which committed the LHA to housing assistance payments on the tenant's behalf. Responsibility for finding an apartment, however, lay with the tenant; the LHA could assist only in hardship cases.

The new regulations significantly reduced the role of the LHA in leasing. While the LHAs determined tenant eligibility and issued certificates, they had little operation responsibility unless they contracted with the owner to perform managerial services. Otherwise, their principal functions were to conduct an initial inspection of the premises and to process the housing assistance payments. They also retained final control over eviction proceedings.

The Housing Act of 1974 made some major additions to the new administrative regulations. "Low" and "very low" income were defined for housing purposes as 80 percent and 50 percent respectively of the median income for the area; "large" and "very large" families were defined as containing six and eight minors. These definitions provided a base for determining rent levels. Families that were very large or had very low incomes (or medical expenses equal to 25 percent of income) were required to pay 15 percent of income *before deductions* for rent; all other families were charged 25 percent of income *after* deductions. No family could pay less than 15 percent of income for rent. The deductions allowed were modest: $300 per minor child, medical expenses in excess of 3 percent of gross income, and "unusual" costs. Each family was given a small utilities allowance. Thirty percent of the families in leased housing were to come from the very low income group.

The certificate of eligibility was made valid for a sixty-day period, and an additional sixty days were authorized if the tenant had made a serious effort to locate housing. Each family was to be allowed a "shopping incentive credit," defined in a way calculated to baffle even the most ardent bureaucrat:

(b) The amount of the monthly Shopping Incentive Credit shall be the dollar amount equal to that percentage of the Gross Family Contribution which the Rent Savings is of the Fair Market Rent. The Rent Savings is the amount by which the Fair Market Rent (1) exceeds the approved Contract Rent (plus any applicable allowance), or (2) exceeds the initially proposed Contract Rent (plus any applicable allowance), if that be higher than the approved Contract Rent (plus any applicable allowance).[c]

The net effect, apparently, is a monthly reduction in rent equal to the percentage of the fair market rent saved by the tenant. That is, if the fair market rent is $200 per month and the tenant obtains the unit for $190 per month, the 5 percent saving translates into a $5 per month rent decrease for the tenant.

[c] See *Federal Register*, vol. 40, no. 87 (May 5, 1975), *Section 8 Leased Housing Assistance Payments Program*, Existing Regulations, para. 882.115. The regulations were simplified somewhat in March, 1976.

The 1974 act further increased the owner's control over the leasing program. He could now evict tenants with LHA approval, and approval was apparently contingent only on the legitimacy of the owner's interpretation of the contract. HUD also agreed to pay up to 80 percent of the rent for a period of sixty days if the tenant vacated the unit in violation of the lease; this was a significant reduction in the amount of risk assigned to the owner. Housing quality was defined in more detail. The full effect of the act on the leasing program remained uncertain even at the end of 1976. Some changes are clear. The authority of the LHA was much reduced, the tenant's responsibilities were increased, and the owner controlled the bulk of the operation. Indeed, the LHA was specifically enjoined from any action that would "directly or indirectly reduce the family's opportunity to choose among the available units in the housing market." Yet it seems reasonable to assume that the prime limit on the individual's "freedom of choice" is likely to be the inability of the LHA to intercede on his behalf. While not quite so serious as refusing to allow a physician to choose his patient's medicine, much the same principle seems involved in both areas. The potential bargaining power of the LHA as collective purchaser and government agent was given away deliberately. Granted the LHA's potential had not been fully exploited, the potential remained important even if unused. Finally, the search and lease arrangements were almost an open invitation to collusion between owner and tenant at the expense of the public treasury. For if the fair market rents were high enough so that the owner was adequately rewarded from the subsidy payment alone, as seems the case in practice, then the owner's interests would best be served by retaining the tenant regardless of the rent actually collected (by the owner, under the terms of the act). Such arrangements would be almost impossible to detect. Finally, carelessness or bias in the inspection of units would have the effect of converting the program into a support system for marginal local slums with little possibility of forcing an improvement in quality or terminating the lease.

Construction for Lease

The Housing Act of 1965 clearly intended that leasing should apply only to the existing supply of housing; it would serve as an adjunct to the conventional housing program. That intention was transposed or transformed by HUD into active support for construction of new housing for lease and for rehabilitation of existing housing. The reasoning used to justify the change would do credit to a correspondence school lawyer. HUD argued that once new housing is built it becomes part of the "existing" stock and, thus, can be included in the program. Moreover, since the LHAs were creatures of state, not federal, law, nothing prevented them from entering into an agreement with a developer to lease as yet unbuilt property for use in the low-income housing program. Congress, instead of resenting or resisting such blatant flouting of intent, changed its legislation in 1970 to legalize the administrative modifications. The LHA was allowed to commit its annual contributions in advance; the developer could then use them as a base for obtaining financing. The LHA could commit the contributions for eight successive five-year periods, a total of forty years (reduced to twenty years in the 1974 Housing Act).

The result of the HUD interpretation was a sharp increase in the amount of new construction for lease, particularly in states where public housing was difficult to site. Between 1969 and 1974, some 61,000 units of housing were added to the lease program; of that number, more than 75 percent (46,123) were new construction, fewer than three hundred were substantially rehabilitated, and 24 percent (14,500) were part of the existing housing stock (table 1-1). This caused some anxiety among program supporters, and an effort was made to maintain an even balance between new construction and lease of existing housing.

Until the Housing Act of 1974, the regulations governing administration of new construction were the same as those applied to lease of existing stock, but the owner of the new apartment complex was in a much stronger position vis-à-vis both tenant and LHA than his counterpart who owned existing housing. Most of the differences were due to programmatic needs generated by the effort to finance new construction or rehabilitation. The rule that limited the LHA to leasing 10 percent of the units in any one complex were clearly inapplicable to projects built specifically for LHA use. Similarly, financing could not be obtained if HUD gave priority to developments in which fewer than 20 percent of the units were leased by an LHA. The same problems appeared if subsidy payments stopped during vacancies created by tenant violations of lease provisions. HUD maintained these rules through 1973 in the face of bitter protests from owners, but financing requirements did force some concessions. An automatic adjustment in rent was incorporated into the rules, and further changes were allowed if inflation turned sharply upward—thus waiving the stabilizing effect of leasing on operating costs. The owner retained total managerial control over new construction units and could contract with either an LHA or a private firm for managerial services. In effect, lease of new housing provided for the reintroduction of the traditional landlord system with only minor modifications. The owner paid for taxes, utilities, and other services, was responsible for all maintenance, processed applications, selected tenants, and collected rents. After 1974, he also determined tenant eligibility, verified it periodically, set the amount of family contribution and subsidy, and terminated tenancy subject only to minor delay by the LHA.

The LHA's functions in the new construction for lease program were minimal. It could serve as a cosponsor of a development but could then exercise no managerial function over the property. When it did manage, it was at the owner's request. HUD regulations made joint sponsorship complex and difficult, and the central administration clearly favored direct applications from developers and individual state agencies. Selection of developers, site and plan approvals, and fiscal arrangements were all made entirely through the local HUD office. The language of the regulations allowed but did not require HUD to notify the LHA when a new construction-for-lease program was announced—a basic indicator of impotence in the bureaucratic world. While the LHAs have some broad supervisory functions with respect to lease of existing housing, the April 1975 regulations governing lease of new property did not contain even one numbered paragraph enumerating the responsibilities of the LHAs for the program.

The key to a strong construction-for-lease program is the method of financing available and the opportunity for profits it provides. From the point of view of the developer, access to capital at preferred rates or the right to depreciate the investment quickly and thus generate tax losses is the key to success. Both of these techniques found a place in the construction-for-lease program, often combined in the same development. To obtain preferred borrowing rates, the LHA's power to issue tax-free bonds was exploited and the creation of state agencies with similar powers was encouraged. One common procedure was to create a nonprofit corporation that was a creature of the LHA; that corporation built the apartments and then leased them to the LHA under an agreement that transferred ownership to the LHA at the end of twenty years. The corporation could issue tax-exempt bonds because of its special relation to the LHA. Since local corporations pay local taxes, that method of financing proved popular with local governments whose tax bases were declining. The same tax break is obtained if the LHA loans the developer the capital needed for construction using funds acquired from issuing tax-free bonds. The completed development is then leased to the LHA in the normal manner. More than thirty states created financing agencies with the power to issue tax-exempt bonds for specific purposes; they can provide capital for developers using the LHA's pledge of payment as security for a loan at a favored rate of interest.

Even more spectacular returns to the developer are produced by "equity syndication," a procedure developed for use with Section 236 housing. The key to success here is the Internal Revenue Service's willingness to allow accelerated depreciation on multifamily properties intended for use by low-income families. In effect, the IRS ruling allows the developer to depreciate the combined value of his "up front" investment *and* his mortgage in a very short time, usually five years. Since this is generally more depreciation credit than one person can use unless his annual income is enormous, a portion of the depreciation credit can be sold or assigned to members of a limited liability company formed specially for that purpose. As an example, a developer who invests $500,000 of his own money and borrows $4,500,000 more to build a $5 million project (a common ratio of investment to borrowing in the industry) can depreciate the property at a rate of $1 million per year for the first five years of operation; in effect, he buys $100,000 worth of depreciation per year for each of five years for only $50,000. He need only find individuals with large personal incomes and sell them the depreciation he has cumulated in the development. For the person with a large income, the depreciation is a good buy; the developer, obviously, can charge rather more than his own investment. At the end of five years, when the property value is reduced to nil, the project can be sold and the return treated as capital gains, taxed at a much lower rate than personal income. Even though the "rollover" provision that allowed Section 236 developers to defer taxation on profits simply by reinvesting in new construction (as a private homeowner can avoid taxes on profit from sale of a house by purchasing another) was not extended to construction for lease, it remained a very attractive investment for persons in the higher tax brackets more concerned with the gain from depreciation losses than with regular income from tax-exempt securities. Properly funded, however, construction-for-lease can serve both sets of interest.

REPRISE

The public housing program in the United States was seriously damaged if not mortally wounded in the decade between 1965 and 1975. The justification for abandoning the effort that is heard most often, particularly from former supporters of the program, is "we tried it and it didn't work." But the businessman or executive who tried a particular brand of machinery in various plants throughout the country without providing enough resources to maintain it properly, and knowing that the knowledge required to operate it properly was not available, then announced that the machinery was no good, sold it at great loss, and purchased far more expensive and less effective substitutes would, if exposed, be rightly denounced and discharged by the stockholders. Yet that is precisely the kind of condemnation without trial that public housing has suffered. In this case, both the stockholders (the tax-paying general public) and the consumers (the tenants) have a genuine grievance against the policy-maker. At the national level, the program has been characterized by lack of foresight, ignorance, failure to learn, and dogmatic adherence to principle in despite of the observable consequences of action.

At the beginning of 1976, the public housing program had effectively been divided into three parts and had lost much of its original impetus. The working poor, the original target population for public housing, had long since lost interest in the facilities. The dependent poor who replaced them in the mid-1950s were a poor risk and lacked clout; by mid-1976 they were increasingly herded into conventional housing developments that resembled nothing so much as downtown Indian reservations presided over by Indian agents and some few collaborators. The elderly poor, who became the primary target of the turnkey construction program in the 1960s and 1970s, occupied the lion's share of the newer apartments. The third main arm of public housing, the leasing program, transferred program control to the private landlord in very large measure. Moreover, policy could be expected to squeeze both the very low income tenant and working tenant out of public housing, other things equal. The Brooke amendment of 1969 had that effect in practice, and the requirement that LHAs collect at least 20 percent of tenant income in rent has the same impact. Program regulations tend to press the landlord to seek higher—income tenants within the limits of his discretion since that policy will maximize income and minimize collection losses over time. While the stated aim of the federal government has been the promotion of economically mixed public housing, the net effect of detailed policy has been to force out more and more of the working poor.

If trends apparent by mid-1976 continue, public housing will be transposed into a direct rent subsidy program within a private market framework. That is precisely the situation that public housing was originally intended to remedy. It involves loss of the economies attainable through collective purchasing and of the ability of the collectivity to deal with landlords on an equal footing. Further, the possibility of increasing the available knowledge of how best to provide decent housing for the poor with improved efficiency must also be discarded. In those circumstances, the facilities available for the poor are likely to decrease over the long run. Failure by the private sector to generate enough construction to take care of replacements and population expansion, which is likely given the vagaries of the industry and the different economic conditions found in different regions of the country, will impose enormous hardship on those in society least able to withstand it. The target population for the program as it appeared in 1976 was one solid notch higher in income level than was the case in the 1960s; that difference, though slight, spells significant deterioration in the housing available to the very poor and an increase in its real cost.

The history of public housing in the United States is most discouraging for anyone seriously concerned with the willingness and capacity of the democracies to deal with fundamental human problems. Clearly, the institutions responsible for the decisions that guided the development and operation of public housing failed miserably. Worse, they seem incapable of pursuing identifiable goals persistently or improving their performance with experience. They have not learned. And behind the failure of particular institutions lies the grim specter of a society utterly unwilling to accept the social and economic burdens required for even a modest effort to redress the more grievous inequities in the established order. Here, perhaps more than anywhere else, is where public housing's failure was decided. Until genuine changes are made in society's fundamental priorities, efforts to alleviate the suffering of the unfortunate will continue to fail, or at best succeed imperfectly and be expensively disguised as solutions to other problems that society *is* willing to tackle—with the additional risk that such accomplishments will be taken as surrogate for the humane considerations that ought to guide collective action in these spheres. Of those changes, there is no sign whatsoever.

The "horse" theory of social melioration remains as the best guide to the social actions of the federal and local governments. That is, if humane social action involves the transfer of grain from the public granary to the unfortunate sparrows, the horses who control the granary are unwilling to make distributions except by feeding the grain through intervening horses, most of which seem to be Percherons capable of heroic feats of constipation. The system is operated by horses and guided mainly if not entirely by awareness of the benefits that accrue to horses. The sparrows are necessary, but only because the rules of the game forbid direct feeding at the public trough and hence require a justification which the sparrows, like the concept of national defense, can supply. And anyone seeking to feed the sparrows directly is quite likely to be kicked through the walls of the stable in which the principal horses are housed. It is a most unlovely parable.

REFERENCES AND BIBLIOGRAPHY

Books and Articles

Aaron, Henry J. (1972) *Shelter and Subsidies: Who Benefits from Federal Housing Policies?* Washington, D.C.: Brookings Institution.

Bingham, Richard D. (1975) *Public Housing and Urban Renewal: An Analysis of Federal-Local Relations*. New York: Praeger.

Burchell, Robert W., J. Hughes, and George Sternlieb (1970) *Housing Costs and Housing Restraints*. New Brunswick, N.J.: Center for Urban Policy Research, Rutgers University.

Compilation of the Housing and Community Development Act of 1974, Public Law 93-383 (1974) Subcommittee on Housing of the Committee on Banking and Currency, House of Representatives, 93rd Congress, Second Session, (October).

De Leeuw, Frank, assisted by Eleanor L. Jarutis (no date) *Operating Costs in Public Housing: A Financial Crisis*. Washington, D.C.: Urban Institute.

————, and Sam H. Leaman (1972) *The Section 23 Leasing Program: Progress Report*. Washington, D.C.: Urban Institute.

————, assisted by Sue A. Marshall (1973) *Operating Expenses in Public Housing: 1968–71*. Washington, D.C.: Urban Institute.

Downs, Anthony (1973a) *Federal Housing Subsidies: How Are They Working?* Lexington, Massachusetts: Lexington Books.

———— (1973b) *Opening Up the Suburbs: An Urban Strategy for America*. New Haven: Yale University Press.

———— (1974) "The Successes and Failures of Federal Housing Policy." *The Public Interest* (Winter): 124–45.

———— (1973) *A Section 23 Primer*. Washington, D.C.: Section 23 Leased Housing Association.

———— (1975) *1975 Supplement to the Leased Housing Primer* (2nd ed.) Washington, D.C.: National Leased Housing Association.

Edson, Charles L. (1976) "Leased Housing: Evolution of a Federal Program." In Robert E. Mendelson and Michael A. Quinn (eds.), *The Politics of Housing in Older Urban Areas*. New York: Praeger.

Ellickson, Robert (1967) "Governmental Housing Assistance to the Poor." *Yale Law Journal* 76 (January): 508–44.

Fisher, Ernest M. (1975) *Housing Markets and Congressional Goals*. New York: Praeger.

Fisher, Robert M. (1959) *Twenty Years of Public Housing*. New York: Harper.

Freedman, Leonard (1969) *Public Housing: The Politics of Poverty*. New York: Holt, Rinehart, and Winston.

Friedman, Lawrence M. (1968) *Government and Slum Housing: A Century of Frustration*. Chicago: Rand McNally.

Gilson, R. J. (1970) "Public Housing and Urban Policy: *Gautreaux v. Chicago Housing Authority*." *Yale Law Journal* 79 (March): 712–29.

Hartman, Chester W. (1975) *Housing and Social Policy*. Englewood Cliffs. N.J.: Prentice-Hall.

————, and Margaret Levi (1973) "Public Housing Managers: An Appraisal." *AIP Journal* 39 (March): 125–37.

Isler, Morton L., Robert Sadacca, and Margaret Drury (1974) *Keys to Successful Housing Management*. Washington, D.C.: Urban Institute.

Long, Norton E. (1976) "The City as a System of Perverse Incentives." *Urbanism Past and Present* (Summer): 1–8.

Mandelker, Daniel R. (1973) *Housing Subsidies in the United States and England*. New York: Bobbs-Merrill.

Meehan, Eugene J. (1971) *The Foundations of Political Analysis: Empirical and Normative*. Homewood, Ill.: Dorsey.

———— (1975) *Public Housing Policy: Myth Versus Reality*. New Brunswick, N.J.: Center for Urban Policy Research, Rutgers University.

———— (1975) "Looking the Gift Horse in the Mouth: The Conventional Public Housing Program in St. Louis." *Urban Affairs Quarterly* 10 (June): 423–63.

Muth, Richard F. (1973) *Public Housing: An Economic Evaluation*. Washington, D.C.: American Enterprise Institute.

Newman, Oscar (1972) *Defensible Space*. New York: Macmillan.

Prescott, James R. (1974) *Economic Aspects of Public Housing*. Beverly Hills, Calif.: Sage Publications.

Pynoos, John, Robert Schafer, and Chester W. Hartman (eds.) (1973). *Housing Urban America*. Chicago: Aldine.

Rainwater, Lee (1970) *Behind Ghetto Walls: Black Family Life in a Federal Slum*. Chicago: Aldine.

Reeb, Donald J. and James T. Kirk, Jr. (1973) *Housing the Poor*. New York: Praeger.

Rydell, Peter C. (1970) *Factors Affecting Maintenance and Operating Costs in Federal Housing Projects*. New York: The New York RAND Institute.

Sadacca, Robert, Suzanne B. Louz, Morton L. Isler, and Margaret J. Drury (1974) *Management Performance in Public Housing*. Washington, D.C.: Urban Institute.

Scobie, Richard S. (1975) *Problem Tenants in Public Housing*. New York: Praeger.

Solomon, Arthur P. (1974) *Housing the Urban Poor: A Critical Evaluation of Federal Housing Policy*. Cambridge, Mass.: MIT Press.

Starr, Robert (1973) "A Reply." *Public Interest* (Spring): 130–34.

Sternlieb, George (ed.) (1972). *Housing 1970–71*. New York: AMS Press.

———— (ed.) (1974) *Housing 1971–72*. New York: AMS Press.

Taggart, Robert, III (1970) *Low Income Housing: A Critique of Federal Aid*. Baltimore: Johns Hopkins University Press.

Urban Institute (1973) *A Working Paper: The Development of a Prototype Equation for Public Housing Operating Expenses*. Washington, D.C.: Urban Institute.

Welfeld, Irving H. (1973) *America's Housing Problem: An Approach to its Solution*. Washington, D.C.: American Enterprise Institute.

Wolman, Harold L. (1975) *Housing and Housing Policy in the U.S. and the U.K.* Lexington, Mass.: Lexington Books.

———— (1971) *The Politics of Federal Housing*. New York: Dodd, Mead.

Government Documents

The basic legislation includes the Housing Acts of 1937, 1949, 1961, 1965, 1968, 1969, 1970, 1971, and 1974. Some of the basic governmental circulars and reports include:

RHA *Section 23 Leased Housing*, (10/6/65).

RHA 7430.1 *Leased Housing*, (11/69).

RHM 7465.8 *Leased Housing*, (2/21/71).

FHA 7430.3 *The "Flexible Formula"*, (9/24/71).

HM 7475.1 *Financial Management Guide*, (3/72).

HM 7475.12 *Subsidies for Operations*, (11/28/72).

HUD 7495.3 *Low-Rent Housing Homeownership Opportunities*, (11/74).

HM 75-20 Appendix 1, Subpart A: *Performance Funding System*, (5/75).

RED 75-380 *Report to Congress: Leased Housing Programs Need Improvements in Management and Operations*, (7/11/75).

HUD, *Housing Allowances: The 1976 Report to Congress*, (2/76).

Tulsa Housing Authority, *Experimental Housing Allowance Program: Final Report*, (10/75).

※ *Chapter 2*

A Prescription for Reducing Housing Costs[a]

Joseph M. Davis

A national goal for over two decades has been to ensure a decent home in a suitable living environment for every American family. Satisfying the great American dream has been the aim of a variety of federal government programs designed to create more and better housing through the establishment of favorable conditions for the home-building industry and the home purchaser.

Unfortunately, there is a growing national concern that the American dream of homeownership is becoming just that—more of a dream than an obtainable reality.

HOUSING'S DILEMMA

Rising Expectations

Part of housing's dilemma derives from the fact that our affluence has expanded our expectations of what constitutes a "house." The standard house used to be three bedrooms, one bath, and about 1000 square feet of living area (*Arizona Republic,* 1976a). There is little basis on which to compare a typical house of today with that of twenty, forty, or sixty years ago. For readily understandable reasons, there has been a steady transition from the fine detailing and craftsmanship of the older homes to today's preassembled structures with complex mechanical, electrical, and plumbing systems and appliances. The real comparison between housing costs of fifty years ago and today should be based upon the total amenities

[a] This paper is reprinted, with revisions, from *Arizona Business* 24 (January 1977): 17–26, with the permission of Arizona State University College of Business Administration, Tempe, Arizona.

offered by the house. Frankly, what we consider necessities, such as dishwashers, air conditioning, central heating, carpeting, patios, two-car garages, landscaping, and many other features, were luxuries available only to the very wealthy fifty years ago. When our expectations as to what constitutes a decent home rise, the cost increases accordingly. In the future as we add security systems, microwave ovens, decorative lighting, and sunken tubs and expand our list of "necessities," the cost of housing will rise for no other reason than that we are buying more housing.

Rising Production Costs

According to a recent *Wall Street Journal* article, most families must stretch their budgets to be able to make that purchase of a first home because the price of housing has been escalating faster than family income. The price of new homes has skyrocketed; the median price today is $39,000, whereas ten years ago it was $20,000 and twenty years ago it was $13,400. According to a survey by Investors Mortgage Insurance Company in Boston, the median family income of nearly 16 million couples in the age group twenty-five to thirty-four was about $14,800. With interest rates at 8.5 percent, that income would qualify a buyer for an 80 percent, thirty-year conventional mortgage on a $38,125 home. With rates at 9.5 percent, the same buyer could afford to pay only $34,687, or $4313 less than the current median new home price (Simison, 1975).

The National Association of Realtors reported in November 1976 that the median sale price of an existing single-family home in September was $38,700, 8.1 percent above that of one year before. A rise of 10.8 percent had been recorded in 1974 and 10.4 percent in 1975. Although 8.1 percent is significantly below the previous two years, at an annual rate of 8 percent, the price of a house will double about every nine years.

According to the National Association report, the September 1976 median price in the West was $47,800, about $6900 above a year ago. In the North Central region, the median price was $33,400, up $2800 in a year. The median was $43,000 in the Northeast, about $2100 higher. Finally, the $36,200 median price recorded in the South was $1700 above a year ago (*Realtor,* 1976b).

The continued increase in median sale price reflects another decrease in the proportion of homes selling in the low and moderate price classes and an increase in the percentage of transactions in the upper price ranges. Fewer houses than last year are selling under $30,000, about the same percent sell in the $30,000 to $40,000 range, and a much larger percent are now selling for more than $40,000 (*Realtor,* 1976a).

The trend of rising housing prices is likely to continue in rough proportion to changes in the nominal incomes of families and inflation. Unfortunately, for a dozen years or so now, housing costs generally have been climbing faster than the over-all price level and family income (First National City Bank, 1976).

Housing cost reduction alternatives are: (1) to reduce the cost of a standard unit of housing—some proposals will be discussed later; (2) to allow housing expenditures to consume a greater portion of the family budget; or (3) to provide less housing through lower-quality construction, fewer amenities, and smaller lots than in the past. Of these three alternatives, allowing housing expenditures to consume a greater portion of the family budget would be the most undesirable from a social viewpoint because many low-income and median-income families are already forced to scrimp on the necessities of food, clothing, and other basic items.

Other Housing Costs

The price of the house itself does not reflect the full cost of housing. While the home-building industry is concerned primarily with the initial purchase price of a home, the monthly cost of ownership is a more meaningful measure of an individual's ability to afford a home.

The other "real" monthly costs of owning a home would include: the interest payment on the mortgage; maintenance and repairs; property taxes and insurance; income foregone on the down payment and settlement costs invested in the home; and other recurring shelter expenses that might be associated with owning a particular home, for example, pool maintenance or a recreational assessment paid to a neighborhood association. For the homeowner, there will be a "monthly income tax savings" that offsets these costs because the interest portion of the mortgage payment and the property taxes are deductible against one's federal and state income tax liability.

Two studies (Lozano, 1972 and Thompson, 1973: 247–60) that have analyzed the full costs of homeownership have concluded that the initial purchase price of a home amounts to only about 25 percent of the total housing cost over the mortgage period. Nearly *75 percent* of the total cost is related to interest payments, property taxes and insurance, maintenance and repairs, and utilities, with interest as the largest single component of the housing expense. According to the study by Lozano (1972), interest accounted for 40 percent of all costs. The study by Thompson (1973) indicated that interest contributed 33.5 percent to the total cost.

Over the period 1955 to 1975, mortgage interest rates climbed from 4.8 percent to 9 percent and, according to John C. Hart, president of the National Association of Home Builders: "With every one percent rise in borrowing costs . . . eight percent of potential buyers are eliminated—or about eight of 10 over a 10-year period" (*Arizona Republic,* 1976b).

Property taxes and insurance add nearly as much to the cost of housing over the mortgage period as the initial purchase price. Lozano (1972) attributed 24 percent of the total housing cost to property taxes and insurance. During 1955 to 1975, real estate taxes soared 341 percent and insurance premiums increased 321 percent (*Arizona Republic*, 1976b).

Maintenance and repair outlays are those expenditures the homeowner routinely makes on upkeep. Maintenance and repair costs are difficult to estimate for a particular house. They vary because of the age of the house, the type of construction, and external factors. Rough estimates usually comprise .75 to 1 percent of the value of the property per year. A $400 per year maintenance and repair bill would be reasonable for a median price contemporary home. Maintenance and repair costs over the mortgage period might approximate 7 percent of the total housing costs, or about one-third as much as property taxes and insurance. These expenses have climbed 269 percent between 1955 and 1975 (*Arizona Republic*, 1976b).

Utility costs also have increased rapidly since 1970, with the most rapid increase taking place between 1974 and 1975, a rate jump of approximately 30 percent for the nation as a whole (Federal Power Commission, 1975: 6). Utilities only went up 199 percent during the 1955 to 1975 period (about 10 percent per year); in fact, in the early 1960s there were even some decreases in utility rates due to economies of scale in production. Lozano (1972) and Thompson (1973) both indicated that utilities represented about 14 percent of all housing costs. In the future, a much bleaker picture is forecast. It is not uncommon to hear comments to the effect that our utility bills soon will equal our mortgage payments. If utility rates continue jumping at 30 percent per year, utility bills will double every two and one-half years. Housing costs will increase sharply as utility rates escalate, and utility costs will become a larger and larger component of the total.

THE NATURE OF THE HOUSING INDUSTRY

The instability of residential construction caused by cyclical swings in mortgage financing is widely recognized. Since World War II there have been at least five major shifts in the housing market. From 1963 to 1966 the market declined, recovered from 1966 to 1969, declined from 1969 to 1970, recovered from 1970 to 1973, and started to decline again in 1974. Once again there is a housing boom starting. In September 1976 new home starts were at the highest level since February of 1974. Apartment starts continue to be the weak link in a total housing recovery as multifamily construction continues to lag in this most recent upturn in the housing cycle.

Housing Trends

In 1966, 65 percent of all housing built consisted of single-family detached homes. This ratio fell to 54 percent in 1969 as mobile homes and apartments greatly increased their share of the market. The single-family detached home was written off in the early 1970s as uneconomical and inconsistent with a new life-style that supposedly was sweeping the country. Many observers argued that a mobile, young population and smaller average household size would continue to boost the demand for multifamily housing (First National City Bank, 1976).

Recently, the single-family detached home has made a remarkable comeback. The fact remains that most families apparently continue to want to own their own home and a plot of open space. A survey undertaken by *Professional Builder* magazine indicates that consumers prefer, by more than 94 percent, a home of their own (*Arizona Republic*, 1977).

Housing Construction

Most housing in the United States is built by approximately 100,000 localized builders who average only thirty-five full-time employees. The 112 firms identified by *House and Home* as the nation's largest builders in 1975 constructed 124,793 units, 10.6 percent of the total U.S. production for that year. These 112 were selected for the "biggest builders" list if they produced five hundred or more housing units in 1975 (*House and Home*, 1976).

Large building firms such as U.S. Home Corporation and Singer Housing Company can achieve significant cost advantages over small firms through large-scale developments, sophisticated management, bulk purchase of materials, and efficient production methods. However, the development of additional large-scale firms is restricted by market fluctuations and related difficulties in achieving and maintaining the continuity of large volumes of work. The cyclical swings in the housing market have been too short to allow big firms with their more efficient practices to become more dominant in the industry. Small firms, which are free from the overhead of long-range financial commitments, large management and sales staffs, extensive plant and equipment facilities, and material inventories, are often better able to cut back and survive in rough times.

The industrialization of housing would require an enormous capital investment combined with a high level of management skills, both of which require the long-range forecasting of production costs and sales volume. Because of cyclical activity, the housing industry has been forced to achieve flexibility through the use of unspecialized labor, small fixed capital, and mobile entrepreneurs.

Technological advancements on a major scale have been slow in coming to the housing industry; these innovations for the most part have been limited to factory production of wall, floor, and roof components, which ordinarily represent no more than 25 percent of the total cost, thus leaving only a small margin for cost reduction. Many of these innovations were initially blocked by local building codes (Weimer, Hoyt, and Bloom, 1972; 668–70).

Building codes tend to be presumptive in nature, attempting to assure proper construction through detailed specific regulations. They assume that every site and construction condition can be anticipated and covered by a single fixed ordinance. Insofar as new construction concepts differ from those on which the building codes were based, such regulations restrict innovation. The alternative to presumptive standards is performance standards that specify the performance to be achieved by various components of the building, but not the manner in which this performance is to be achieved.

Restrictive union work rules have also hampered many innovations in the mechanical, electrical and plumbing elements of housing. The National Commission on Urban Problems, after a careful, objective investigation of many specific charges, found that while unions have been involved in breakthroughs involving new products and methods, many restrictive practices that vary greatly from place to place and trade to trade do exist and hinder adoption of greater cost efficiencies. However, they also found that many of the practices could not be eliminated unless the construction industry was expanded and stabilized through a constant demand for labor year round (National Commission on Urban Problems, 1968: 465–75).

Housing Starts

The recent upward trend in housing starts appears to signal a halt to the severe two-year slump in home building. Housing starts in December 1976 ran at an annual rate of 1,940,000 units, up 51 percent from the earlier year's rate of 1,283,000. December's production boosted total actual housing starts for 1976 to 1,540,000 units from the depressed level of 1,160,000 in 1975. This was the largest output since the two million-plus annual production years of 1971, 1972, and 1973 (*Wall Street Journal,* 1976). Single-family construction accounted for some 70 percent of the industry's total activity in 1976, as compared to 55 percent in the early 1970s.

The recent housing recovery has been triggered by at least three economic factors:

1. Savings, accumulated by consumers who were reluctant to purchase durable goods during the recent period of economic uncertainty, have

provided the means by which people can make commitments to mortgages or make higher rent payments.

2. Heavy inflows of savings into mortgage lending institutions have tended to enlarge the supply of mortgage funds and thus ease the cost of mortgage credit.

3. Reduced inflationary pressures have allowed construction labor and material prices to fall or at least stabilize. Unemployment in the construction industry tended to reduce labor costs as workers competed for jobs (Leyer and Starr, 1976).

These three economic factors, along with revived consumer confidence, have lent a major impetus to the boom.

Figure 2-1 illustrates housing starts over the period 1959 to 1976. Aside from the importance of total housing starts, the graph clearly points out the drastic swings that have occurred in the housing market. The peak in housing production occurred between late 1971 and early 1973 when starts averaged 2.4 million at a seasonally adjusted annual rate. During the whole of the 1971–73 housing boom, private housing starts averaged 2.2 million per year, 35 percent higher than the previous three-year record established in the 1950–52 period. The 1950s averaged 1.5 million starts annually and the 1960s, 1.4 million (First National City Bank, 1976). Except for brief periods, production seldom exceeded 1.8 million, the proposed target advocated by the trade associations of the private building and private mortgage finance industries (Cohan, 1975).

It is reasonable to expect that total housing starts will continue to advance and that 1977 starts will be at a minimum annual rate of around 1.8 million. By past standards, 1977 may turn out to be a good year in terms of contributing to our housing needs.

Mortgage Financing

An absolutely essential ingredient in the housing market is credit availability. Only consumer expectations concerning the general economic future even come close to rivaling credit availability in importance. Since World War II, mortgage borrowing has placed the largest demand on long-term capital funds. The tremendous demand for mortgage money has not always been readily satisfied because adequate funds were not available at acceptable interest rates. The interaction in the economy among the private sector, fiscal policy, and monetary policy has often placed a severe strain on the mortgage market, especially during periods of tight money.

The private sector's decision whether to save or consume during a given period may be influenced by psychological rather than economic factors. Therefore, their savings versus consumption decision may be

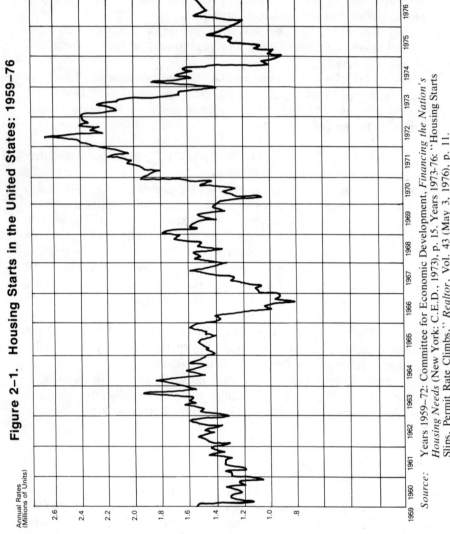

Figure 2–1.   Housing Starts in the United States: 1959–76

Source: Years 1959–72: Committee for Economic Development, *Financing the Nation's Housing Needs* (New York: C.E.D., 1973), p. 15. Years 1973-76: "Housing Starts Slips, Permit Rate Climbs," *Realtor,* Vol. 43 (May 3, 1976), p. 11.

contrary to public economic policy. When inflationary pressures caused by consumer demand are present in the economy, restrictive monetary and fiscal policy are usually necessary. The mortgage market is directly affected by the success with which savings associations, commercial banks, mutual savings banks, life insurance companies, and other mortgage-lending institutions can compete for scarce funds. Because of structural problems, government regulations, methods of operation, and other reasons, the mortgage-lending institutions, especially recently, have failed to provide adequate funds when needed at an acceptable interest rate.

The housing market is unusually vulnerable to cyclical fluctuations because of difficulties in attracting adequate financing. The ultimate borrowers of mortgage credit—households—appear to be more sensitive to interest rate increases than business borrowers. As interest rates rise, demand for residential mortgage funds falls. During a period of rising interest rates and tight monetary conditions, the thrift institutions, savings and loan associations, and mutual savings banks, which account for about 60 percent of all residential mortgage lending, suffer losses of loanable funds as depositors pull their funds out and place them in high-yield securities and short-term money markets. When credit conditions ease, sharp inflows of funds into these institutions create wide fluctuations in the opposite direction and an easing of mortgage interest rates.

Theoretically, the housing market can act as a counterbalance wheel for the economy. Residential housing construction stimulates the economy when interest rates are falling as the economy slows. As the economy recovers, housing construction drops off as families are no longer capable of competing with businesses at higher interest rates.

Unfortunately, during the last recession (1974–75), despite a record net flow of saving into thrift institutions, interest rates remained high relative to previous levels, according to John C. Hart, president of the National Association of Home Builders, "defying the law of supply and demand" (*Arizona Republic,* 1976b). As a result of such behavior in the mortgage market, the Federal Reserve Board's Philip Jackson has called for new ways to diversify the narrow base upon which housing credit exists (Wilson, 1976).

PERCEIVED BARRIERS TO HOUSING COST REDUCTIONS[b]

Past attempts at reducing housing costs have been hampered by biased opinions as to the appropriate cost reduction approach. For example,

---

[b] Most of this section is taken from Kelly (1975) and is used with the permission of the Texas Real Estate Research Center, Texas A & M University at College Station, Texas.

Operation Breakthrough assumed that mass production and technology would be the answer to "industrializing" house building. An obvious assumption of Operation Breakthrough was that we should produce houses similar to the existing stock because people would prefer to live in dwellings like the ones they had purchased in the past. Genuine innovation was eliminated from the project because the objective was to take an old idea about housing and do it better.

Builders' Conception of the Housing Market

Housing, lacking some of the sophisticated market research techniques utilized by other major industries, seems to base its future plans on past sales more than some industries. What has sold is an established fact; what will sell is mere speculation. This approach instinctively rejects all innovation; the public is forced to buy what is for sale and has no choice of new ideas in housing, about which it has no knowledge.

Several housing concepts are widely accepted as having the potential for reducing costs. Among these are industrialization of the building process, modular factory construction, and more dense housing forms such as cluster and townhouses. Many of these are rejected by developers as unacceptable to the market as they know it. Such perceptions of the market block not only the utilization of new ideas, but also the search for them. So long as old ideas sell and new ideas seem risky, builders avoid cost-reducing innovations.

Builders are reluctant to build in the price range below $20,000 because they feel that those families with incomes too low to buy more costly homes would be unwilling to buy a home with the amenities and quality level achievable for $20,000. Historically, builders have been reluctant to build small-unit, low-cost housing because their overhead per unit was high and their profit low. While in the past there has been a sufficient market for higher-priced homes to sustain the building industry, more recently the trend has been toward smaller homes with fewer amenities because soaring home prices have forced larger segments of lower-middle-income families out of the housing market.

Perceiving a market reluctance to accept innovation and then basing plans almost entirely on tested concepts, builders patronize their customers. The lower the price of the house, the more builders assume the market to be unsophisticated and the more emphasis is placed on decorative gimmicks to the detriment of construction quality.

When rising costs or other factors have made the utilization of innovative materials or techniques unavoidable, the most common practice among builders and materials manufacturers has been to disguise the new approach, to make it look like a conventional one. Many industrialized systems are aimed at producing houses that look and function like conventional houses. This preoccupation with making the unconventional seem conventional adds costs, reduces quality, inhibits the full development of innovative concepts, and adulterates the real merits of new products. Innovation in housing will not occur until builders perceive their market differently or are forced by industry conditions such as falling sales or rising costs to abandon established practices.

Enchantment with the Single-Family Home

The great American dream of homeownership is more often than not synonymous with the concept of owning a single-family detached home. In today's crowded environment, regardless of the size of the house, the single-family detached home requires a lot of land and achieves a low density of development.

In search of land on which to build single-family homes, developers move to the urban fringes, where land is cheaper. This low density, leapfrog growth pattern is costly for the city and the tax-paying homeowner. The further homes are spread apart, the greater the quantity of streets, water mains, sewers, and gas and electric lines required to link them together. Similarly, public services such as police and fire protection, and amenities such as parks and libraries, are extended and made increasingly more costly.

The single-family detached home is in itself a costly and inefficient proposition when compared with other housing forms. Relative to housing that clusters living units together in some manner, a single-family home requires more perimeter wall, which means more construction materials and labor and more exposure to the weather. This generates a need for more heating and cooling equipment, more energy consumption, and more exterior maintenance. Occupying more land, the single-family home requires investment in site improvements, landscaping, and maintenance.

It is widely assumed that those who live in single-family homes have a higher degree of privacy than those who live in attached dwellings such as cluster homes, townhouses or apartments. Perhaps if every home had a three-acre site there would be some merit to this assumption, but it does not hold for typical tract houses planned five or six to an acre. Merely placing homes on separate lots is no assurance of privacy at all.

It is also assumed that single-family homes offer much more outdoor space for gardening and play area for children. Measured in terms of square feet of space, this is obviously true; each family has access to more privately owned exterior space. The question is: "How usable and used is this space?" Front yards and side yards tend to be purely decorative in nature, having too little privacy for family use or entertaining and too little space and too much landscaping to be a real play area for children.

Perhaps the American dream needs to shake loose from its rural antecedents and seek out housing forms more suited to the content of twentieth-century urban America. No one really contends anymore that the suburbs offer the best of life in both the country and the city. Maybe we should now question whether suburbia and the single-family home offer much of either.

Prescriptive Zoning and Building Codes

Prescriptive zoning and building codes attempt to assure proper planning or construction through specific detailed regulations. Zoning utilizes such devices as minimum lot size, building setbacks, height limitations, and maximum densities. Building codes specify fire safety requirements such as exiting, structural requirements, and the use of materials in areas such as plumbing and electrical systems. The problem for new housing concepts with such prescriptive zoning and code regulations is precisely that they are "prescriptive."

Zoning reflects the widely held notion that low-density housing is good and high density, if not bad, is at least much less good. The American dream, the single-family detached home, is, in fact, given by law the number-one priority in the development of a zoned city. What we have unwittingly done is to require by law suburban sprawl and all the related problems of traffic congestion, air pollution, high-cost public services and utilities, squandering of land, and loss of community.

To avoid conflicts among different activities such as housing and industry, zoning isolates each in an area containing only other similar uses. The result has been fragmentation of normal patterns of daily life—houses here, offices over there, stores down the road—and the attempt to reassemble them with automobiles and freeways. Both building codes and zoning ordinances are obstacles to new cost-reducing directions in housing. Ultimately, zoning may prove the most difficult to revise, for it is firmly rooted in American tradition and thinking, and changes would undoubtedly generate political turmoil in every city.

PRESCRIPTION: A SHOPPING LIST OF REMEDIES

Many of the woes of housing are directly traceable to problems of providing adequate financing for residential construction. It is almost impossible to overemphasize the degree to which housing is affected by fiscal and monetary policies. Expansionary policies are often instituted to stimulate employment at the expense of increased inflation. Increased inflation drives up the price of construction materials and labor and, consequently, the cost of housing. Interest charges rise, the money market tightens, and the interest cost of housing, already the biggest item, makes homeownership prohibitive. Thus, residential construction plunges.

Coordinate Monetary, Fiscal, and Housing Policies

Alignment of monetary and fiscal policies consistent with our housing goals is needed desperately. The objective of this alignment should be to provide adequate mortgage financing for whatever our socially determined housing starts goal will be, whether the target is 1.8 million annual starts or the 2.6 million originally suggested as our annual housing needs by the Kaiser Committee Report (President's Committee on Urban Housing, 1968: 39–50).

The supply of funds for mortgage financing is provided primarily by the individual propensity to save part of one's disposable income in any one of a number of savings or thrift institutions. Demand for these funds arises from four major areas: business borrowing; mortgage loans; consumer and personal loans; and governmental financing, which includes federal, state, and local borrowing. Business borrowing tends to vary directly with profits; as profits decline, so does the demand for capital. As the economy slows down, the demand for consumer credit also slackens.

Monetary policy carried out through open-market operations, discount rates, reserve requirements, margin requirements, or moral suasion normally provides a stimulant to a weak economy and restraint to an overheated one. Fiscal policy through deficit or surplus spending should exert an appropriate contractionary or expansionary influence on the economy. Theoretically, both fiscal and monetary policy should be countercylical.

The rate of interest, which is the price of borrowed money, is the linkage by which monetary and fiscal policies influence the housing market. Interest rates result from the relationship between the supply and demand for funds. Historically, interest rates have peaked near the top of the business cycle, declined throughout the downturn, and then rebounded as business activity began to expand.

The housing market, acting as a counterbalance wheel for the entire economy, has responded with a high degree of sensitivity to fluctuations in interest rates. Housing starts increased as the economy cooled and interest rates dropped, and housing starts decreased as interest rates rose from an overheated economy. Unfortunately, as figure 2-1 clearly shows, the cyclical fluctuations have been too severe to allow the housing market to adopt efficient, large-scale production techniques. Through interest rates, determined by monetary and fiscal policies, cyclical disruptions in housing finance should be curtailed or at least ameliorated.

Broaden Sources of Mortgage Funds

One of the criticisms mentioned earlier was that the housing industry is too dependent on thrift institutions. The justification for the criticism apparently was based upon the fact that in recent months, when the savings and loan associations experienced large inflows of funds, interest rates did not decline adequately to meet housing's needs. Recently, builders have been plotting a strategy to tap pension funds for mortgages. According to Preston Martin, president of PMI Corporation, a San Francisco insurer of conventional mortgages: "Over the next five years pensions are going to be *the* major new source of funds for housing" (Wells, 1976).

Tapping additional mortgage funds has been an objective of the housing industry for a number of years. Mortgage-backed securities issued by the Federal Home Loan Mortgage Corporation (FHLMC), the Federal National Mortgage Association (FNMA), and the Government National Mortgage Association (GNMA) are examples of previous attempts which have had some degree of success in stabilizing the mortgage market.

Until recently, real estate investment trusts (REITs) were viewed as a potential means by which the base of loanable funds could be broadened. Those REITs that were able to survive the recent recession may become viable organizations in the future once they have made the necessary adjustments in their operations based upon what was learned during the recession.

The existing instrumentalities for channeling funds from the securities market to the housing sector have considerable potential for moderating cyclical instability in residential mortgage investment and for augmenting the supply of mortgage loans in the long run. The interregional flow of mortgage funds has already been facilitated by FHLMC, FNMA and GNMA. In the future, real estate backed securities should provide access to larger nationwide capital pools. Efforts to interest private and public pension funds in direct residential mortgage investment span two decades and have had relatively meager results. Whether or not these recent attempts to attract pension funds into financing housing will be successful remains to be seen.

Revamp Mortgage-Lending Institutions

The thrift institutions that put up most of the money for mortgages have to borrow on short term the money they lend long term. This is one of the most significant reasons for the feast-and-famine problem in mortgage finance. When money is tight, institutions find themselves stuck with a mortgage portfolio paying such low interest that they find it hard to bid in the open market for new money to lend.

Variable interest rates would allow mortgage-lenders to avoid the profit squeeze and remain in the capital market during tight money periods. To the home-buyer with a variable interest rate mortgage (VRM), an increase in interest rates would result in higher monthly payments and/or an extension of the amortization period, depending upon the terms of the contract. The converse applies if interest rates were to decline. One side effect of the VRM could be increased interest costs paid by the borrower, thus increasing his housing costs. On the other hand, available mortgage funds might stabilize housing production and reduce initial home cost.

Savings and loan associations in several states have experimented with VRMs. California appears to be leading in their adoption by several of its major savings and loan associations. Comments with regard to its acceptance have been very favorable; in fact, California banks are beginning to follow major state-chartered savings and loan associations into VRMs. The first to do so was Wells Fargo Bank of San Francisco, but the giant Bank of America is also looking into variables (Keene, 1976).

If interest rate ceilings were removed on mortgages and on savings accounts, interest rates could vary with changing market conditions. By being able to raise rates paid on savings, savings and loan associations could attract additional deposits during periods of tight money. As it now stands, the Federal Home Loan Bank Board must consult with the Federal Reserve and the Federal Deposit Insurance Corporation before altering the ceiling. Government ceilings on rates paid by savings and loan associations have prevented them from competing for funds during periods of rising interest rates.

State usury ceilings also present serious problems for the rates that could be charged if mortgage rates were determined through market competition. If feasible, these provisions should be removed or raised well above the average rate over recent years.

One final suggestion made by the Committee for Economic Development (CED) for revamping mortgage-lending institutions was to extend the responsibility of the federal intermediaries in protecting against cyclical disruption. CED urged that a clear set of guidelines be developed for the federal intermediaries (FNMA and GNMA), setting out as precisely as possible their roles and responsibilities as part of a coherent national housing policy (CED, 1973: 18).

Attack Total Housing Costs

As mentioned earlier, total housing costs over the life of the mortgage are composed of several elements, with interest rates accounting for about 40 percent. Interest rates were discussed in the preceding section as the linkage connecting monetary, fiscal, and housing policies. Some suggested approaches to attacking the other housing cost barriers are listed below:

1. Reduce the initial cost of housing to reflect initial cost savings as well as future savings since the initial cost is the basis of determining interest, taxes, and insurance.
2. Increase initial outlays to lower maintenance, repair, and utility bills.
3. Increase the density of dwellings to reduce walls, landscaping, and land costs as well as associated labor and material costs.
4. Curb the speculation in undeveloped land through land banking so that speculative exchanges of property do not drive up land prices.
5. Reduce carpentry expense by using factory-assembled components and panels whenever feasible.
6. Experiment with new technology and materials.
7. Eliminate the restrictive union work rules which set wages at higher than competitive rates and tie any future wage increases to increases in productivity.

If most of the elements of housing costs are attacked simultaneously, the studies by Lozano (1972) and Thompson (1973) have concluded that total costs could be reduced by only about 15 percent or less.

The efficiency of the building industry can also be improved through more effective management, which includes planning, organization, motivation, and control. Unprofitable builders create waste, which drives up the cost of housing. Many home-builders who have gone out of business might have survived if they had possessed adequate management and financial controls.

Currently, the size of a typical house is being reduced and amenities are being eliminated in order to provide a "basic" house at an affordable price. If the market becomes dissatisfied with a basic house lacking design and amenities, the home-building industry will be forced to be creative in providing a *new* house through land-use planning, design, materials, and technology.

SUMMARY

The right to own one's home is viewed as fundamental to the American way of life with citizenship and homeownership mutually supportive and necessary to our democratic system. Private enterprise is primarily responsible for providing housing for our citizens; where it fails it becomes the social responsibility of government to support our housing goals. Unfortunately, the government has often been responsible for the failure of private industry to respond adequately to housing needs. Failure to curb inflation caused by government spending has hiked construction costs. Inflation and high interest rates have driven purchasers from the housing market. The irony of this situation is that as a result of inflation caused by government spending, the government has had to institute costly public housing programs to supplant private industry.

The home-building industry and mortgage-lending institutions have fulfilled the American dream for many families. The problem with the housing industry is that it is very deeply committed to current methods of planning, design, construction, marketing, and financing. It seems highly improbable that the industry will either seek or accept new housing technology or forms of housing as long as the present forms are still marketable in sufficient quantities.

The rising cost of utilities, insurance, and property taxes will force innovation upon the housing industry. Already the size of the typical house is being reduced and many amenities are being removed to make the price more affordable. Any dissatisfaction with such a "basic" house will force the home-building industry to develop a *new* dwelling using different land-use planning, design, materials, or technology.

It seems quite unlikely that any of today's housing cost problems will be alleviated by a single stroke of technological genius. The problem is much more pervasive. Solutions must be sought not only in technology, but over the full gamut of design and planning, financing, taxes, insurance, maintenance, and utility costs.

REFERENCES

Arizona Republic (1976a) "Most Housing Woes Involve Rising Costs." (29 February).
———— (1976b) "20-Year Cost Rise in Home Upkeep Put at 303%." (10 March).
———— (1977) "Industry Poll Shows Consumers Seek Privacy, Security." (23 January).
Cohan, Miles L. (1975) "Should There Be an Annual Target for New Housing Starts?" *The MGIC Newsletter* (December): 1–3.
Committee for Economic Development (1973) *Financing the Nation's Housing Needs.* New York: Committee for Economic Development.
Davis, Joseph M. (1977) "Reducing Cost Barriers in the Housing Market." *Arizona Business* 24 (January): 17–26.
Federal Power Commission (1975) *Typical Electric Bills.* Washington, D.C.: Federal Power Commission.
First National City Bank (1976) *Monthly Economic Letter* (January): 11–15.
House and Home (1976) "What Does 'Biggest Builder' Mean?" 49 (March): 70.
Keene, Jenness (1976) "Southern California Banks Test the S & L's Variable-Rate Mortgage." *House and Home* 49 (March): 28.
Kelley, Frank S. (1975) "Construction Technology and Low Cost Housing in Texas." Report prepared by OMNIPLAN of Dallas, Texas and sponsored by the Texas Real Estate Research Center, Texas A & M University (August).
Leyer, Richard R. and Mark Starr (1976) "Bouncing Back-Mortgage Availability, Consumer Confidence Spur Housing Upturn." *Wall Street Journal* (April 5).

Lozano, Eduardo E. (1972) "Housing Costs and Alternative Cost Reducing Policies." *Journal of the American Institute of Planners* 38 (March): 176–81.

National Commission on Urban Problems (1968) *Building The American City*. Washington, D.C.: Government Printing Office.

President's Committee on Urban Housing (1968) *A Decent Home*. Washington, D.C.: Government Printing Office.

Realtor (1976a) "Home Sales Prices Climb Again in March." (2 May).

———— (1976b) "Single-Family Home Sales Rise in September." (8 November).

Simison, Robert L. (1975) "Out in the Cold: Many House Hunters Find New Homes Are Beyond Their Means." *Wall Street Journal* (December 10).

Thompson, J. Neils (1973) "Assessment of the Character and Trends of Housing Technology and Industrialized Building of Housing in the United States." Austin, Texas: The Center for Building Research, University of Texas at Austin.

Wall Street Journal (1976) "Housing Starts Last Month Hit 3½ Year High." (19 January).

Weimer, Arthur M., Homer Hoyt, and George Bloom (1972) *Real Estate*. New York: Ronald Press Company.

Wells, H. Clarke (1976) "Big Builders Plot New Strategy to Tap Pension Funds for Mortgages." *House and Home* 51 (February): 9.

Wilson, Stan (1976) "Fed's Jackson Warns: Too Little Housing and It's Too Expensive." *House and Home* 51 (February): 5.

❋ *Part II*

The Environment

✳ *Chapter 3*

The Dynamics of
Neighborhood Change[a]

James T. Little

As general objectives of national housing policy, a "decent
home" and a "suitable living environment," are admirable;
in practice, they offer no substantive guide to policy development. The adjectives "decent" and "suitable" are both value terms, and
although some agreement has been reached as to a definition of acceptable
physical standards, we are still unable to define "suitable living environment" with any precision. Moreover, only very recently has the role of
the neighborhood environment in the operation of the housing market
been investigated in any depth. That neighborhood environment is an
important consideration in residential decisions is so obvious that it is
natural to question why it has not been included in formal analysis of
housing market behavior. The most important reason is that economists
do not fully understand the operation of markets characterized by inter-
dependency of consumption. Neighborhood effects inherently involve
locational interdependencies that under fairly general conditions produce
violations of the conditions required for equilibrium in competitive markets. Thus, insofar as formal analysis is concerned, the introduction of
neighborhood effects into the analysis of housing markets involves the
study of unfamiliar allocation mechanisms and disequilibrium behavior
for markets. Yet if the goal of a "suitable living environment" is to be at
all meaningful, these issues must be addressed. An understanding of the
nature and significance of locational externalities in the housing market is

[a] Much of the research on which this paper is based was done in collaboration with Hugh
Nourse and Donald Phares of the University of Missouri-St. Louis. I am also indebted to
Charles Leven of Washington University and Louise Taylor of the Maxwell School, Syra-
cuse University, for their comments on an earlier version.

63

not only essential for defining neighborhood quality. It is also necessary if the over-all effects of policy decisions are to be predicted with any degree of accuracy.

While many of the technical problems remain open, we have progressed to the point where we can describe broad outlines of a theory of residential location decisions which take neighborhood interdependencies into account. Our purpose here is not any further extension of this theory, but rather to summarize where we stand at present and to note the more important policy implications. In particular, we will attempt to answer two central questions:

1. Which locational characteristics are important in households' residential decisions and how important are these relative to the physical quality of units? Or put another way, how do the households themselves define "suitable living environment" and to what extent do such considerations determine prices and individual locational choices?
2. What are the interactions between neighborhood characteristics and the neighborhood succession process[b] and to what extent is succession a function of these neighborhood effects as opposed to the physical nature of the housing stock?

We begin by describing the general nature of the housing market in which housing is taken as a multidimensional bundle of characteristics, with neighborhood characteristics representing one set of dimensions, and consider the implications of existing empirical evidence on the nature of households' tastes. Next, a model of neighborhood succession—the arbitrage model—is described, and finally we comment on empirical studies based on this model.

THE MARKET FOR HOUSING ATTRIBUTES

In purchasing or renting a dwelling unit, a household receives the right to use the physical structure and land parcel (subject to constraints imposed by zoning and building codes), the right to consume the goods and services produced by the local government, and the responsibility for associated tax liabilities. In addition to the legal rights, the household receives a bundle of attributes that can be described as *site specific*. These include access to employment and commercial centers, ambient air quality, noise levels, and other externalities associated with the use of adjacent sites. In very general terms, any attribute of the site which affects

---

[b] Defined as a change in a neighborhood's socioeconomic composition. Refer to Leven, Little, Nourse, and Read (1976) for more detail.

households' evaluations of alternative sites would be included in this bundle. Thus, if households have well-defined tastes for the socio-economic status of their neighbors, neighborhood characteristics such as income level and racial mix of the surrounding area become dimensions of the bundle of attributes. This bundle for any residential site includes five basic groups of characteristics: the physical features of the structure and parcel, access, the local public sector, the neighborhood, and the environment. It is this collection we refer to as the housing bundle.

Thus, rather than being a single homogeneous commodity, housing is differentiated by the attributes contained in the housing bundle, and the housing market is more properly described as the market for residential sites or the market for housing bundles. Furthermore, when taking this approach, it is improper to speak of quantities of housing consumed by an individual household. However, once it is asserted that households have preference rankings for alternative bundles, the natural measuring device becomes this preference order. Thus, more housing can be interpreted as better housing according to individual preferences.

At any point in time, a household will evaluate the available supply of housing in terms of its tastes and determine a maximum price it is willing to pay for a given site. This maximal bid for a site will depend not only on preferences over housing bundles, but also on preferences for other commodities, and the household's income. It would be expected that if a household prefers housing bundle A to bundle B, then its bid for A will exceed its bid for B. Similarly, sellers establish a minimum price (the reservation price) at which they will sell. Effectively, the market reduces to trades between a single buyer and seller with the price established between the maximal bid, and the reservation price and the final trading price determined by competition from other potential trading partners. Buyers will choose trading partners so as to maximize the difference between their bids and market price, while sellers maximize the difference between final sale price and their reservation price.[c]

Two important characteristics of this process should be noted. First, any participant who is both a potential buyer and a potential seller has the option of choosing himself as a trading partner. This implies that he will

---

[c] This market can be modeled in the framework of a trading game. As strategies, players choose trading partners, and by definition no mixed strategies are allowed. Payoffs for buyers are the difference between maximum bids and market price; payoffs for sellers are the difference between reservation price and market price. Both buyers and sellers will choose trading partners so as to maximize their payoffs. It is through prices that equilibrium is achieved; as prices adjust, payoffs adjust. Each buyer is matched with a single seller so that each is maximizing his gains from trade. The market prices that produce this equilibrium are, in general, not unique. This corresponds to the fact that in actual markets there is some room for negotiation between buyer and seller. A fairly elementary exposition of such games is given in Shapley and Shubik (1972).

choose another site only if his net payoff from selling his initial site and buying another is positive. Thus, any household that trades its unit for another must be better off. It does not, however, imply that the household considers the second housing bundle superior to its initial bundle but means only that the household's utility from consumption of all goods and services has increased. However, some information as to households' preferences can be inferred from behavior. If a household chooses to move, then it must prefer the chosen unit to those with lower prices. Put very simply, if a household purchases site A for $25,000 when site B is selling for $15,000, then it must prefer A to B.

So far we have assumed that buyers are certain as to the housing bundle associated with a particular residential site. For some attributes, this is a reasonable supposition. The size of the land parcel is given; the structural characteristics are relatively fixed and are in any case under the control of the household. However, even in the short run, the household cannot be certain as to the neighborhood attributes associated with a site. These attributes depend on the market process itself; that is, on who lives where. Thus, from the point of view of the individual household, neighborhood characteristics are uncertain, and thus the utility of occupying a particular site is itself uncertain. A similar argument holds with respect to sellers: the reservation price that is established will depend on the expected (in the sense of mathematical expectation) utility of the site. Thus, bids and reservation prices will depend on participants' perceptions of the likelihood of various outcomes; a higher perceived probability of a less desirable bundle will lead to lower bids and reservation prices. Furthermore, if the market participants are risk averse, we would expect that greater uncertainty (in the sense of a larger variance in outcomes) would, ceteris paribus, lead to lower bids and reservation prices and consequently to lower market prices. Thus, both market prices and the assignment of households to residential sites will depend on households' preferences and income and their expectations of the attributes of residential sites. As we shall see later, these expectations play a critical role in rapid neighborhood change.

While the attribute approach does increase the realism of our description of the allocation process, it would contribute little to our understanding if households' decisions were dominated by structural attributes, with neighborhood and local public sector considerations entering only at the margin. However, evidence based on observed choices indicates that neighborhood and local public sector attributes are important elements in households' decisions. A study of market behavior in the St. Louis SMSA suggests the following (Little, 1976):

1. Of all neighborhood attributes, median income of residents is more important than racial composition for households' decisions.

2. Households are willing to pay a premium for sites at a distance from concentration of nonwhite population and, by inference, prefer neighborhoods with a low probability of socioeconomic change.
3. Households reveal themselves to be somewhat more sensitive to the racial composition of adjoining neighborhoods than the racial composition of their own neighborhood.
4. While structural attributes are important in decisions, they are considered in combination with neighborhood and local public sector attributes; households place substantial premiums on units in "desirable" locations and discount low-income, low public service neighborhoods.

An immediate and important implication of the findings is that a housing policy based on the filtering notion—in particular, one that seeks to improve housing by an upgrading of the stock via new construction—can produce locational shifts and changes in residential patterns that offset physical improvement through their effects on neighborhood and local public sector attributes (Leven, Little, Nourse, and Read, 1976). Putting it another way, if we ignore location-specific attributes, we might conclude that improved physical quality has high value. Whereas, in fact, a substantial portion of the observed premium for sites of high physical quality results from the high quality neighborhood and local public sector attributes that often accompany these units. Thus, failure to recognize the importance of all dimensions of the housing bundle will result in an overestimate of the benefits of a filtering strategy, lack of recognition of the possible deleterious relocation effects induced by such a strategy and, perhaps more important, a policy strategy that neglects the potential of the neighborhood and public sector dimensions in improving over-all housing quality.

THE ARBITRAGE MODEL OF NEIGHBORHOOD SUCCESSION

One clear implication of the foregoing analysis is that neighborhood succession—defined as change in a neighborhood's socioeconomic composition—is a synergistic process. Neighborhood succession will alter the position of a set of units in households' preference hierarchies, and since these ranks determine demand patterns, they may in turn produce another round of succession. More generally, neighborhood succession is one manifestation of housing market dynamics, with succession itself as one of the important factors in inducing locational change.

The arbitrage model provides a framework within which market dynamics can be analyzed. This model has several precursors; most notably, the work of the "human ecologists" (Park, Burgers, McKensie, 1925; Hoyt, 1939) and the model of housing market equilibrium in the presence of racial aversion developed by Bailey (1959). The basic assumptions of the arbitrage model are (1) other things being equal, all households prefer neighborhoods having higher-income residents to those with predominantly lower-income households; (2) whites have a preference for neighborhoods with a low proportion of nonwhite; and (3) all households are risk averse in the sense that they have a preference for neighborhoods with low (perceived) probabilities of socioeconomic change. It is assumed that households can be classified into groups according to their race and income, with this classification in turn defining "submarkets" on the demand side of the overall housing market.

As a simple illustration, consider a case in which there are only two submarkets—high and low income—and all units are identical except for the neighborhood component. Under the assumption that all households prefer to live in areas of high average income, two equilibrium residential distributions can occur. In one, each income group is equally distributed over all neighborhoods; since the average income of neighborhoods is then the same, households are indifferent among all sites. However, this equilibrium is unstable in the sense that any perturbation will send the system toward the second equilibrium, and thus it is unlikely that the market would reach such a distribution. The second equilibrium is one in which each group lives in an exclusive neighborhood. This equilibrium is characterized by a price system in which the highest price prevails in the interior of the high-income area with successively lower prices as one moves from the high-income side of the boundary (between the high-income and low-income area) to the low-income side of the boundary to the interior of the low-income area.

Now suppose the system has achieved the second equilibrium and let this equilibrium be disturbed by a reduction in the supply of sites in the low-income area. The direct effect of this reduction in supply is an increase in price in both the interior and at the boundary of the low-income area. If the boundary price rises sufficiently, it will become profitable for owners of property on the high-income side of the boundary to shift these units to the low-income submarket. Thus, we would observe an increase in the price of high-income boundary units which in turn would induce an increase in price in the interior of the high-income area. The increase in price in the interior of the high-income market (and the corresponding shortfall in supply of high-income sites) will induce the purchase of new housing, thereby increasing supply.

The effect of the reduction in supply in the low-income market then is the "arbitraging" of boundary units from the high-income market to the low-income market in response to the higher price (and therefore higher profit) in the latter. However, there is an important secondary effect; the transfer of boundary units to the low-income market shifts the boundary toward the interior of the high-income area. As a result, a group of units that prior to arbitrage were in the interior of the high-income area and therefore commanded a premium are now on the boundary between the two submarkets and will be priced as boundary units. Even though the reduction in supply in low-income areas may have raised the price of sites generally, there is a possible *decline* in price (and capital losses for their owners) for these sites which were formerly in the interior of the high-income area.

To summarize, the reduction in the supply of sites in the low-income submarket has the following effects: (1) an increase in prices in the low-income submarket; (2) the shifting of units from the high-income side of the boundary into the low-income submarket in response to higher values; (3) the movement of the boundary toward the interior of the high-income submarket; (4) a reduction in the price (and capital value) of sites made part of the boundary market as a result of the shift; and (5) a general upward pressure on prices for sites other than those in the new boundary market. Thus, the net effect is to increase prices (which results in capital gains) for units in the interiors of the newly defined submarkets, with a reduction in price and capital losses for units in the boundary market.

This description of the adjustment process also applies when the stimulus is an increase in demand in the low-income market or an increase in supply in the high-income market. In both cases, the boundary will move towards the interior of the high-income area. The one difference occurs with an increase in supply in the high-income area. Rather than a general increase in prices, we would expect a decline. Thus, rents decline as do capital values. However, owners of units shifted from the interior of the high-income area to the boundary experience an additional decline in capital values resulting from proximity to the low-income area.

This analysis is simplified in the extreme, for it involves only two submarkets. However, it can be extended to any number of submarkets so long as the assumptions concerning the nature of household preferences are valid. In this more complex system, we would expect a series of exclusive neighborhoods with the same kind of general relationships between boundary and interior price; that is, the highest prices prevailing in the interior of the highest-ranked neighborhoods with boundary markets at each interface of a higher and lower ranked area. Clearly, the dynamics are also more complex; for example, a shift in the boundary between any two submarkets will have effects on other submarkets. For instance, if there are three income groups, a shift in the boundary between the low-income and middle-income area would also affect the demand at the boundary between the middle-income and high-income area and would result in a shift of this boundary as well. Thus, a change in the supply-demand conditions in a single submarket will trigger a series of capital gains and losses. But what is most important is that these capital gains and losses will be concentrated in particular neighborhoods; that is, all units transferred to the boundary of a submarket at a lower level in the market hierarchy will experience a capital loss.

The potential for capital losses as a result of boundary shifts suggests a role for expectations in the process. Consider the position of an owner-occupant living not on, but close to, the boundary. If the boundary should shift towards him, his unit would become part of the boundary market. Should he remain in the unit, he will be worse off, since he would be living in proximity to a socioeconomic group that is, to him, less desirable. However, if he were to relocate after the shift of the boundary, he would suffer a capital loss. The alternative to the less desirable housing bundle or a capital loss is to move deeper into the interior of his submarket's area *in advance of the shift in the boundary*. But if all potential purchasers of this site have similar expectations as to movements of the boundary, the market price of the unit must decline. The higher the perceived probability of a shift in the boundary or the more risk averse are potential buyers, the larger this decline. The fall in prices for units proximate to the boundary must result in price declines for boundary units themselves, and as the difference between prices on either side of the boundary decreases, the boundary will in fact move. Thus, expectations of a change in the boundary are self-realizing. Furthermore, once the boundary has changed, the same process may be repeated for sites not actually in, but proximate to, the new boundary. This suggests that a market characterized by frequent shifts in boundaries may become dynamically unstable as a result of expectations. That is, even if the original supply-demand factors that produced the initial boundary shifts are no longer operative, expectations in and of themselves may lead to rapidly shifting boundaries, changing prices, and rapid turnover in neighborhood occupancy.

The instability of the boundary and near-boundary markets is compounded by the impact of uncertainty on the lending decisions by financial institutions. In making a real estate loan, the financial institution faces two risks: first, that the borrower will be unable to meet the terms of the loan; second, that should default occur, the value of the collateral—the market value of the unit—is uncertain. Given that financial institutions are risk averse, increased uncertainty as to price or the expectation of lower future prices will result in more stringent lending terms. Since at some point these terms will increase the probability of default, increased price risk will ultimately lead to a refusal to make loans. As price expectations apply to all units in a given area, the refusal to loan manifests itself as "redlining."

To summarize, the arbitrage model views the succession process as driven by two forces acting in combination: changing supply conditions in particular submarkets, and expectations as to shifts in the boundaries between submarkets. To some extent, it is a short-run model in that it takes the physical nature of the housing stock and the general pattern of demand for access as givens. Thus, in the long run, other factors enter into the explanation of neighborhood succession. One important example of such a longer-run factor is the succession induced by a reduction in transport costs throughout an urban area. As is well known, such a decrease will generally lower the amount that households will bid for sites close to employment centers. This shift in the spatial pattern of demand may in turn induce a rearrangement of areas occupied by various submarkets; for example, the replacement of middle-income families by lower-income households in inner city neighborhoods. However, the fact that in the long run other phenomena affect neighborhood succession does not negate the importance of the arbitrage model as an explanation of short-run changes. Furthermore, it is these short-run changes that are of greatest significance from a policy standpoint. Perhaps the most important conclusion to emerge from the model is that succession can occur even in the absence of changes in fundamental supply and demand factors. In the presence of high levels of uncertainty and with no market for the trading of these risks (other than that provided by real estate speculators), the market cannot operate efficiently. The decay and abandonment of neighborhoods with a high quality housing stock which has occurred in many cities is one symptom of this inefficiency.

THE TRANSITION HOUSING MARKET[d]

The arbitrage model predicts that as the boundary between two submarkets shifts, the initial effect is an increase in price for the sites that are shifted from one submarket to another. In fact, it is these higher prices which induce the transfer. However, as the increase in supply works itself through the submarket to which the transfer has occurred, some moderating of boundary prices is to be expected. In addition, if the boundary shift involves the movement of a lower-level submarket into the area occupied by a higher-level submarket, we would expect a decline in the price of units on the new boundary. Furthermore, if uncertainty is operative, we would also expect a decline in the price of units that have become proximate to the new boundary. Rapid price declines will in turn be associated with a lowering in the economic status of neighborhood residents, racial change, or both.

An example of the operation of arbitrage is provided by the behavior of

[d] This section draws from Little (1973).

the housing market in University City, Missouri (a suburb of St. Louis) over the period 1961 to 1971. During the second five years of this period, University City experienced fairly rapid racial change accompanied by a modest decline in the economic status of its residents. What makes University City appropriate for a study of the market process is that it can be divided into six fairly homogeneous neighborhoods using census tract definitions. However, substantial differences exist across these neighborhoods in the age and quality of the housing stock and in the initial socioeconomic status of neighborhood residents. Furthermore, since all neighborhoods are contained in a single political jurisdiction, public goods and service levels are the same for all neighborhoods. Figure 3-1 shows neighborhood definitions and select housing and neighborhood characteristics.

Three indices were constructed to measure patterns of housing market behavior. The first is the turnover rate for owner-occupied units and is measured as the sales of such units in each year as a percentage of all owner-occupied dwellings. The second measure is an index of housing prices by neighborhood. This index is based on a sample of transactions which includes all sales insured under the FHA and VA programs and a sample of conventionally financed mortgages. Using multiple regression techniques, prices were standardized for differences in the structural attributes of the units. The price index was then computed by averaging the standardized price for all transactions in a census tract in a given year, converted to a base 100 index (using the average standardized price in tract 2157 in 1961 as the base). Thus, the index measures relative prices (undeflated) of a standard unit across tracts and over time. The final measure is an index of neighborhood socioeconomic status developed by Nourse and Phares (1974). This index is based on the occupation of household heads from a sample of properties in each neighborhood. These occupations were placed in decile ranks of the national income distribution as derived from federal census data. The index number is the median decile rank for each neighborhood sample. These three indices are listed year-by-year in table 3-1.

In 1960, University City was an upper middle to upper income community with virtually no nonwhite residents. However, by this time the area to the immediate east of University City (the west end of St. Louis City) and the area to the northeast (Wellston) had experienced substantial racial and income status change (figure 3-1). Thus, the two eastern tracts of University City, tracts 2160 and 2161, can be taken either as boundary neighborhoods or neighborhoods proximate to the boundary. It is significant, then, that these two tracts had the lowest relative prices in 1961. This in spite of the fact that tract 2161 had the highest socioeconomic status as measured by median decile rank. In 1962 and 1963, as the first

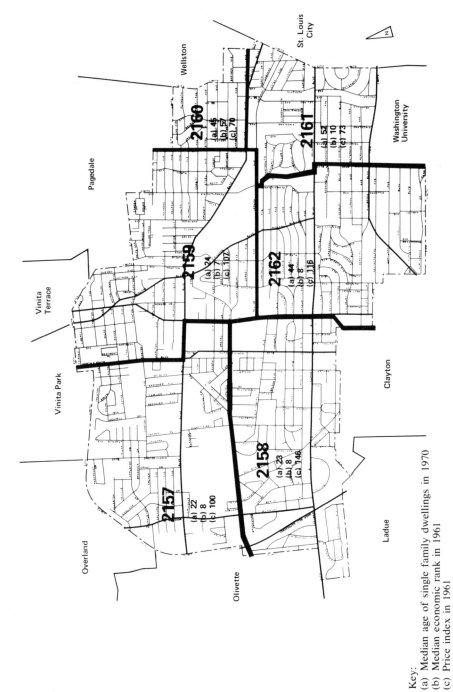

Figure 3–1 University City by Census Tract

Key:
(a) Median age of single family dwellings in 1970
(b) Median economic rank in 1961
(c) Price index in 1961

Table 3–1.   Select Indices of Housing Market Behavior in University City by Census Tract: 1961–71

| | Census Tracts[a] | | | | | | | | | | | | | | | | | |
| | 2157 | | | 2158 | | | 2159 | | | 2160 | | | 2161 | | | 2162 | | |
YEAR	T	P	R	T	P	R	T	P	R	T	P	R	T	P	R	T	P	R
1961	4.8	100	8	4.6	146	8	5.9	107	7	4.6	70	8	7.1	73	10	4.6	116	8
1962	6.0	98	8	6.3	110	8	4.5	91	7	4.6	73	7	2.8	92	10	6.7	116	8
1963	5.7	76	7	3.1	110	9	6.6	81	7	9.3	84	7	12.8	91	10	8.3	105	8
1964	6.1	88	—	10.5	107	—	6.2	76	—	6.2	76	—	8.1	85	—	5.5	101	—
1965	8.9	91	8	8.8	139	9	11.6	96	6	16.9	86	7	9.0	81	10	9.5	114	8
1966	7.8	91	8	9.7	124	8	11.3	94	6	12.9	52	7	9.0	96	10	9.5	105	8
1967	13.5	99	8	10.6	136	8	13.1	95	6	13.9	81	8	9.0	87	9	8.5	112	8
1968	11.0	96	7	6.6	136	8	13.8	93	6	16.5	85	7	10.0	100	9	5.7	131	8
1969	11.5	97	7	9.4	134	8	11.6	92	6	13.9	70	6	11.9	83	7	7.9	112	8
1970	12.3	96	7	7.8	113	8	9.3	86	6	7.7	71	4	11.9	81	9	8.9	110	8
1971	12.0	89	7	7.0	119	8	10.3	84	6	10.3	81	4	11.9	80	10	2.2	112	7
Change in Percent Nonwhite 1960–70	26.3			8.3			39.0			46.1			14.7			4.8		
Percent Change in Price 1961/62 to 1970/71	−6.6			−5.7			−14.0			7.7			−1.2			−4.3		

[a]T = owner-occupied turnover rate
P = price index
R = median income rank
— = no data available

nonwhites began to move into these tracts, we observe that, as expected, prices increased.[e] At the same time, this shift of the arbitrage boundary led to decreases in price in the other four tracts during this period. We also note that as the two eastern tracts were absorbed into the arbitrage boundary in 1964 and 1965, prices declined slightly, also as the model would predict. The same pattern is repeated for tract 2159; with the first shift of the arbitrage boundary into this neighborhood in 1964 and 1965, prices increased but then declined moderately as more of the area was absorbed into the boundary market. The pattern repeats once again in tract 2157 beginning in 1966.

Thus, we see rather clear evidence of price changes associated with the absorption of the northern tier of census tracts into the boundary. This is confirmed by substantial racial change and modest declines in socioeconomic status. Furthermore, we note that the three southern tracts, although not significantly absorbed into the boundary market, experienced price declines over the ten-year period. This fact gains added significance when it is noted that the prices on which the index is based are nominal prices and thus would reflect any general effects of price level increases. This provides further evidence as to the effect of proximity to the boundary market and the increased uncertainty that accompanies proximity on market prices.

To summarize, we find that experience during the period of racial change is precisely that predicted by the arbitrage model. Furthermore, we see evidence pointing to the significance of expectations; areas not absorbed into the boundary market experienced price declines. Relative to experience in other communities, the story of change in University City has a happy ending. Since 1971, it has stabilized significantly. While the reasons for this are complex, a strong and well-enforced housing code and general tightness in mortgage markets were certainly contributing factors. The stabilization of the market was accompanied by a sharp rise in housing values, with the largest change occurring in the southern tracts. These increases can be viewed as the result of a lower (perceived) risk of further shifts in the arbitrage boundary. That is, while the northern tracts remained boundary areas (with something approaching an equal racial mix), the perceived risk of these areas becoming completely absorbed into the lower status market and of the boundary shifting into the southern tracts had fallen.

However, University City provides the only example of a neighborhood in the St. Louis area that has stabilized as a boundary neighborhood. More prevalent is the experience of Wellston, the suburb immediately to

[e] Phares (1971), using a different set of sales observations for the period 1958–67, reaches somewhat similar conclusions.

the northeast of University City. In the early sixties, Wellston experienced a first round of arbitrage similar to that of University City. Rather than stabilizing, Wellston experienced a second round of change as it was absorbed completely into the lower-status market. Median income fell sharply as did real estate values, and in the terminal stage the frequency of abandonment rose. A similar series of events has been documented for the west end of the city of St. Louis (Leven, Little, Nourse, and Read, 1976: chapter 6). Thus, we must conclude that the stabilizing of University City does not significantly alter the argument that boundary markets are fundamentally unstable.

LONG-RUN PATTERNS OF TRANSITION

It has often been argued that past development patterns and the aging of the housing stock are largely responsible for the neighborhood succession process. Another frequently cited explanation for the succession of inner city neighborhoods is a shift in preferences on the part of the middle class toward a "suburban" life-style. Still another explanation is the rise of the automobile as the dominant transport mode and the resulting decentralization of both population and employment. These factors are examples of what we classified earlier as "long-run" influences on the succession process. They clearly serve as stimuli to the arbitrage process, but it is also possible that, independent of arbitrage, such long-run factors may have been the major force in neighborhood succession over the past several decades.

The question of the relative importance of arbitrage versus more long-run phenomena in explaining succession has been addressed by Nourse and Phares (1974). In this study, transition patterns, market values, and socioeconomic status for a sample of fifteen communities in the St. Louis metropolitan area were examined over a forty-year period. The neighborhoods were chosen so as to ensure considerable variation in initial socioeconomic status, vintage of the housing stock, and proximity to transition areas. The main conclusion of this analysis is that transition per se (change in racial occupancy or decline in median income rank) is overwhelmingly associated with proximity to the arbitrage boundary. In only one case out of the fifteen sampled did a neighborhood distant from the main path of transition experience a significant drop in median income rank. Also, there was no systematic relationship between the age of the housing stock and transition. While some of the oldest areas did experience transition, neighborhoods with a relatively recently constructed housing stock (for example, two of the three University City transition neighborhoods) also experienced change. Furthermore, one of the fifteen communities with relatively old and small housing actually experienced a significant *increase* in its median income rank. The effect of proximity to nonwhite neighborhoods was also ambiguous. The main path of transition in the St. Louis market has been associated with racial change, but some neighborhoods proximate to stable nonwhite neighborhoods did not experience rapid change and in one case actually increased in socioeconomic status.

The one effect of long-run factors which became apparent was a general decline in housing values, relative to the SMSA median, for those neighborhoods close to the central city. For example, all neighborhoods in the first ring of suburbs of the city of St. Louis, had relative housing values fall between 1950 and 1970. In some cases, transition to lower income levels did occur, but for others socioeconomic status was stable or even rose slightly. This general decline in relative values probably reflects a declining value placed on access to the central business district as a result of lowered costs of transportation and decentralization of employment and commercial centers.

This study provides fairly strong empirical evidence that the most important causal factors in neighborhood succession, as it is currently observed, are those identified by the arbitrage model. Furthermore, the analysis reinforces earlier findings as to the primacy of expectations. One additional result of the Nourse-Phares study which should be noted is that, in most cases, transition was associated first with racial change and was followed by declines in the socioeconomic status of neighborhoods. This, together with other evidence, suggests that while preference for neighborhoods may depend primarily on the neighborhood income level, expectations are formed largely on the basis of proximity to racial change. That is, market participants view declines in neighborhood income as the inevitable consequence of racial transition.

These findings have two general implications for policy. The first is that housing programs that focus on supply or demand in particular submarkets will alter the geographic configuration of these markets. For example, a program such as a housing allowance is likely to raise prices initially in the low-income submarkets and lead to a shift of boundary units into this market. Clearly, if this leads to an improvement in the physical quality of housing for low-income households, the primary objective of the program will be achieved. Yet it must be recognized that this shift in the boundary will produce capital losses for owners of units brought into the boundary and may set off another round of arbitrage through the effect of a boundary shift on expectations. The limited evidence we have suggests that the only *market* forces which might abate the process are increases in the supply price of new housing (via higher land and construction costs) and tightening of mortgage markets. The second implication is that extensive neighborhood integration is unlikely to occur unless expectations can be stabilized. Much of the transition observed in the St. Louis area has been initiated by the movement of middle-income blacks. That the market interprets this as a signal of impending economic down-ranking of the neighborhood has meant that, with the sole exception of University City, the process has continued with a second round of transition in which socioeconomic rank falls precipitously. The end result of the process is the decay and abandonment of neighborhoods, not because of a substandard housing stock, but rather because in the view of virtually all households the neighborhood itself is substandard.

REFERENCES

Bailey, Martin (1959) "Note on the Economics of Residential Zoning and Urban Renewal." *Land Economics* 35 (August): 288–92.

Hoyt, Homer (1939) *The Structure and Growth of Residential Neighborhoods in American Cities.* Washington, D.C.: U.S.G.P.O.

Leven, Charles L., James T. Little, Hugh O. Nourse, and R.B. Read (1976) *Neighborhood Change: Lessons in the Dynamics of Urban Decay.* New York: Praeger.

Little, James T. (1973) "Housing Market Behavior and Household Mobility Patterns in a Transition Neighborhood." St. Louis: Institute for Urban and Regional Studies, Working Paper HMS1, Washington University.

Little, James T. (1976) "Residential Preferences, Neighborhood Filtering, and Neighborhood Change." *Journal of Urban Economics* 3 (January): 68–81.

Nourse, Hugh O., and Donald Phares (1974) "Socioeconomic Transition and Housing Values: A Comparative Analysis of Urban Neighborhoods." In Gary Gappert and Harold M. Rose (eds.), *The Social Economy of Cities.* Beverly Hills, Calif.: Sage Publication Inc.

Park, R.E., E.W. Burgers, and R.D. McKensie (eds.) (1925) *The City.* Chicago: University of Chicago Press.

Phares, Donald (1971) "Racial Change and Housing Values: Transition in an Inner Suburb." *Social Science Quarterly* 51 (December): 560–73.

Shapley, L.S., and M. Shubick (1972) "The Assignment Game I: The Core." *International Journal of Game Theory* 1: 111–30.

Chapter 4

Redlining in Perspective: An Evaluation of Approaches to the Urban Mortgage Dilemma[a]

**Michael Agelasto, II and
David Listokin**

Few housing issues have aroused so much controversy in the last few years as the charge leveled by some community groups and politicians that financial institutions are hastening the death of many American urban neighborhoods by arbitrarily denying them mortgage credit.[b] These accusations are denied with equal vehemence by lenders, who claim they merely adhere to sound lending practices and do not unjustifiably discriminate. This "redlining" issue has caused the federal government and several states and cities to promulgate rules and actually to enact or at least consider legislation that ranges from simple requirements that financial institutions disclose where they grant loans to more stringent measures such as credit allocation.

The urban mortgage controversy has been characterized more by extreme rhetoric than by sophisticated analysis (Redlining Rag; Taggart, 1974; U.S. Senate, 1975a). Even balanced analyses have failed to explore the subject sufficiently (Bradford and Rubinowitz, 1975; Bill Moyer's Journal, 1976; Federal National Mortgage Association, 1976; Duncan, Hood, and Neet, 1975). This chapter, in attempting to introduce a bit of theory to the credit problem, examines its causes, the current federal, state, and local responses, and possible future responses that are likely to serve as ameliorative strategies. The Home Mortgage Disclosure Act of 1975, which President Ford signed into law on December 31, 1975, is discussed in detail, with major emphasis placed on the data needed to

---

[a] The research contained in this chapter is current through December, 1976.

[b] Several hearings held on redlining can serve as references on the subject; refer to U.S. Senate (1975a), U.S. House of Representatives (1975), and U.S. Department of Housing and Urban Development (1976).

meet congressional intent. We also examine the regulations promulgated by the Federal Reserve System as of late 1975 to implement the act.

It is important to clarify the terminology employed in order to avoid the problem in semantics that so often characterizes discussions of the redlining issue (U.S. Senate, 1975a: 874; U.S. House of Representatives, 1975: 2102). *Urban credit crunch* or *mortgage dilemma* serve as neutral descriptive phrases referring to the difficulty faced by some urban residents in certain *mortgage-short* neighborhoods in obtaining institutional mortgages or other loans for purchasing, refinancing, or repairing properties. These terms make no implication as to why a credit shortfall exists. For this purpose, two additional terms will be employed. *Redlining* refers to those lending practices that constitute an arbitrary denial of financing not justified on the basis of economic criteria such as risk or rate of return. The term *disinvestment,* in contrast, refers to credit shortfall motivated by justifiable economic or investment standards.

It is particularly important to make these distinctions because the residential financing dilemma has spawned emotive terms that make it inherently difficult to discuss the issue objectively and clearly. Redlining, for example, conjures up an image of some cabal of lenders delineating in red ink on a city map those areas that will receive no credit. Such a conspiracy may or may not exist, but an examination of the controversy cannot be made with phrases that presuppose motivation. Consequently, we use *credit crunch* or *financing dilemma* as a neutral description of the facts, while *redlining* and *disinvestment* refer to the alleged causes for the urban credit shortage.

THE URBAN MORTGAGE CRUNCH: ANALYSIS OF THE PROBLEM

The urban credit crunch is not new. For New York City, three separate studies over a twenty-five year period illustrate the financing dilemma that has troubled certain of the city's neighborhoods. A study examining real estate activity in the city from the 1910s to the 1930s reported: "In every borough and numerous large areas (mortgage) terms are so strict as practically eliminating funds for the construction of a new house or the purchase of an existing home" (Swan, 1944: 213). A study of neighborhoods on the West Side of Manhattan in the 1950s arrived at a similar conclusion (Rapkin, 1959). And slightly more than a decade later Sternlieb examined the New York City housing market, as part of a study of the city's rent control law, and his findings paralleled the somber conclusions of the earlier studies (1971). Based on interviews with both financial institutions and building-owners, Sternlieb reported that new mortgage money was not only expensive, but was extremely difficult to obtain. The only seemingly bright note in his analysis was a reported decline in the number of second mortgages. But upon closer examination this too reflected a weakening in the market, for it indicated that certain speculators were no longer willing to take risky loans.

Newark stands out as another city with continuing and accelerating urban lending problems. A 1966 analysis showed that residents of many of this city's neighborhoods were finding it difficult to obtain institutional mortgage financing and, when they obtain loans, had to pay a high cost (Sternlieb, 1966). A follow-up study in 1971 showed that these problems had intensified and that the basic pace of the market had slowed drastically (Sternlieb and Burchell, 1973).

Other studies conducted in the 1950s and 1960s explored residential financing problems, especially as they relate to minority loan applicants (Abrams, 1955; McEntire, 1960; Chicago Mayor's Commission on Human Relations, 1962). More recently, a number of monographs have discussed the urban credit crunch, including a 1971 study on abandonment which documented a credit shortfall in seven communities across the country, and Case's study of nine cities which revealed that many areas, especially inner city neighborhoods, suffered the effects of a dearth of institutional mortgage loans and other financing (National Urban League, 1971; Case, 1972). Studies of New York City, Milwaukee, Chicago, Baltimore, Hartford, and other cities have reported that a growing number of neighborhoods in these communities are experiencing a credit crunch (Agelasto and Listokin, 1975).

Some Parameters of the Problem

Past studies of the urban financing dilemma show that the problem can assume many forms.

1. *A reduction in the total number of new or refinance loans originating in certain neighborhoods.* Studies in Chicago, New York, and other urban centers have indicated this downward trend (*Kansas City Star,* 1975; Phoenix Fund, 1975; Naparstek and Cincotta, 1976; Sternlieb, 1966). Such a decline can have a major adverse impact on neighborhood stability and maintenance, since property owners can maintain and rehabilitate their units only if loan funds are available. Also, new investors who wish to buy and existing owners who wish to refinance are unable to get mortgages. Refinancing is especially important to both current homeowners and landlords, for it is their primary way to recapture equity. As one author notes for Newark, most of the return on residential real estate comes from the capacity of the owner to remortgage his building, capturing the amortization and improving his cash flow yield (Sternlieb, 1971).

These sales, resales, and refinancing transactions all characterize a sound housing market. Credit availability, therefore, is a sine qua non for neighborhood preservation or improvement; the credit crunch cuts this capital lifeline and contributes to neighborhood deterioration. Limiting the supply of mortgages to governmentally insured loans may have a similar effect. This decline in conventional loans to certain areas may largely be caused by lenders' targeting and restricting subsidized FHA programs to these neighborhoods (Case, 1972; U.S. House of Representatives, 1975: 201 ff).

2. *Lower appraisal of urban properties vis-à-vis their suburban competition is another feature of the mortgage financing dilemma, thus creating a dual market favoring suburban development.* Until 1967, officials of the Federal Housing Administration (FHA), following standards in the FHA appraisal manual, valued suburban homes at a premium compared with properties in core urban areas (National Commission on Urban Problems, 1969: 100). Critics charge that lenders still engage in these practices today and that they reflect underappraising rather than a justifiable recognition of market conditions. A frequent charge is that appraisers use arbitrary criteria, such as age of the house, which produces the discriminating impact of effectively eliminating entire neighborhoods from the lending process.

Lower appraisals force a potential purchaser to make a larger down payment. In addition, the buyer may have to resort to costly secondary mortgage sources, such as those offered by private companies or individuals (Stegman, 1972: 199). These factors tend to weaken the urban resale market by limiting the pool of available buyers and/or by forcing residents to sell to speculators who can obtain financing because they offer a bulk market and are willing to pay high interest rates for their short-term holding. Alternatively, the existing property-owners, unwilling to sell at lower prices, will often let their property deteriorate, or rent it out.

Defining risk through appraisal and underwriting standards and procedures is at the crux of the mortgage dilemma. Real estate appraisal is both an art and a science; few people have attempted to set definitive quantifiable criteria, and as a result the profession relies heavily on individual judgment. Although general standards have been discussed by real estate professionals for many years, the entire topic has come to the public's attention only recently. Prior to 1976, most of the debate and literature on redlining placed little emphasis on issues relating to the assessing of risk. Today, observers are recognizing the fundamental need to establish appraisal and underwriting standards that are more objective and precise (Governor's Task Force on Redlining, 1976). Simple solutions to this complex issue, however, are not likely to occur, and future public debate can be expected to be intense, as illustrated by the Seattle Reinvestment Task Force, which was so strongly divided on what criteria should be used in defining risk that the lenders and community members filed separate reports (City of Seattle, 1976).

The issue may partially be resolved by the courts. On April 16, 1976, the Justice Department filed a complaint in the U.S. District Court for the Northern District of the Illinois, Eastern Division, alleging that four appraisal and mortgage-lending groups were requiring or encouraging undervaluation of homes in racially mixed neighborhoods. The defendants are the American Institute of Real Estate Appraisers (a subsidiary of the National Association of Realtors), the Society of Real Estate Appraisers, the U.S. League of Savings Associations, and the Mortgage Bankers Association. These groups have denied the charges, stating that their practices are based solely on economic criteria.

3. *Granting urban mortgages with short terms and high interest rates.* Urban loans, compared to suburban loans, must often be paid back comparatively faster and at higher interest rates, or they require the payment of additional points at closing (Rapkin, 1959; Sternlieb, 1966). Points raise the initial cost of the house, while higher interest rates increase the over-all cost of housing. Both phenomena price out low-income and moderate-income households from purchasing or adequately maintaining their property. For the multifamily investor, the high-cost urban loan may reduce cash flow to a point where maintenance must be kept at a bare minimum, just to break even. Confronted by a high debt service, the owner of the single or multifamily urban property may decide to free himself of his real estate burden. But sale is impeded by the financing dilemma, forcing the owner to forestall needed maintenance or to sell to a speculator who has his own line of credit. In the extreme case, the owner simply abandons his parcel.

4. *The presence of noninstitutional financing in some urban neighborhoods, such as land installment contracts (LIC) offered to a purchaser by a private seller, is another characteristic of the financing dilemma.* Studies in Baltimore and elsewhere have shown that in some areas private loans are the most prevalent type of credit and are contributing factors to neighborhood decline (Stegman, 1972; Rapkin, 1959; Contract Buyers League of Chicago, 1968). Since equity is not built up until the loan is paid off, this type of loan incurs a high cost and offers the purchaser little protection.

Noninstitutional mortgages, or ''contracts to buy,'' are frequently the only type of credit available in ghetto areas, imposing a burden on black families. For the black contract buyer, this spells hardship, suffering, exhaustion, and despair. Contract buying often means they must choose the lesser of two evils: either continue to pay even greater rents compared to possible LIC payments, or buy on contract with the hope that someday they might own their own home.

5. *Another contributor to the financing dilemma is the removal of lending institutions from the inner city.* This can occur when an institution moves its central office to the suburbs, as has happened in communities in California and Illinois (Marshall, 1974; Urban-Suburban Investment Group, 1974). In other cases, central city lending institutions may merge and subsequently close down one of the offices or open a branch in the suburbs which de facto assumes the major functions of the institution.

Effects of the Urban Mortgage Crunch—Homeowners, Legitimate Investors, and Speculators

The scarcity of financing adversely affects existing owners. They feel abandoned by the banks and may fear there is little chance to recapture even their initial investment, let alone secure a profit. As Sternlieb and Burchell concluded in their Newark analysis:

> If the banks, savings and loan companies, insurance companies and the like are willing to lend in an area, then owners can have confidence that their investments in properties are redeemable through ultimate resale or re-mortgaging. Without this assurance, landlords become locked in; they know that capital improvements and investment will add little to the ultimate value of their properties; they may very well view even positive cash flows and operating profits from their properties as nothing more than the liquidation of capital values (1973: 237).

Given this defeatist attitude, existing owners are likely to keep their maintenance expenses to a minimum, making the chances for rehabilitation practically nil. They ask: "Why should we keep throwing in money, adding to already sunk costs, when we know the entire investment will soon become a total loss?" Rather than rehabilitating, the discouraged owner keeps maintenance outlays low and foregoes urgently needed repairs.

The existing owners' pessimism feeds the "sharks" of a declining neighborhood—speculators interested in short-term profits acquired through deferring maintenance and "milking" a piece of property. Sometimes using such tactics as blockbusting to force panic sales, speculators are attracted to credit-short neighborhoods where they can induce cheap and multiple sales from existing owners who are glad to rid themselves of property they view as a continuing source of expense. Once the speculators infiltrate a neighborhood, the level of maintenance and rehabilitation tends to plummet further as deterioration in the delivery of public services and an increase in crime sets in. Many minority and low-income house-hunters, unable to afford housing in other areas, are "steered" to these neighborhoods. Because of the primary role of homeowner income in determining property value, the influx of poor tends to speed up the decay process (Nourse and Phares, 1975). In a short time, once viable neighborhoods soon become known as both slums and ghettos.

Areas experiencing or threatened by a credit shortfall find that potential "legitimate" investors interested in long-term gains and tenure have little motivation to invest. They are afraid of being burdened by a high debt service cost and, even more critical, fear that they will become "locked in" to their investment, unable to sell the property because of the lack of demand caused by the absence of mortgage financing.

Despite an area's drawbacks, a small-scale "legitimate" investor may decide to purchase properties in disinvested areas. Such an investor may be unable to buy in white neighborhoods because of racial or ethnic discrimination, or may be unable to afford more expensive properties in more desirable areas. Whatever the motive for the purchase, the new owner will be hard pressed because of his mortgage's stringent amortization, especially if his purchase was financed by a private source such as an LIC.

An absence of institutional loans means that costly private financing will increasingly tend to dominate the neighborhood. Expensive debt service is not conducive to adequate maintenance and makes rehabilitation even less practical. Speculators, on the other hand, are not nearly so concerned with high debt service costs, because they will drastically reduce even necessary maintenance and repairs and increase rental income through means such as subdividing existing apartments.

Another class of potential buyers in a declining neighborhood is the young professional household, usually white and often at the prefamily stage with both husband and wife employed. This class is largely responsible for the private renewal that is occurring today in many cities (Urban Land Institute, 1976). Although their actions may sometimes drive out minorities and the poor (Georgetown, Capitol Hill, and Adams Morgan, in Washington, D.C.), the net result is the revitalization of a once declining urban neighborhood. This audience of potential rehabilitators needs financial backing for their renovation, and the urban mortgage crunch can squelch the restoration ambitions of this new cadre of urban "homesteaders," "brownstoners," and others interested in restoring old neighborhoods.

EXPLAINING THE MORTGAGE CRUNCH: REDLINING OR DISINVESTMENT?

Few will dispute that adequate residential financing, among other factors such as sufficient levels of public services and public safety, is essential to the health of a neighborhood. Most agree that in the past some lenders avoided certain urban neighborhoods, especially black and racially transitional areas. This policy, encouraged by the Federal Housing Administration (FHA), was not unique to financial institutions, was supported by much of the real estate and insurance industry, and was implicitly condoned by the general public (Orren, 1974; Fried, 1971; Levin, 1976). Furthermore, many agree that there is substantial variation in the volume and type of credit made available in different areas and that some urban neighborhoods, especially inner city locations, have seen a decline in the level of conventional financing. A subject of intense controversy is the motivation underlying the tightening of credit for these urban areas. Many charge that the urban mortgage crunch is due to redlining, the denial of credit for such unjustifiable reasons as racial discrimination. Lenders retort that the urban financing shortfall has been prompted by legitimate economic concerns, in other words, disinvestment.

The Redlining Hypothesis

Proponents of the redlining hypothesis view the mortgage crunch as one additional manifestation of residential housing discrimination in the United States. They attribute the growing inner city credit shortfall to an increased minority and lower-income concentration and to the discriminatory policies of lenders who are reluctant or refuse outright to grant mortgages to minority and low-income applicants. Proponents of the racial hypothesis recognize that economic factors are sometimes legitimate criteria for loan denials but believe that economic considerations usually play a minor role and are overwhelmed by racial factors.

Allegations of redlining come from a number of community-based organizations and public interest groups who support their charges with studies of varying quality.[c]

1. The National Committee Against Discrimination in Housing (NCDH), in examining the pattern of mortgages issued in Oakland, California, documented distinct geographical belts of loans. They found considerable differentials in the volume of bank loans, which varied according to the percentage of blacks in individual census tracts: the larger the black population, the more scarce was institutional financing. NCDH accused lenders of discriminating against black areas.

2. The Northwest Community Housing Association, Inc. has charged

---

[c] Studies undertaken or supported by community-based organizations which are discussed in this section include National Committee Against Discrimination in Housing. Inc. (1972), Northwest Community Housing Association. Inc. (1973). Devine (1973). Orren (1974). Center for New Corporate Priorities (1975). Vitarello. Balko. and Washington (1975). and U.S. Department of Housing and Urban Development (1972). For other studies. refer to Agelasto and Listokin (1975).

that racial discrimination was the reason that northwest Philadelphia, an area with a changing racial population, has experienced a large drop in the volume of mortgages granted by institutional lenders. Another neighborhood, northeast Philadelphia, very similar in terms of resident income, education level, and age of the housing stock, had maintained its white population and consequently still had access to institutional loans, so the report concluded.

3. Richard Devine has hypothesized that financial institutions in the Bronx reacted to demographic changes in the borough by selectively refusing to grant new or refinanced mortgages in those community planning districts that had become more and more dominated by blacks or Puerto Ricans. Using regression analysis to explain the absence of lending in the Bronx, he concluded that financial institutions were indeed discriminating on the basis of race.

4. Karen Orren has examined mortgages granted by life insurance companies in Chicago. She found that until 1955 black areas received practically no loans. This situation has improved in recent years, but white areas continue to receive the lion's share of life insurance credit. Orren concluded that the concentration of loans in white areas was due to racial not economic reasons.

5. The Center for New Corporate Priorities analyzed all the loans granted in Los Angeles by state-licensed savings and loan institutions over a six-month period. After examining the Los Angeles mortgage data by census tract, they concluded that there was an "immediate correlation between minority areas and redlining." The Center charged that minority residents received fewer loans and the mortgages they did obtain had higher interest rates and lower loan-to-value ratios.

6. The (Washington) D.C. Public Interest Research Group analyzed lending practices of District savings and loan associations over a three-year period (1972–74). The group observed that these institutions made fewer loans in Washington itself than in its suburbs and that black neighborhoods received a small share of the financing that was made available in the District. They charged: "There is little doubt that the great majority of the D.C. savings and loans have failed to make *local, home loans to minority neighborhoods* in Washington, D.C."

7. A 1972 Department of Housing and Urban Development (HUD) survey of over 15,000 lending institutions demonstrated that at least some of them considered factors that either directly or indirectly would work to the disadvantage of minorities. Almost 900, or 6 percent of the total, stated that they considered neighborhood racial or ethnic characteristics before granting a loan. Another 6 percent considered the presence of low-rent public housing projects to be a negative factor. Over 10 percent took into account the income level of *neighborhood* residents in evaluat-

ing loan applications in a particular area. Such criteria certainly could make it harder for a minority loan applicant to secure a mortgage.

The HUD survey also revealed that a substantial number of institutions contacted (29 percent) made fewer than 5 percent of their loans to minorities even though they were operating in cities with between 16 and 74 percent minority populations. Other banks had more minority business, but such financing still constituted a negligible proportion of their overall lending volume.

The Disinvestment Hypothesis

Lenders often vehemently deny the charges outlined above and claim their decisions to lend are based purely on a consideration of objective risk factors. Furthermore, they state that community groups charging redlining oversimplify the complex problem of urban decay by attributing the entire decline in lending to the financial community. Lenders argue that they have reduced their urban loan portfolio because such loans have often become relatively poor investments and that fiduciary responsibilities force them to seek out alternative investment avenues in the interest of their savers.

Some potential economic difficulties that would account for the existence of credit-short neighborhoods include:

1. *Higher administrative costs:* Various studies have found that for a number of reasons a bank's administrative costs are usually higher for urban loans (Case, 1972; Rafter, 1975). Servicing costs, which often are fixed, constitute a relatively greater burden on a small loan than on a large mortgage; since urban mortgages are sometimes smaller than suburban loans, their relative servicing cost is higher. Another factor affecting administrative costs is the periodic inspection of a lender's foreclosed properties. This can prove time-consuming, expensive, and on occasion even dangerous. Periodic visits are also required to investigate delinquent debt service payments by a property-owner. Follow-up actions as a result of repayment difficulties can also prove time-consuming and expensive. Factors increasing the complexity and cost of appraisal work in the inner city include special provisions to insure the personal safety of the appraiser and special attention given to code violations, compliance certificates, and zoning violations.

2. *Repayment difficulties:* An even more serious problem is that the repayment of urban loans often falls behind schedule or ceases entirely (Von Furstenberg and Green, 1974a; Sternlieb, 1971; New Jersey Department of Community Affairs, 1975: 37). Many lenders fear urban loan delinquency, and to them foreclosure trends indicate the start of a chain of events that can lead to severe financial hardship. Although there is no proven causal relationship, these trends may in part account for inner city

banks branching out to the suburbs. Lenders can absorb some bad losses, but high urban loan delinquency and default rates often prove unbearable. In addition to perceived and actual repayment difficulties, lenders are aware that foreclosing a mortgage can be expensive and time-consuming (McElhone and Cramer, 1975).

The life insurance industry's $2 billion Urban Investment Program, which operated during the late 1960s, illustrates the high delinquency and foreclosure rates sometimes associated with urban financing. Urban property loans in this program had a foreclosure rate eight times that of nonprogram mortgages and had delinquencies ten times higher than normal life insurance mortgages.

3. *Loan security and property disposition:* Urban lending problems do not end with delinquency and foreclosure. The ultimate security for a real estate loan is the mortgaged property. When its condition is poor, market value falls below the outstanding loan balance and the entire loan is in jeopardy. Urban properties in declining areas are often considered poor collateral. Case's inner city financing study revealed that lender fears over the security of mortgaged properties was one of the major restraints to their granting credit to urban areas (Case, 1972). In California, for example, lenders defended their suburban credit focus on the grounds that the typical inner city property offered for security was far below the quality and maintenance level of property in the suburbs. In Memphis, mortgage brokers cited physical depreciation of urban property, which diminished its security, among the reasons they avoided urban lending (Case, 1972).

Numerous factors account for a heightened fear that urban properties constitute poor loan collateral. Many structures are old, offer few amenities, and yet require expensive repairs. Vandalism is a constant threat which, if left unchecked, can lead to rapid housing deterioration. Additionally, properties may be hard to insure against fire, despite the fact that Fair Access to Insurance Requirement (FAIR) plans have been established in twenty-six states, the District of Columbia, and Puerto Rico (Levin, 1976). And in certain localities like New York City, rent control may reduce building income to the extent that the property loses its economic attractiveness (Sternlieb, 1971).

The cumulative impact of this array of social and economic forces on the urban housing stock cools enthusiasm by banks to extend credit in such areas. This pessimistic view of the city, especially of the inner city, is revealed in the testimony of the president of the Harlem Savings Bank explaining why his institution reduced its flow of mortgages to the Bronx (U.S. Senate, 1971: 1368–69):

> The plain fact is that at the present time investment in housing in such areas is becoming totally unattractive to private enterprises. Primarily, it is

financially unattractive. . . . First of all, the housing inventory itself . . . is old, and is subject today to harder usage in its old age than when it was new and could better absorb usage.

Second, it is regulated directly or indirectly by a myriad of municipal agencies and their administration has not been distinguished by too much efficiency. Formulas for increases in rent are unnecessarily complex. Tenant militance has grown rapidly in recent years and has become quite popular . . . drug addiction and crime are on the increase. Rents are more difficult to collect.

The plain fact is . . . that these difficulties render the operation of a multi-family apartment house in certain urban areas of the Bronx no longer attractive . . . some areas where blight is worst, it is difficult, if not impossible, to attract a capable superintendent of the building, or a capable agent who is willing to undertake rent collection and maintenance.

In addition to future loan repayments that are foregone in the event of foreclosure, lenders must also meet certain other costs. Few things are more distasteful to lending institutions than owning and running foreclosed real estate. Lenders, viewing their role as financiers, are not normally equipped to own and manage real estate. Such operations are time-consuming, expensive, and can lead to adverse publicity in the event that tenants must be evicted. Also, financial regulatory agencies have sometimes considered inner city property as a questionable legitimate asset for securing depositors' savings.

Aggravating the economic phenomena discussed above are the "opportunity costs" incurred by foregoing other more profitable investments. Lenders might be willing to grant urban loans despite the potential problems, if few competing alternative investments existed, or if these investments had an equal risk. Yet this is most often not the case for financial institutions such as commercial banks, which find other investments more lucrative. Even savings and loan institutions, restricted by law primarily to residential lending, still prefer to grant suburban mortgages, which they view as far less risky. For example, lenders in the Northeast go to the "Sunbelt" as a more lucrative market.

In specific cases lending institutions may be willing to make urban loans, but their general opinion is that the return is not commensurate with the perceived risk of the investment. The potential urban loan applicant may not be able to afford the interest rate that banks would require to compensate for the risk. Also, state usury laws that set limits on loan interest rates prohibit banks from making the higher charges they might feel are necessary to balance the higher risk of an urban mortgage (Brophy, 1970).

Finally, in certain instances lending institutions willing to make loans may find that, due to effects of national economic cycles, mortgage money is not available. In other cases, the secondary mortgage market intermediaries (Federal National Mortgage Association, Government National Mortgage Association, etc.) may be hesitant to purchase possible risk-prone urban loans, making it difficult for the local lender to resell the mortgage.

Redlining—An Historical Note

Redlining has been an issue of contention between community organizations and financial institutions for several decades. Over the years the focus of the controversy has shifted. To illustrate, studies in the 1950s sought to determine why blacks received few FHA loans. In more recent years, however, minority areas have been flooded with FHA mortgages. The question now of concern is whether or why this occurs and does such "FHAing" hasten neighborhood deterioration (Fried, 1971; Boyer, 1973).

Today, community groups in Chicago are at the forefront of the anti-redlining forces. In 1969 a group of community organizations on Chicago's West Side formed the West Side Coalition (WSC), which sponsored demonstrations in local banks seeking an end to alleged redlining practices. The Coalition brought pressure on City Hall to pass an ordinance requiring banks with city deposits to disclose where they were granting mortgages. WSC also lobbied for the creation of a governor's commission on redlining and for empowering the state's Legislative Investigating Committee to study lending practices. The West Side Coalition's influence extended far beyond Illinois. It conducted numerous national conferences, and at a 1972 meeting it formed two bodies, the National Training and Information Center (NTIC) and the National People's Action on Housing (NPAH). The former acts as a national information center and also helps coordinate grass-roots organizing activities to fight redlining. The latter acts as a "national people's lobby on urban issues" with a focus on the redlining controversy.[d]

Scores of local groups across the country have followed WSC's example. Most are neighborhood citizen organizations, such as the Alliance of Concerned Citizens (Milwaukee), People Acting Through Community Effort (Providence, R.I.), Coalition of Neighborhoods (Cincinnati), Coalition to End Neighborhood Deterioration (Indianapolis), Toledoans Against Redlining (Toledo, Ohio), and the Oak Park Community Organization (Oak Park, Illinois). In addition to citizens' groups, a number of research and civil-rights organizations have also accused lenders of redlining. These include the NAACP, the National Urban League, the Center for National Policy Review, the National Committee Against Discrimina-

[d] The Chicago organizations provide a variety of information to community groups around the country under the umbrella of the National Training and Information Center, 121 West Superior, Chicago, Illinois 60610.

tion in Housing, the Center for Urban Ethnic Affairs, and the Center for New Corporate Priorities.

The response by financial institutions has primarily taken the form of rebuttals by national lender organizations such as the American Bankers Association, the National Savings and Loan League, the U.S. League of Savings Associations, and the Independent Bankers Association of America. Lenders have uniformly cited "sound lending economics" as the reason for mortgage-short neighborhoods and have noted that the deterioration of urban neighborhoods has caused them millions of dollars in bad loans.

The redlining versus disinvestment controversy intensified in mid-1972 when the first National Housing Conference was held in Chicago. The tactics of the antiredlining camp first focused on pressuring individual lending institutions to expand their urban credit line. This emphasis changed in 1974–75 to lobbying for federal and state legislation requiring disclosure of mortgages granted. In 1976 there appears to be the beginnings of cooperative efforts between community groups and lenders to develop programs to assist mortgage-short neighborhoods.

Redlining Versus Disinvestment: Limitations of Citizens' Studies

Our review of the empirical literature suggests that as yet neither the redlining nor the disinvestment hypothesis has been substantiated definitively. Most of the recent empirical analysis in the area has been done by groups alleging that lenders are denying mortgages to certain areas arbitrarily or for racial motives; these studies suffer from numerous deficiencies.

First, many of them start out with an explicitly expressed bias against lenders, reflecting perhaps the public's dislike, or at best grudging tolerance, of lending institutions. Verbal confrontations between neighborhood groups and lenders have occurred quite often, with the former seeing the stakes as life or death for their neighborhoods and the latter resenting what they feel is an unfair attack against their past and current practices. While some studies do present an objective appraisal of bankers and their activities, most prejudge the banks to be arbitrary and discriminatory and search for evidence to support this view.

Other drawbacks to local studies are that they are often isolated, contain limited analysis, and are based on questionable assumptions. Most of the recent disinvestment literature examines lending at only one point in time. At best, a few studies examine mortgage patterns over a span of years (frequently using census data for 1960 and 1970). Such a limited approach does not reveal the complex dynamics of the urban lending scene.

There are further drawbacks. Basic social and economic data are usually available only from the decennial census, which often does not reflect the very rapid change in the socioeconomic characteristics of transitional neighborhoods. Such redlining studies, therefore, rely on outdated data or data that are available much too infrequently.

Many studies also fail to consider the diverse forces affecting the lending environment. Some of these are subtle but nevertheless exert a powerful influence. Professional concerns, for example, help explain lender hesitation to grant loans to marginal areas and applicants. A banking institution is sometimes penalized for giving mortgages outside the lending territory that the federal or state regulatory agency considers "secure." The agencies' displeasure can range from warnings during regular audits to an outright refusal to consider the urban loans as reserves against deposits. The individual lending officer also works under pressures that might discourage him from approving loans to urban neighborhoods or minority mortgage applicants. A major determinant of his career advancement is the track record of the loans he has approved; high foreclosure rates stand as a black mark against him. In addition, the Case inner city housing study found mutual distrust and lack of communication between bank lending officers and urban minority loan applicants (Case, 1972).

Analysis in many of the redlining studies is quite limited. Some of them have a degree of statistical rigor, but these are the exceptions (Orren, 1974; Devine, 1973). In most cases no statistical analysis is even attempted. Rather, lending data often are merely listed for certain census tracts (or zip codes) along with a few socioeconomic characteristics from the census. Where multiple regression techniques have been employed, the volume or number of mortgages per zip code (or census tract) is the dependent variable, with racial and economic factors the independent variables. These studies, which try to demonstrate that the "racial" variables are significant in explaining variation in mortgage volume or amount, also suffer from certain drawbacks. The statistical model is incorrectly specified because all the economic factors influencing lending variables are not entered into the regression analysis as independent variables. Another statistical problem is the high intercorrelation among the independent variables. For example, high minority proportion neighborhoods tend to have relatively lower family incomes and a more deteriorated housing stock. This intercorrelation makes disentangling the racial explanatory variables from the economic factors very difficult.[e]

[e] Interactive problems among the dependent variable loan volume and independent variables, i.e., housing condition, may also be expected. To illustrate, if the economic thesis is valid we would expect that the condition of the housing stock in a zip code or census tract—an independent variable—should affect the volume of mortgages—the dependent

A typical redlining study uses the following methodology: count the loans made in a particular area; identify the social and housing characteristics of the specific neighborhoods; and then compare the volume of loans across different areas. In some instances another step is added which calculates the volume of neighborhood deposits and examines the ratio of loans to deposits. Redlining is said to exist if there are relatively fewer mortgages in black areas or if the ratio of loans to deposits is very low in predominantly minority locations.

This methodology assumes that a certain loan volume should exist in a particular area and that a certain level of parity in the volume of loans in different neighborhoods also should exist. A low or reduced volume of loans in a particular area, especially a minority enclave, is seen as resulting from unjustified decisions by lenders not to advance credit to a certain neighborhood. There is, however, no basis for assuming parity in loan volume across different neighborhoods. To the contrary, volume can be expected to vary according to loan demand, which itself is a function of such factors as number of eligible mortgage applicants, new construction and renovation activity, and housing turnover. In part, older urban neighborhoods may receive relatively few mortgages because they have less housing construction or fewer eligible mortgage applicants than the suburbs. A particular black neighborhood may receive relatively less mortgage money, not because of racial reasons, but due to "neutral" economic or demand factors. Thus, gross lending data for different areas is in itself an inadequate data base from which to prove the existence of redlining. This possibility was noted as long as fifteen years ago in hearings before the U.S. Civil Rights Commission (1962: 340).

This methodology also assumes that applicants for loans in a neighborhood resemble existing residents and that the property for which the applicant is attempting to obtain financing resembles existing neighborhood parcels. Based on such assumptions, redlining studies examine applicants for urban mortgages and their properties by studying demographic and housing census data.

The presumption that the socioeconomic background of the mortgage applicants in an area parallels the socioeconomic profile of its residents is untrue, especially in areas experiencing rapid racial change, either through blockbusting (in which minorities are coming in rapidly) or rapid redevelopment (in which minorities are forced out).

---

variable. A prime facie argument could be made, however, that the availability of mortgages in a prior time period (period t-1) affected the condition of housing at the current period (period t) which in turn influences mortgage volume. In the prior time period (t-1) mortgage availability served as the independent variable and housing quality as the dependent variable, exactly the reverse of the relationship at time period (t). This interactive, interchangeable regression relationship calls into question the validity of using ordinary least squares regression analysis—the statistical technique frequently used in empirical/analytical redlining studies.

Without detailed knowledge of the race and economic class of mortgage applicants, it is almost impossible to verify whether redlining or disinvestment is the cause of the mortgage crunch. The same is true with reference to the type and condition of the properties for which the loan is being sought; it does not follow that an applicant's property resembles other parcels in the area. Quite possibly, applicants desire mortgages on new properties which are in better condition than existing units. Conversely, a parcel may be in relatively worse condition if a loan is intended for substantial rehabilitation.

Another assumption is that there should be some balance in deposit-loan ratios among different areas. That an excessively low ratio reveals a "draining" of resources from a particular location is questionable. Financial institutions have a fiduciary responsibility to make investments with the least risk and a greatest return. These investment opportunities may or may not be located in areas from which deposits have flowed. The argument that deposit flow is indicative of neighborhood economic health is also dubious, because deposits in a particular area are often made by persons working rather than residing there.

We do not mean to state that redlining does not exist but rather to point out that the existing studies have not substantiated that the mortgage crunch is caused by arbitrary or racially motivated factors. Any criticism of redlining studies must, however, note the difficulties that community groups have experienced in obtaining adequate data for research. With few exceptions, financial institutions will not release information on their mortgage-lending activities, data that quite possibly could help to support their assertion that redlining is not a widespread phenomenon.

To obtain such information, researchers have been forced to use real estate directories or title registration files for recording the type and location of each mortgage. This is very laborious and time-consuming and explains why many studies examine only a small sample of loans or look at lending activity over only a limited number of years. Furthermore, up-to-date housing and socioeconomic data usually are not available. Unless a city planning department or similar body has commissioned a more recent study (which is rarely done), the most recent census serves as the most current, comprehensive source of data on housing and socioeconomic characteristics.

Other data are almost impossible to obtain. Redlining studies are criticized for not examining mortgage demand, but it is very difficult to determine loan demand for a specific location. Examining proxies for demand, such as the number of newspaper ads of houses for sale or building permits issued, only indirectly indicates the strength of the housing market and are themselves difficult to differentiate neighborhood by neighborhood. The general public does not have access to socioeconomic profiles on successful and unsuccessful applicants and the characteristics of the housing for which these two groups wished to obtain mortgages. Lacking precise data, researchers have assumed that those seeking to buy houses in a certain neighborhood resemble the existing residents of that area.

Even though redlining studies are far from definitive, their consistent findings that urban neighborhoods across the country, especially those of high minority concentrations, have experienced a steady decline in the number of mortgages they receive, are most disquieting; to date they have not been empirically rebutted. Financial institutions may attempt in the future to answer the specific redlining charges with studies of their own rather than offering a simple denial that the accusations are unfounded.

THE FEDERAL RESPONSE: DISCLOSURE

Two recent federal responses to the redlining/disinvestment controversy are surveys of lending practices undertaken by regulatory agencies and the passage of the Home Mortgage Disclosure Act of 1975.

Survey and Pilot Project

The HUD 1972 survey of lenders has already been described. Another early survey was conducted in 1971 by the Federal Home Loan Bank Board (FHLBB) (1972). The results of a questionnaire returned by seventy-four savings and loan institutions indicated that, on the average, 12 percent of their loan portfolio consisted of loans in low-income or minority neighborhoods. Some lenders had stricter standards for neighborhoods: 30 percent disqualified neighborhoods because they had low-income or minority residents; 58 percent felt redlining certain urban neighborhoods was unimportant; and 57 percent felt that a group of savings and loan institutions working together could make a significant impact on revitalizing deteriorated neighborhoods. A third survey of lending institutions was undertaken by the Federal Home Loan Bank in 1973. Because mortgage demand data were not included, the scope of the data was insufficient to permit any detailed analysis (Federal Home Loan Bank of Chicago, 1974).

In 1974, the four major federal financial regulatory agencies, the Federal Home Loan Bank Board, the Board of Governors of the Federal Reserve, the Federal Deposit Insurance Corporation (FDIC), and the Comptroller of the Currency, began to explore ways in which housing lending activities could be monitored, especially to determine how minority applicants fared. These agencies conducted a joint survey entitled the Fair Housing Lending Practices Pilot Project. The survey was designed to determine whether and how data on lenders and borrowers could be used to monitor compliance with antidiscrimination requirements of Title VIII of the Civil Rights Act of 1968.

The four agencies used three different survey instruments. Form A, developed by the FHLBB, sought information on the sex, age, race, and marital status of a loan applicant on a census tract basis. Form B collected data on the race of applicants and provided for an open-ended, noncoded response regarding reasons for loan denial. It was administered jointly by the Federal Reserve and FDIC. Form C, developed by the Comptroller of the Currency, was the most comprehensive survey. It collected information on the economic status of the applicant which included income, years at occupation, debts, monthly debt payments, assets, the amount of the loan, purchase price, census tract location of property, race, marital status, sex of applicant, whether the property was to be owner-occupied, and date of denial or reasons for applicant's failure to submit a written application.

The three forms were administered in eighteen Standard Metropolitan Statistical Areas (SMSAs) between June 1 and November 30, 1974. A total of 105,000 applications for loans were collected. The results of the Pilot Project Survey, released during the first part of 1975, indicate that the data gathered were insufficient for resolving the redlining versus disinvestment controversy (U.S. House of Representatives, 1975: 890). One major flaw is that the forms elicited only a small portion of the data necessary for legitimately examining loan patterns. To illustrate, Form B listed by zip code the number of loan applications and the number of successful and unsuccessful minority and nonminority loan applicants. The survey revealed a higher rejection rate for minorities, but this tells us very little because information on the type and condition of the applicant property as well as the income and resources of the applicant is unknown. The absence of such information precludes drawing a conclusion on whether the higher minority rejection rate is significant.

Form C, used by the Comptroller of the Currency, was much more meaningful; it obtained data on the income and assets of successful and nonsuccessful, minority and nonminority applicants. The Comptroller's survey revealed a higher minority rejection rate. This finding held true when examined by applicant income, assets, employment record, property purchase price, and other variables. Use of the Comptroller's data is limited, however, by factors such as nonuniform compliance with instructions in filling out the form as well as considerable missing, invalid, or inconsistent information. In addition, certain crucial items such as the condition of the applicant's parcel and the nature and quality of surrounding housing were not requested.

Given the deficiencies in the data collected and the fact that certain information was never asked for, the Fair Housing Lending Practices Project yielded only limited insight into the mortgage crunch problem and must therefore be viewed as a first-step effort at obtaining an empirical base for studying urban lending patterns. The real value of the survey has been that it emphasized the difficulties of designing an operational and meaningful disclosure survey instrument.

The Home Mortgage Disclosure Act of 1975

The Home Mortgage Disclosure Act of 1975 (P.L. 94-200) was first introduced by Senator William Proxmire on March 22, 1975. The sponsor's intent was to advance urban revitalization through local action on the part of consumers encouraging the investment of mortgage funds in their communities. In May, six weeks after introducing the bill, Proxmire, as chairman of the Senate Committee on Banking, Housing and Urban Affairs, held four days of hearings on his proposed legislation. Representatives from community groups and civil rights organizations testified in favor of disclosure. The testimony of a Chicago community organizer typifies the argument repeatedly made by antiredlining campaigners:

> The redline is there because the bankers made a decision that they would no longer make conventional loans in my community. The only effective way the neighborhoods, cities, and Congress can deal with this redlining crisis is full mandatory national disclosure, so that every case . . . can be exposed and the pattern of redlining documented (U.S. Senate, 1975a: 170).

Put on the defensive, representatives from federal regulatory agencies and the institutional lenders generally denied the allegations. They concurred with the explicit objectives of the bill but questioned the wisdom of disclosure as a means of preserving older urban neighborhoods. As William A. Beasman, Jr. of the National Association of Mutual Savings Banks testified:

> Mr. Chairman, we fully share the view expressed in the statement accompanying the introduction of S. 1281, in which you identified the decay of America's great cities as one of the central problems of our time. . . . We respectfully disagree, however, that S. 1281 would further these objectives.
>
> We are concerned about the incorrect and misleading inferences which might be drawn from such information. In particular, we are deeply disturbed by two possible implications of this legislation.
>
> First, S. 1281 appears to hold depository institutions primarily responsible for inadequacies in the availability of mortgage funds to inner-city borrowers, without taking into account the higher risks and administrative costs frequently involved in such lending. In our judgement, it is not proper to place such burdens on depositors. Nor is it practical, since lenders will be restrained from participation in high-risk and high-cost lending by supervisory authorities or by their own depositors who are free to shift their funds to other institutions able to offer higher returns.
>
> Second, S. 1281 appears to suggest that geographic fragmentation of

financial markets is a desirable social objective. At the extreme, the proposed reporting requirement could be construed as implying that there should be some fixed relationship between the amount of savings deposits and volume of mortgage lending in any particular narrow geographic area. This conflicts with longstanding efforts to encourage the free flow of credit and to establish a truly nationwide mortgage market for the benefit of borrowers throughout the country (U.S. Senate, 1975a: 812).

On the House side, Joe Moakley, congressman from Boston, introduced a disclosure bill similar to Proxmire's on May 1. Several other House bills on disclosure were introduced, with some forty-five cosponsors. Legislative hearings in July focused on HR 8024, introduced by the chairman of the Subcommittee on Financial Institutions Supervision, Regulation, and Insurance, Fernand J. St. Germain of Rhode Island. Title III of the bill concerned mortgage disclosure, while the other two titles dealt with other aspects of financial institution regulation. The subcommittee and full banking committee marked up the bill and produced a clean bill (HR 10024) which was debated, amended, and passed by the House. Eight weeks earlier, the Senate had passed the Proxmire bill, also as amended on the floor.

The evolution of the House and Senate disclosure bills toward the final version (P.L. 94-200) is shown in table 4-1. After more than four-thousand pages of published testimony, debate, and reports, the law was passed by Congress upon recommendation by the House-Senate Conference Committee which resolved differences between bills passed by the House and Senate. The Home Mortgage Disclosure Act of 1975 was signed into law by President Ford on the last day of 1975 and was welcomed enthusiastically by community groups.

Several key factors, apart from the merits or substantive content of the legislation, account for the congressional support the legislation received. First, the cost to taxpayers was minimal. In contrast to the legislation that authorized categorical housing programs in the 1960s or the block grants for community development in 1974, the 1975 act would require no federal appropriation. Federal government costs incurred by the act would be virtually nonexistent. This was undoubtedly attractive to a cost-conscious Congress that was witnessing many of its major legislative initiatives being struck down by presidential veto. In its first six months, the ninety-fourth Congress was unable to override any of the president's vetoes. By the close of the first session, seventeen bills had been vetoed, with only three successfully overridden. In addition to being conscious of presidential criticism of "wanton spending," Congress had just established new budget processes to promote better planning. Legislation without a price tag would receive far less scrutiny than proposals with a budgetary impact.

Table 4-1. The Evolution of P.L. 94-200: A Comparison of Major Features of Federal Disclosure Bills, 1975

Bill	Sponsor	Date	Findings/Purpose	Type of Loan or Account	Required Data
S 1281	Proxmire	3/22/75	FI sometimes failed to provide loans in deposit areas and disclosure information to public	savings account, residential real property loans, FHA/VA, absentee	for current and future FYs: (a) FIs located in an SMSA: dollar amount and total number of loans and savings accounts by zip within SMSA, by county outside SMSA (b) FIs located outside an SMSA: same data, by zip within state and by state for outside state
HR 6596	Moakley	5/1/75	same as S 1281	S 1281 plus adds commercial property and home improvement loans	same as S 1281
S 1281*	S Comm. on Banking	6/6/75	same as S 1281	eliminates savings accounts from S 1281	eliminates FI outside SMSA—by CT if within SMSA, by county if outside SMSA
HR 8024	St. Germain	6/18/75	same as S 1281	same as HR 6596	FI located in SMSA: by CT if in SMSA, by county if outside
HR 9520	Symington	9/21/75	same as S 1281	same as S 1281*a	CT for principal city in SMSA, zip for other areas in SMSA; zip for SMSA under 350,000 population by state if outside SMSA
HR 9897	Jacobs	9/29/75	same as S 1281	same as S 1281*a	adds number of loan applications received by FI
HR 10024	HR Comm. on Banking	10/3/75	added purpose: shall not encourage credit allocation or unsound lending practices	SF/MF residential and home improvement loans, originated or purchased, FHA/VA, absentee	FI located in SMSA: for loans outside SMSA, dollars and total number; for loans in SMSA, by CT when available at reasonable cost, otherwise zip for prospective years only
S 1281*a	S Bill as amended; includes comm. amendments	9/4/75	same as S 1281	S 1281 plus adds originated or purchased and home improvement loans	Zip, not CT for prospective years only; by state, if outside SMSA
HR 10024a	HR bill as amended, including committee amendments	10/31/75	same as HR 10024	same as HR 10024	same as HR 10024
S 1281*c	Conference committee—became Public Law 94-200 on 12/31/75	12/15/75	same as HR 10024	same as HR 10024	same as HR 10024

Table 4-1. continued

Bill	Regulations/ Enforcements	Studies/ Reports	FIs Covered	State Laws	Expiration Date	Place Data Maintained
S 1281	regulations by Fed; FTC to enforce	*	state and federally chartered FI, not excluding mortgage bankers	*	*	at each office of FI
HR 6596	same as S 1281	*	mortgage bankers excluded; includes trust and insurance companies and pension funds	*	*	post sign in each office giving data
S 1281*	same as S 1281	Fed. report on FI disclosure outside SMSA; info. study on saving acct. down payment data use	same as S 1281	exempt FIs where state laws determined to be sufficient	*	same as S 1281
HR 8024	regulations by HUD	HUD summarizes data sends to Congress; Census also to study	state and federal chartered banks, S&Ls, homestead assn's, unions not included	adds building and credit to S 1281*	*	same as S 1281
HR 9520	same as S 1281	*	same as S 1281*a	same as HR 8024	same as S 1281*a	same as S 1281*a
HR 9897	same as S 1281		same as HR 9520, where portfolio exceeds $500,000	same as HR 8024	same as S 1281*a	same as S 1281*a
HR 10024	regulations by Fed. FHLBB may compensate for costs	HUD submits data findings to Congress with legislative recom; FHLBB finding on match CT with address	same as HR 8024; exempts FI of assets under $25 million	same as HR 8024	expires in two years, effective in 90 days	same as S 1281
S 1281*a	same as S 1281	*	Federal FIs; state FIs determined by Fed	same as HR 8024	expires in 3 years effective in 90 days	records maintained for 5 years; data kept in applicable FI
HR 10024a	same as HR 10024	Fed submits data (not findings) within 15 months, then annually	exempts FI of assets under $10 million	state-chartered FI may be exempted if state law sufficient	expires in 4 years, effective in 180 days	at home office; at any branch to extent of activity there
S 1281*c	same as HR 10024	Fed regarding non-SMSAs; everyone on matching CT and zip areas	regulated federal FIs and state FIs as determined by Fed	same as HR 10024a	same as HR 10024a	same as HR 10024a for 5 years

Second, unlike previous Great Society and antipoverty legislation, the major outcomes of the 1975 act would not benefit just one particular race or economic class. Witnesses who testified at the hearings did not represent core city, poverty, or minority-impacted neighborhoods. Rather, they generally came from white ethnic or integrated middle-class neighborhoods. These are the transitional areas, more appropriately labeled "gray" than "disaster," which by standard underwriting criteria would still appear to be lendable. Citizens expressing their dismay over disinvestment came from urban ethnic neighborhoods or inner suburbs, not the urban ghetto.

A third reason for the popularity of the redlining issue is that the hearings provided community groups a public forum with national media coverage and an opportunity to question the policies of mortgage lenders, policies generally exempt from public scrutiny. The popularity and emotional quality of the hearings and testimony, however, did have a tendency to force discussion into oversimplification. For example, the distinction between redlining and mortgage disinvestment—arbitrary versus reasoned decision making—was rarely made clear. The Senate hearings in particular were unable to sort out the complexity of the problem being confronted.

The hearings also offered legislators an opportunity for oversight of HUD programs; their predominant focus was the negative effects of FHA policy on communities. The term "FHAing" a neighborhood was used to describe the withdrawal of conventional mortgage money from areas dominated by FHA insurance programs. To many, FHA housing implied poorer quality construction and lower risk standards for applicants. The favorable financing terms available under FHA, such as low down payment, tend to raise price-value relationships to levels that discourage buyers with substantial equity.

The disclosure law appealed to Congress on three other grounds. A year earlier, the Housing and Community Development Act of 1974 had been enacted. This act expressed concern over the decay occurring in urban neighborhoods and emphasized rehabilitation as the primary national housing strategy. The mortgage crunch was viewed as a major obstacle to neighborhood preservation and Congress embraced disclosure as a strategy for promoting an adequate flow of credit into urban neighborhoods. This would forestall further deterioration and encourage rehabilitation.

Second, over the past several years the federal strategy for dealing with the problems of inner city decay has refocused its emphasis away from the planning and management of programs by Washington toward funding and other aids to encourage local initiatives. The Home Mortgage Disclosure Act, by providing data that could be used by local community groups, was consistent with this "new federalism."

Finally, the act, when considered as consumer legislation, accepts the premise that disclosure will inform neighborhood savers whether or not their funds are being made available within their own community for mortgage loans. Given information, consumers can better decide whether the policies of local financial institutions are in the community's best interest. If they determine that savings are not being invested locally, they can attempt to force local investment through the threat of withdrawal of funds.

The Home Mortgage Disclosure Act: Implementation, Data Needs, and Non-needs

The preamble to the Home Mortgage Disclosure Act does not declare that Congress acknowledges the existence of universal redlining. Rather, the wording reflects that the hearings failed to provide sufficient evidence on the redlining/disinvestment issue (P.L. 94-200, Sect. 302[a]):

Congress finds that *some* depository institutions have *sometimes* contributed to the decline of *certain* geographic areas by their failure pursuant to their chartering responsibilities to provide *adequate* home financing to *qualified* applicants on *reasonable* terms and conditions [emphasis added].

The stated purpose of the act is to "provide the citizens and public officials of the United States with *sufficient information* to enable them to determine whether depository institutions are fulfilling their obligations to serve the housing needs of the communities and neighborhoods in which they are located" (P.L. 94-200, Sect. 302[b]). This goal is to be attained through the disclosure of mortgage-lending information by certain financial institutions located within urban areas. The minimum information to be collected and made publicly available includes the number and dollar amount of residential mortgage and home improvement loans by geographic area, the breakdown between loans to owner-occupied versus absentee-owned housing, and whether the mortgage loans are FHA or VA insured. In assigning implementation of the law to the Federal Reserve Board, Congress gave it broad flexibility to exceed the minimum requirements of the act. The statute provides only the skeleton of a disclosure program. For example, the Board may determine the exact unit (postal zip code or census tract) for collecting data, the type and amount of any additional data required, and which state-chartered institutions will be required to collect data or be exempted.

In regulations proposed on March 31, 1976 and issued in final form on June 14, 1976, the Federal Reserve Board specified the exact type of data and manner of presentation required of lending institutions (table 4-2). The regulations require institutions making any federally related mortgage

Table 4–2. A Comparison of Federal and State Disclosure Requirements

Jurisdiction:	Federal	California
DISCLOSURE STATUTE, DIRECTIVE, OR BILL	Home Mortgage Disclosure Act of 1975, Title III of P.L. 94-200	Admin. Code Title 10, Ch. 2 Sub. ch. 23.
WHO DISCLOSES	depository institutions (savings and loan association, commercial bank, savings bank, or credit union) with assets of $10 million or more located in an SMSA and making "federally related mortgage loans."[a]	state-chartered savings and loan associations
WHICH MORTGAGES REQUIRE DISCLOSURE	"mortgage loan"—loan secured by residential real property or a home improvement loan[b]	loans secured by a lien or real estate
BREAKDOWN OF REQUIRED MORTGAGE DATA	I. mortgage loan data (number and dollar amount), divided into two categories: *originations*—loans originally made by the depository institution. *purchase loans* II. within each of these categories the data must be segregated between loans on property located within the *relevant SMSA* (i.e., the SMSA where a home or branch office is located) and loans on property outside of the relevant SMSA. Each of these segregations must be further itemized to show the number of loans of total dollar amounts of different categories of mortgages (i.e., FHA and VA loans) [c] III. loans located within the "relevant" SMSA must be further itemized by either census tract or zip code	I. data on successful and unsuccessful loan applications including race of applicant, purpose, type of property, loan amount, value of units of mortgaged property, loan interest rate, and loan terms II. location of successful and unsuccessful loan by census tract

DISCLOSURE UNIT	by census tract where readily available and reasonable costs are determined by the Federal Reserve, otherwise by zip code. The Board has tentatively decided to require disclosure by census tract.	census tract
DISCLOSURE MONITORING BODY	Federal Reserve	California Business and Transportation Agency
OTHER FEATURES	for institutions with offices in only one SMSA, data are to be made available at the home office and one branch office. A depository institution with offices in more than one SMSA would be required to make data available in at least one branch office in each SMSA. The Board can grant exemptions to state-chartered institutions subject to local disclosure laws that are substantially similar to the federal requirements.	California has required some disclosures since 1964 in its Loan Register.

Table 4-2. continued

Jurisdiction:	Massachusetts	New York	Pennsylvania
DISCLOSURE STATUTE, DIRECTIVE, OR BILL	Publication 8260-9-555-7-75 CR of the Massachusetts Commissioner of Banks	Supervisory Procedure G107 and appendices (February 18, 1976)	Pennsylvania House Bill No. 447
WHO DISCLOSES	state-chartered banks and credit unions having $20 million in deposits and having main offices located within the Boston SMSA.	state-chartered banks, trust companies, savings banks, and savings and loan associations with assets of $50 million or more. Disclosure is also required of national banks and federally chartered savings and loan associations located in New York.	"Every banking institution subject to regulation by the Pennsylvania Department of Banking and every person who holds himself out to be in the business of securing mortgage commitments or selling mortgages."
WHICH MORTGAGES REQUIRE DISCLOSURE	mortgages	loan secured by a mortgage or other lien upon real property, whether residential or otherwise.	first mortgages placed on residential real estate.
BREAKDOWN OF REQUIRED MORTGAGE DATA	I. number of mortgages granted, average interest rate, outstanding balance, number of applications, average down payment, and number of foreclosures segregated by: a. zip code areas for all cities and towns within the Boston SMSA b. total for all other areas within Massachusetts c. total for all out of state d. census tract areas for selected towns and cities. II. within each of these categories the data must be segregated by FHA/VA loans, non-FHA/VA loans, loans on all other buildings designed principally as residences, home improvement loans, and all other mortgages.	I. data on written mortgage application including: a. SMSA census tract of the subject property on which a mortgage loan is sought b. background data on mortgage applicant and property[d] c. disposition of application d. reasons for denial or mortgage loan II. data on financial institutions and other operations[e] III. disclosure of location of mortgage loan by zip code or census tract giving total number and aggregate amount of loan. Loans are to be segregated into various categories.[f]	zip code, down payment, interest rate, size, and terms of all loans

	Massachusetts	New York	Pennsylvania
DISCLOSURE UNIT	1. zip code 2. census tract 3. in Massachusetts but outside Boston SMSA 4. outside Massachusetts	by census tract for loans secured by property located within (and deposits received from) SMSAs; by zip code areas in the case of all other mortgage loans or deposits	zip code
DISCLOSURE MONITORING BODY	Massachusetts Commissioner of Banks	New York Banking Department	Pennsylvania Department of Banking
OTHER FEATURES	deposit information is also required including the number and amount of savings. Time, new, and demand accounts must be segregated into zip code, census tract, in state, and out-of-state categories.	a sample of deposits (number and amount) will be disclosed by either zip code or census tract. Loan and deposit data are to be submitted in a computer readable format.	

---

a A first-lien mortgage loan on 1–4 family residences that is federally insured or an original loan that is insured or guaranteed by HUD or intended to be sold to FNMA, GNMA or FHLMC.

b Includes loans on single-family homes, residences from 1–4 families, and multifamily dwellings, loans on individual units of condominiums and cooperatives, and both secured and unsecured home improvement loans. Junior mortgages as well as senior mortgages would be covered and a participating interest in specific mortgage loans would be disclosed to the extent of the participation. A refinancing involving an increase in the unpaid principal amount would be considered a new mortgage.

c The specific loan breakout includes: (a) originated or purchased FHA, FMHA, and VA loans; (b) originated or purchased mortgage loans made to mortgagors not residing in the mortgaged property; and (c) originated or purchased home improvement loans. Data for loans on multifamily dwellings (4 units or more) would be separately itemized but would not require the loan breakout (i.e., FHA, home improvement) described above.

d Includes applicant gross annual income, years at present employment, amount of outstanding debts, monthly debt payments, assets, amount of loan requested, purchase price of subject property, and whether subject property will be owner-occupied.

e Includes type, size, total real estate loans and participation on properties located in and outside New York State, total number of construction loans, total number of FHA/VA loans and participations (segregated by in-house and outside servicing and location within and outside New York State), aggregate dollar amount of GNMA pass-throughs, etc.

f Includes number of mortgaged properties presently under foreclosure action, value of purchase money mortgages, average rate of interest, average loan-to-value ratio. These data are to be further segregated into various categories such as conventional vs. FHA/VA, own vs. outside serviced loans.

loans to disclose aggregate data on number of loans and total dollar amount with respect to mortgages and home improvement loans on single-family and multiple-unit dwellings. For the fiscal year ending prior to July 1, 1976, these data are to be reported for postal zip code areas and made publicly available by September 30, 1976. After the initial year, information is to be reported by census tract, except for those counties not tracted.

The proposed regulations fall short of meeting the intent of Congress (as expressed in the act) to obtain "sufficient information" to prove or disprove redlining patterns. This task, as discussed earlier, requires data on:

1. condition of the property;
2. credit worthiness of mortgagor (income and credit rating);
3. demand for loans; and
4. lending practice for mortgagee (its valuation of risk, its preference for certain geographical areas, opportunity costs of certain alternative investments foregone, requirements to diversify portfolio, and other regulatory constraints).

Data on the availability of mortgage money, at the regional level, and the condition of property, at least on the census tract level, are obtainable from published sources and need not be collected through the regulations. While the required data may yield some useful information on the extent of mortgage lending within an SMSA or census tract, information on the causal factors of disinvestment or whether redlining exists will not be obtained.

Data concerning loan demand are missing. Witnesses representing federal agencies and lending institutions repeatedly made the point that the demand data necessary for analysis do not currently exist. One bill attempted to address this point by requiring data on the number of loan applications received, although telephone and informal inquiries would not have been covered.

By making the census tract the unit of observation, the regulations will not provide data adequate to ascertain variation within a census tract or zip code area. For example, an institution reports thirty-five home improvement loans with a total principal amount of $35,000. This aggregate figure fails to provide statistics on the variation; the mean figure of $1,000 may be misleading, especially in the case where one loan was for $25,000 and the rest *totalled* $10,000.

The regulations require that data be collected for the current fiscal year and future years but do not require any data on past years. These data are necessary for two reasons. First, disinvestment must be considered as a dynamic process. Traditionally, actual disinvestment is preceded by a number of forces operating over a period of time. If only current data are considered an analyst must wait a decade or more before being able to say to what extent or at what stage disinvestment is occurring. Second, current lending activity must be related to past activity. For example, the absolute number of loans for a given year must be related to activity over past years.

Comments from both the Senate and the House imply that their respective committees failed to understand fully the need for time-series data. The Senate committee tightened up the bill's language to restrict data collection to future years only, in response to lenders' objections about the costs of collection. The data needs of the analyst were not considered. The House committee concluded that prospective disclosure would by itself be sufficient to identify the beginning stage of redlining.

An issue of debate during the congressional hearings was whether data should be reported by census tract or zip code. Proponents of census tracts stated that for analytical purposes census tracts were more appropriate because they conformed better to neighborhoods, were smaller than zip code areas, and were the unit frequently employed in social science research. Those advocating zip codes stated that bank information already included the zip code but not the census tract information, and that because the methods of matching addresses to census tracts by computer would be costly and highly susceptible to error, the use of census tracts was not feasible.

The statute provides for disclosure by either zip code or census tract. Choosing one rather than the other can mean a tremendous difference in the cost, difficulty, and meaningfulness of disclosure. Identification by zip code is much easier and cheaper since such information is almost universally found on mortgage applications. However, zip codes were established for postal convenience, are most often not homogeneous neighborhoods, and usually contain a potpourri of high-cost and low-cost housing and residential and commercial buildings.

Census tracts, in contrast, tend to conform more closely to neighborhoods and are a frequent unit of analysis in social research. But requiring disclosure by census tract necessitates the conversion of addresses into tract areas. This can be done manually, at great cost and with much error. More efficient are computer routines such as the ADMATCH system of the Census Bureau. But even ADMATCH and similar computer address-census tract conversion methods are far from perfect. Updating to account for changes in street names and census tract boundaries is one problem. Another is proper setting up of the computer conversion system. Even with computer methods, anywhere from about 5 to as much as 50 percent of the mortgage addresses may be rejected. Those rejected would still have to be coded by hand.

The Conference Committee temporarily solved the question of tract versus zip code by accepting the House language permitting Federal Reserve Board discretion in determining which unit of observation should be used (U.S. Senate, 1975b). The regulations require an institution to disclose by zip code for the current fiscal year and by census tract in the future. The act recognized that improvements were needed to facilitate reporting by census tract and that federal agencies "shall develop, or assist in the improvement of, methods of matching addresses and census tracts to facilitate compliance by depository institutions in as economical a manner as possible with the requirements of this title" (P.L. 94-200, Sect. 307 [a][1]).

The cost of disclosure, a subject that repeatedly came up during the hearings, remains unknown. The director of the Bureau of the Census testified that, based upon an input of 50,000 items, coding of addresses to census tracts by computer would cost from 3.7 to 8.7 cents per item (U.S. House of Representatives 1975: 504). Conversion in areas where an address-census tract coding guide was not available would cost $1.50 per case. Others have projected far higher outlays. Peat, Marwick, Mitchell, and Company, in a study conducted for the First Federal Savings and Loan Association of Chicago, estimated an initial cost of $2 per mortgage to establish a reasonably accurate disclosure system and approximately 70 cents per mortgage to maintain and generate this data annually (U.S. Senate, 1975c: 26). The American Bankers Association has estimated costs ranging from 60 to 70 cents per mortgage for disclosure by zip code to $1.40 to $1.60 for disclosure by census tract (U.S. Senate, 1975c: 29).

These are only preliminary estimates. It is imperative that the exact costs be pinned down. If the data-gathering and reporting costs are high, disclosure may entail a major new expenditure for lenders. If disclosure-related expenses accumulate, the lending institutions may even be reimbursed. According to the law: "The Federal Home Loan Bank Board is authorized to utilize, contract with, act through, or compensate any person or agency in order to carry out this subsection" (P.L. 94-200, Sect. 307 [a][3]) Congress, however, has not yet appropriated funds for such activity.

Initially, both S. 1281 and HR 10024 required that data be collected by geographical unit on the total number and dollar amount of *savings* accounts. These provisions were rejected by both committees, which felt that such data would not be relevant, would be costly to gather, and would serve as a foot-in-the-door to credit allocation. The intentional omission of the savings account variable suggests that the consumer orientation of the initial proposal was later replaced by the data needs of policy analysts and public officials. The purpose of the data shifted from serving as a possible weapon for consumers in their fight with lending institutions to informing the public on the extent of the mortgage crunch. This shift was also manifest as differences in focus between the Senate and House hearings, with the latter focusing much more on the content of the disclosure bills. Fewer witnesses from community-based organizations and public interest groups testified in the House. Instead, during much of the hearings, representatives of federal agencies and lending institutions were examined in detail concerning the general intent and specific requirements of the legislation.

The requirement that a savings area match a lending area is not based on statute, nor is the savings variable crucial to disinvestment theory. Its absence serves to eliminate from the redlining/disinvestment controversy a potential red herring.

While financial institutions may resist the disclosure of any additional information, some expansion in scope is necessary if lending data are to be correctly interpreted; the data currently required offer only an incomplete picture and, moreover, can be misleading. Meaningful disclosure requires at least loan volume, location, a socioeconomic profile of successful and nonsuccessful loan applicants, a description of their properties, some indication of loan demand, and consideration of certain exogenous factors.

STATE RESPONSES: DISCLOSURE EFFECTED OR CONSIDERED[f]

Much concern over redlining has also arisen at the state level, especially in California, Massachusetts, and Illinois, where laws or administrative regulations attempt to combat redlining through mortgage disclosure. Several other states, notably New York, New Jersey, Michigan, Wisconsin, and Pennsylvania, have considered similar laws or rules. At the local level, city councils, prompted by citizen antiredlining groups, have held hearings on redlining and, in at least one instance, have passed ordinances directly aimed at curtailing the practice. Citizen groups have also effected the adoption of certain "greenlining" proposals by local lending institutions, directed at encouraging reinvestment in urban neighborhoods (Dorfman, 1975; Movement for Economic Justice, 1975).

[f] Enacted state legislation discussed in this section is Illinois Financial Institutions Disclosure Act [Pub. Act. 79-632, 4 Ill. Leg. Ser. (1975) 978] and Fairness in Lending Act [Pub. Act. 79-634, 4 Ill. Leg. Ser. (1975) 983]. Administrative rules are discussed for Massachusetts (disclosure directives dated August 1, 1975 and June 14, 1976); New York (New York State Banking Department Supervisory Procedure G-107 and Appendices (Feb. 18, 1976); Wisconsin [Wisc. Adm. Code Ch. S-L 13.01(4), May 1, 1974, Ch. S-L 27.05(b) (2) April 1, 1975]; California (California Administrative Code Title 10, Ch. 2, Subch. 23, Fair Lending and Subch. 24, Guidelines Relating to Fair Lending). Proposed 1975 legislation includes bills in California (S1003, A1285, S1048); New York (A6444, B-C-D, A6531A, A6532A, S6252, A7644); New Jersey (S1091); Pennsylvania (H447); and Michigan (H5765). Local ordinances include Chicago, Ill. Municipal Code Ch. 7-30 to 40; Minneapolis Code of Ordinances Ch. 945S (a) (8) (b); and Cleveland Ord. No. 1135-75.

California

Since 1964 state-chartered savings and loan associations have been required to submit a wide variety of lending data to the California Savings and Loan Commissioner. The information collected, which is incorporated into a "Loan Register," includes:

a. loan number
b. date loan entered on books
c. date of recording of trust deed or mortgage
d. name of borrower
e. location of security (by city and state, and by census tract if such information is available)
f. type of improvements
g. purpose of loan (speculative construction, construction for owner, purchase of property, refinance, purchased loan, collateral loan, or other)
h. amount of loan
i. secondary financing, where information is available, indicating:
   1. amount
   2. holder
j. current market value of the mortgaged property
k. selling price of property on loans made for the purchase of property
l. amount of discount or premium on purchased loans
m. interest rate
n. method of repayment (unamortized or amortized)
o. loan fees (not required for purchased loans)
p. maximum loan permitted under loan limitation applicable to the particular property—expressed as a maximum percent of loan-to-value

Regulations effective on July 1, 1975 further expand the information to be supplied for the loan register. In part, this action is a result of statewide hearings on mortgage-short areas and the accusations of community and public interest groups that large sections of Los Angeles were not receiving adequate mortgage financing. The new regulations, issued by the Business and Transportation Agency, require disclosure of the following data for each loan originated or purchased: race of applicant; census tract; purpose (speculative construction, construction for owner, purchase of property, refinance, home improvement); type of property; number of units; loan amount; appraised value; selling price; interest rate; term-to-maturity; fees; discount; and whether or not the loan is a variable rate mortgage, or federally insured. In addition, information on denied loans is collected as well as the status of verbal loan requests where a written application has not been completed.

The regulations call for the creation of two state boards of inquiry to review mortgage loan applications turned down by state-chartered institutions and to consider complaints by borrowers who have been granted credit but at unfavorable terms. The regulations also require that lending institutions wishing to open or close branches, merge, or change location must prepare a neighborhood impact statement. Public hearings on the proposal are also required.

Earlier the agency issued proposed regulations that would also have obtained information on savings accounts. These were severely criticized by representatives of lending institutions. The initial regulations imposed an outright ban on using geography as a lending criteria. The revised regulations present a general rule prohibiting discrimination "because of conditions, characteristics, or trends in the neighborhood or geographic area surrounding the security property" and then offer guidelines on geographic discrimination, appraising, underwriting procedures, and other issues.

In addition to the administrative rules, "antiredlining" legislation has been proposed. One bill, for example, makes it unlawful for a financial institution to discriminate against loan applicants solely because of social, economic, or environmental conditions of the area in which the applicant property is located. Another bill gives borrowers the right to receive a written response to loan applications and requires lenders to keep such records on file for two years.

Illinois

The Illinois Savings and Loan Act of 1974 requires that each loan institution retain rejected loan applicants along with the reasons for rejection for a twenty-four month period. The law provides a definition of what constitutes sound underwriting practices and lists standards that must be followed. It states explicitly that discrimination is prohibited.

During 1975, two state commissions, one executive and one legislative, completed eighteen month studies on redlining. Both commissions held public hearings, with organized support coming from the National People's Action on Housing, the Metropolitan Area Housing Alliance, and the Citizen Action Program, three Chicago-based community action groups. The studies prepared by the citizen groups and the material presented at the hearings paved the way for several legislative proposals which resulted in the enactment of two laws.

First, the Financial Institutions Disclosure Act requires that banks, credit unions, savings and loan associations, insurance companies, and mortgage banking companies operating in Illinois file semiannual statements of deposits and various types of mortgage loans by census tract and zip code area. The legislation applies to counties over 100,000 population and covers residential real estate mortgages, home improvement and construction loans, and FHA and VA insured loans. In April 1976 the Sangamon County Circuit Court granted a temporary injunction sought by the Illinois Savings and Loan league to halt enforcement of the act. The court cited the excessive costs of compliance.

Second, the Illinois Fairness in Lending Act of 1975 prohibits financial institutions from denying or varying the terms of a loan on the basis of geographic location of the property or using lending standards that have no economic basis. Further, it states that nothing contained in the act shall preclude a financial institution from considering sound underwriting practices, defined to include willingness and financial ability of the borrower, market value of the real estate, and diversification of the institution's investment portfolio.

Massachusetts

In a disclosure directive issued on August 1, 1975, the Massachusetts Commissioner of Banks required all state-chartered banks and credit unions to make public data on loans and deposits. After initial resistance, national banks agreed to supply voluntarily the information required of state-chartered institutions. Information in addition to that on deposit accounts is to be collected on residential mortgages, home improvement loans, and FHA and VA insured loans. The data include the number of applications, mortgages and foreclosures, the average interest rate, outstanding balance, and average down payment for loans; all are to be collected for all cities and towns within the Boston SMSA by zip code, except in Boston, where the information must be disaggregated to the census tract level. Deposit data are to be submitted only to the commissioner and then released to the public only as aggregate deposit accounts per city or town.

An earlier disclosure directive, issued in May, had been challenged in a law suit by twenty-six savings and cooperative banks. An out-of-court settlement modified earlier provisions calling for disclosure of information by census tract in cities with populations over 75,000.

As in Illinois, citizen groups in Massachusetts played a major role by focusing public attention on redlining, through collecting and collating mortgage-lending data. The major purpose of the administrative regulations, however, is to produce data that will permit an analyst to prove or disprove the existence of redlining. As the commissioner stated:

> It is important that community groups not be the only ones to analyze bank lending patterns if we are to insure that the data is honestly examined. . . . The banking department will either commission a disinterested

expert to analyze the data collected from the Boston SMSA or will analyze it itself.

In writing this regulation, I have tried to determine what information would be needed for accurate research on redlining (*American Banker,* 1975: 4).

New York

In February, 1976 the superintendent of the New York Banking Department issued comprehensive disclosure regulations. Effective on May 1, 1976 banking institutions were required to fill out a form for each mortgage application listing the socioeconomic profile of the applicant (race, assets, etc.), whether or not the applicant property is to be owner-occupied, and the disposition of the application. If a loan is denied, the lending institution is required to state the reason for the denial. These data are very similar to the information elicited by the Comptroller of the Currency under the Fair Housing Lending Practices Pilot Project; in fact, the form to be used by the New York banks is almost identical to Form C used by the Comptroller.

Additionally, lenders are instructed to provide the superintendent of banking a comprehensive summary of their loan activities from June 1976 onward, including:

Basic lender information: including type of bank (e.g., commercial versus savings) number of branches, assets, and a summary of financial activities including total mortgages granted, total construction loans made, number and dollar amount of loan participations on properties located within or outside New York State.

Mortgage portfolio by categories: (i.e., own-serviced versus outside-serviced loans, conventional versus purchase money or FHA) aggregated by census tracts within SMSAs and zip codes otherwise.

Loan record: (i.e., number of foreclosures and delinquencies aggregated by census tract within SMSAs or zip codes outside. Information to be collected includes aggregate number and dollar amount of foreclosed mortgages, total number and dollar amount of loans where one contractual payment is due and repaid, total number and dollar amount of loans where two contractual payments are due and unpaid, etc.

Deposit record: including total number and dollar amount of deposit accounts and a percentage of deposits located by zip code or census tract. The percentage of deposits to be so identified ranged from 100 percent for institutions with under 4000 accounts to 2 percent for institutions with 500,000 accounts or more.

Loan activity data are to be provided by financial institutions to the superintendent of banking in a computer readable form.

The New York action came several months after a state antiredlining bill failed to pass the Senate. That bill would have permitted savings banks to offer checking accounts in return for their financing of a mortgage-loan pool of up to $3 billion to aid allegedly redlined neighborhoods. A disclosure bill was also introduced, but received no action, during the 1975–76 session.

New Jersey

In 1975, State Senator Joseph P. Merlino of New Jersey introduced a state disclosure bill. The bill commences with a statement that deposit institutions have sometimes discriminated in the granting of mortgage loans. The proposed measure prohibits discrimination in the granting, withholding, extending, modifying, and reviewing, or in the fixing of the rates, terms, conditions or provision of any loan secured by real property because such property is located in a specific geographical area.

To monitor mortgage patterns, the bill calls for state-chartered depository institutions to disclose the number and total dollar amount of mortgage loans originated or purchased by that institution as well as the number and dollar amount of mortgage applications. Loan data are to be listed for each zip code or census tract and catalogued by type of loan (e.g., FHA insured versus conventional).

The New Jersey disclosure proposal is very similiar to the federal disclosure statute. Its purpose is to elicit lending data from state-chartered institutions. The bill is currently being debated by the New Jersey legislature and is given a good chance of passage.

Pennsylvania

A disclosure bill was introduced in the Pennsylvania General Assembly during 1975. It would require lenders to file with the state secretary of banking a statement of the geographic distribution (by zip code) indicating the number of first mortgages placed on residential parcels. The statement was also to give the dollar amount of each mortgage placed, the loan terms, and the total amount of all mortgages placed. Additionally, the total dollar amount was to be broken down into three categories; loans under $12,000, loans under $10,000, and loans under $8,000.

Wisconsin

Regulations in Wisconsin require that state-chartered savings and loan associations retain all rejected loan applications for at least two years, along with a record of the reason for rejection. Fairness in lending regulations also state: "No association may deny or vary the terms of a written loan application on the grounds that a specific parcel of real estate proposed as security for a mortgage loan is located within a given geographic area."

In April 1975, the Madison, Wisconsin Center for Public Representation petitioned the state commissioner of savings and loan to require a detailed annual reporting of each association's savings flow and lending practices on a geographic basis and the collection of additional information at the time of a loan application. The petition was denied in May of 1975.

Michigan

A disclosure bill was also introduced during the 1975 session of the Michigan legislature. Governor William G. Milliken appointed in April 1976 a task force headed by the Financial Institutions Bureau commissioner to report back within two months on the redlining problem and possible remedies. The major finding of the task force is that no standards exist governing mortgage-lending decisions as they relate to the availability of credit and housing opportunity in a geographic area (Governor's Task Force on Redlining, 1976). The task force proposed the development of standards for appraisal, underwriting, and accountability in lending through voluntary or mandatory disclosure.

THE LOCAL RESPONSE TO DISCLOSURE

In June 1974, the Chicago city council adopted an ordinance amending the city code in an attempt to eliminate redlining by financial institutions receiving city government deposits. The ordinance provides that offers to serve as city depositories will be sought from those banks and savings and loan associations (the latter were previously ineligible to be city depositories) satisfying the following conditions:

1. have capital stock and surplus of $500,000 or more;
2. pledge that "within limits of legal restrictions and prudent financial practices" it will not refuse to make mortgages or home improvement loans because of location, age of property, or the race, color, sex, or national origin of the applicant; and
3. report information by census tract on savings and checking accounts; consumer, commercial, home improvement, and construction loans; and on conventional, FHA, and VA mortgages. Data on interest rates and average down payment on mortgage loans are also to be collected for Chicago census tracts and the six-county metropolitan area outside Chicago.

A total of forty-one (about one-half) of Chicago's financial institutions complied with the disclosure regulations, although there was an initial reluctance to do so.

Other local actions have also been taken. The civil-rights ordinance of

Minneapolis contains language that prohibits redlining. The Cleveland city council in May 1976 adopted a disclosure ordinance similar to Chicago's. The Los Angeles board of supervisors recently voted to remove county funds from lenders that redline. Activity in other cities includes: redlining hearing in New York City, Philadelphia, Flint, Michigan, and Toledo, Ohio; consideration of an ordinance in Buffalo; a citizens task force set up in Los Angeles and Seattle; and citizens committees in Rochester, Pittsburgh, Washington, D.C., and Milwaukee to monitor mortgage lending practices.

STATE AND LOCAL RESPONSES: ANALYSIS

It is evident that states, and to a lesser extent localities, are beginning to use their authority to force lenders to disclose far more loan information than is called for by the federal disclosure statute. This is most pronounced in New York, which requires lenders to keep detailed records of all loan applications as well as to reveal the composition and location of their loan portfolio (table 4–2).

The state and local ordinances contain certain similarities. The writing of most of the rules and ordinances was strongly influenced by the research and public demonstrations of community organizations who charged widespread redlining. Many ordinances commence with a statement of findings to the effect that lending institutions are already redlining certain neighborhoods.

Variations across statutes include the amount of detail required of lenders. The New Jersey bill, for example, requires disclosure of far less data than the New York rule. Another variation is coverage. The Chicago statute requires disclosure only by those institutions competing to act as depositories for municipal funds. Most state statutes require disclosure by all state-regulated financial institutions over a particular size. A third source of variation is the existence of ancillary provisions. While most statutes stop at disclosure, a limited number of jurisdictions go further. California, for example, has established a state board of inquiry to examine unsuccessful mortgage applications. Other differences relate to factors such as the disclosure unit (zip code versus census tract), the monitoring body, and the penalities for noncompliance.

An important but often neglected consideration is whether the information required by the emerging state-local disclosure ordinances will generate an adequate data base for determining the causes of a mortgage-short neighborhood. To meet this objective, minimum socioeconomic and housing data for successful and unsuccessful loan applicants are needed. The New York and California regulations come closest to meeting this by requiring data on successful as well as unsuccessful applications. However, even for these two states the data generated are far from sufficient. New York employs Form C, already used by the Comptroller of the Currency. This survey instrument, already discussed above, is not fully adequate. Other state disclosure statutes are even less useful. The New Jersey proposal, which in its present form requires basically the same information as the federal disclosure statute, elicits only selected lending data which are insufficient for meaningful analysis. The Pennsylvania bill and the Chicago ordinance are more extensive than the federal requirements, but they too focus principally on loan volume by area, information that by itself is not meaningful.

The federal, state, and local disclosure requirements do represent a first step toward providing insight into the dynamics of urban lending environments. They should be viewed as first generation approaches to be followed by more refined future requirements, which not only elicit additional information but, more important, seek the data necessary to permit a meaningful analysis of urban mortgage patterns.

EMERGING APPROACHES TO
MORTGAGE-SHORT AREAS

Thus far the response by the federal government, by states, and by localities to the mortgage crunch has focused on disclosure. Even effective disclosure, however, will not resolve the problems of mortgage-short neighborhoods; disclosure only provides a data base for analysis. Litigation and civil-rights enforcement will be necessary to force financial institutions to end discrimination where it is found to exist. In those instances where the mortgage crunch can be traced to legitimate economic concerns, direct remedies addressing urban deterioration are needed. These include neighborhood preservation programs such as neighborhood housing services, mortgage insurance pools, and subsidy and loan insurance programs.

Civil Rights Enforcement

Existing civil-rights statutes that prohibit racial discrimination in lending and penalize violators can be enforced through litigation. The basic provisions requiring federal financial regulatory agencies to act affirmatively to eliminate discrimination in lending are contained in Executive Order 11063. This was issued in 1962 by President Kennedy to insure equal opportunity in federal-assisted housing. Title VI of the 1964 Civil Rights Act prohibits racial discrimination in other programs or activities receiving federal financial assistance.

Executive Order 11063 and Title VI of the 1964 Civil Rights Act have long stood as *potential* weapons against redlining, yet they have never been effective because the plight of mortgage-short areas had not been given the attention it receives today. Also, proving racial discrimination in lending in predisclosure days was nearly impossible. And in the past, some of the federal financial regulatory agencies who were charged with enforcing the safeguards have adhered to a conservative outlook on financing (U.S. Commission on Civil Rights, 1973: 98).

The Civil Rights Act of 1866, originally passed pursuant to the enforcement clause of the Thirteenth Amendment, has been revitalized recently by the 1968 Supreme Court decision *Jones* v. *Alfred H. Mayer Company*. In that decision, the Court applied Section 1982 of that act to the refusal to sell a house to a black. Since then, lower courts have split on the question of the applicability of this section to the practice of charging different prices in the context of an existing dual housing market (Duncan, Hood, and Neet, 1975). The U.S. Fifth Circuit Court ruled in *Love* v. *DeCarlo Homes, Inc.* that the act was not violated unless the alleged discriminatory action fell within the "traditional concept of racial discrimination." A year later, the Seventh Circuit Court opted for a wider interpretation of Section 1982, ruling in *Clark* v. *Universal Builders, Inc.* that a prima facie case could be made if dual housing markets exist because of racial residential segregation and if black buyers were subjected to higher prices and less reasonable lending terms than whites. The Fair Housing Act of 1968, referred to as Title VIII, generally prohibits financial institutions that make real estate loans from discriminating. Section 808(d) requires all federal agencies to implement their programs in a manner that would achieve the fair housing goal and to cooperate with the secretary of HUD, who is charged with the over-all responsibility for administering the program.

During 1972, regulations designed to carry out the provisions of Title VIII were adopted by the six federal financial regulatory agencies. The regulations require that each insured institution indicate in its advertisements that it grants sound real estate loans without regard to race, color, sex, religion, or national origin.

In discussing discrimination at that time, the Federal Home Loan Bank Board stated:

> It is clear that discrimination in lending is illegal when based solely on race, color, religion, or national origin. This does not mean, however, that a lending institution is expected to approve all loan applications, or that it must make all loans on identical terms. Denying loans, or granting them on more stringent terms and conditions, may be justified because of such factors as:
>
>   an applicant's income or credit history,
>   the property's condition, age, or design,
>   the availability of neighborhood amenities or city services, or

the need of the association to hold a balanced loan portfolio, with a reasonable distribution of loans in various neighborhoods, types of property, and loan amounts (Spidell, 1972: 10).

Each of these factors, however, must be applied without regard to race, color, religion, or national origin of prospective borrowers. For example, an association that refuses to make loans in minority neighborhoods because of the age and condition of the housing stock but at the same time makes loans in white neighborhoods on houses of similar age and condition would, in the absence of some other explanation, stand in violation of the law.

Legitimate reasons for denying loans are not always easily distinguished from illegal discriminatory factors (Von Furstenberg and Green, 1974b; Rafter, 1975). Areas of high minority and female-headed household concentrations are often areas of low-income residents with histories of poor credit. Additionally, since city neighborhoods differ in character from more homogeneous, middle-class, suburban communities, the FHLBB in its regulations and in an explanatory memorandum lists "neighborhood amenities" and "balanced loan portfolio" as legitimate criteria for refusing loans; this implies that disinvestment per se is not illegal.

In its regulations, the FHLBB states that

refusal to lend in a particular area *solely* because of the age of the homes or the income level in a neighborhood *may* be discriminatory in effect since minority group persons are more likely to purchase used housing and to live in low-income neighborhoods. (emphasis added)

To clarify further this provision, in an attempt to distinguish legitimate from discriminatory factors, the FHLBB general council's office prepared an internal memorandum in March of 1974. The memorandum stated that "redlining" not based on race, color, religion, or national origin is permissible in certain instances. The burden of proof, however, is on the lender, who must show clear evidence that the practice is a matter of economic necessity and that no less discriminatory means are available to assure sound financial lending.

Laufman v. *Oakley Building and Loan Company*, is the first lawsuit under Title VIII involving discrimination in housing finance. Robert Laufman brought a class action suit on behalf of all property-owners residing in racially integrated or predominately black neighborhoods as well as prospective purchasers of homes in such areas. The suit charged that Oakley Building and Loan Company of Cincinnati had rejected loan applications for houses in a radically integrated neighborhood. The plaintiff averred that the loans were denied for racial reasons and this rejection violated civil-rights guarantees. Oakley retorted that the Civil Rights Act was not applicable.

In February 1976 the U.S. District Court for Southern Ohio ruled that a prospective home-buyer denied a loan because of neighborhood racial composition can bring action under Title VIII of the 1968 Civil Rights Act. The court stated that redlining would violate Section 804 of the act, which prohibits discrimination in the provision of services relating to selling or renting a dwelling, as well as Section 805, which prohibits discrimination in the financing of housing. The Laufman ruling is important because it acknowledges civil-rights litigation as a medium for fighting redlining.

In a suit filed against the four banking regulatory agencies on April 28, 1976, ten civil-rights groups headed by the Center for National Policy Review accused the agencies of failing to carry out their duties under the Civil Rights Act. Specifically, the organizations charged that the agencies have failed to move against housing discrimination despite abundant evidence that such practices are prevalent among lending institutions regulated by them. These charges are in substantial agreement with the findings of a report the Senate Banking Committee issued in June of 1976 (U.S. Senate, 1976).

The limitation of the civil rights enforcement litigation approach is that racial discrimination is difficult to prove and is not easily distinguishable from legitimate reasons for denying loans. However, *Laufman* and other cases will probable sensitize the courts to the redlining/disinvestment issue. The courts are likely to find that areas with concentrations of minority or female-headed households are often areas whose residents have low income and poor credit. The neighborhoods may also lack the amenities associated with more middle-class, suburban communities. Since the urban lending environment involves many highly correlated racial and economic factors, proof of racial redlining becomes difficult to obtain.

Credit Allocation

A number of other approaches are being discussed to remedy the problems of mortgage-short communities. When credit denial is based on economic criteria, the most radical solution proposed—and one given a poor chance of becoming law—is a mandatory allocation of credit, which requires lenders to make a given percentage of their loans in a certain area. A credit allocation bill of this nature was introduced in the Michigan House during 1975, and similar proposals have been discussed by Illinois legislators.

The Michigan bill is a radical solution to the problem of neighborhood decline, a phenomenon only partially caused by lack of credit. The bill prohibits state-regulated lenders from denying residential real estate loans because of the geographical risk of residential real estate. Based on the premise that lending activity in a neighborhood should correspond to the deposits made by that area's residents, it allocates credit to be extended by a branch of a lending institution in a neighborhood according to the amount of deposits by residents in the neighborhood placed in that branch. It is unlikely that such a measure will be enacted at the federal level for two reasons. First, the House Banking Committee inserted specific language in the 1975 act to prevent its interpretation as a step toward credit allocation. Second, the full House also rejected another Banking Committee bill that would have required financial institutions to report on the uses of their credit. If the mere collection and reporting of data on credit use is feared as opening the door to credit allocation, it is doubtful that a law requiring the allocation of credit will be enacted.

Minimum investment requirements undoubtedly would partially alleviate the financing problems of mortgage-short neighborhoods, but they raise many questions, such as what are appropriate ratios and, more seriously, will such investments comprise the fiduciary responsibility of financial institutions (Ahlbrandt, 1975).

POSSIBLE FUTURE RESPONSES

Voluntary Cooperative Programs

The traditional approach for ameliorating the urban credit crunch has been for lenders to establish a voluntary pool of loan funds targeted for mortgage-short areas. Mortgage pools spread the risk of individual loans among the participating institutions so that no single lender is disproportionately penalized for bad loans.

In 1954 the Voluntary Home Mortgage Credit Program (VHMCP) was established, as a joint industry-government undertaking, to facilitate lending in areas (especially small rural localities) avoided by financial institutions and to encourage mortgage borrowing by minorities. An applicant rejected for FHA or VA insurance by two or more lending institutions could apply to a regional VHMCP office which maintained a roster of cooperating banks. Mortgage applicants were then sent on a rotating basis to these institutions until accepted. The federal government's role was limited to providing a small coordinating staff, office facilities, and advice.

A more recent effort was the life insurance industry's 1970 urban investment program. Over 140 life insurance companies made commitments to invest in inner city housing and job-creating opportunities. On a basis prorated according to their assets, these companies invested $2 billion in areas they would normally have avoided.

Other cooperative investment efforts include the New York State pool, the Boston Urban Renewal Group, the Philadelphia and New Haven pools, the Savings Service Corporation in St. Louis, the Mortgage Opportunity Committee in Pittsburgh, the Savings Associations Financial Enterprises, Inc. in Washington, D.C., and the California Savings Associations Mortgage Company, Inc.

The latter, which has operated in the San Francisco Bay Area since 1971, had financed the acquisition or rehabilitation of about 1000 units by 1974, representing total loans of $35.8 million. Affirmative action by individual lenders, often called greenlining, includes the Bank of America's serving as lending intermediary for urban rehabilitation funds in three California cities and a pledge by Midwest Federal Savings and Loan Association of Minneapolis to increase inner city lending. In 1974 the Illinois Housing Development Authority (IHDA) started a pilot program in which it sells securities and lends the proceeds to savings and loan associations and banks that agree to match the funds with an equal amount for loans in their primary service areas.

The voluntary investment efforts have achieved some measure of success. The VHMCP was responsible for placing almost 50,000 mortgages, the urban investments program helped finance the construction or rehabilitation of over 60,000 units, and the New York State pool helped finance many of the Bedford-Stuyvesant Restoration Corporation's housing efforts. Profit was one of the factors that prompted the investment, although the expected return on many of the loans proved to be less than what could be expected on comparable nonurban investments. Other important considerations were protection of sunk investments and a demonstration to the public of the social conscience of the business community.

In 1970, life insurance companies held $15 billion of outstanding central city residential mortgages; savings and loan associations, $17 billion; mutual savings banks, $9 billion; and commercial banks, $6 billion (U.S. Senate 1973: 304). Many of the corporations involved in urban financing programs held considerable commercial real estate holdings, including corporate headquarters and office or warehouse space, in addition to the outstanding loans they held. Business social conscience and concern for urban problems was often expressed during the 1960s by life insurance industry and other executives (Walton, 1967).

But the voluntary approach has severe limitations. The amount set aside for investment is usually small, the noblesse oblige philosophy of some of the past pool participants has troubled urban residents, and the pool investments themselves may be conservative or limited to a particular area, giving rise to charges of discrimination. For example, the IHDA loan-to-lender program, which has provided twenty Chicago banks and lending institutions about $45 million for over two-thousand mortgages, has served low-income and minority areas less well than transitional neighborhoods (Leadership Council for Metropolitan Open Communities, 1976). Another program, where savers at Baltimore Federal may participate in a "Designated Dollar" fund, earmarking where their savings funds will be used for home mortgages, could result in discrimination against certain neighborhoods.

Reducing Urban Lending Risk

Another strategy for reducing the cost and risk of urban mortgage lending is for states to allow localities to use the power of direct sale of abandoned properties rather than judicial foreclosure. The former technique, according to a 1972 Comptroller General report (U.S. General Accounting Office, 1972), is much faster and cheaper, and a switch by those states currently requiring judicial foreclosure would result in direct cost savings. More important, the mortgagee could recover the delinquent parcel quickly, lessening the incidence of vandalism and abandonment that often accompanies the lengthy process of judicial foreclosure. "Fast take" should not be indiscriminately allowed, however. Delinquent mortgagors who are maintaining their parcels should be permitted an adequate measure of forebearance.

Reducing risk also calls for mortgage loan programs, as currently operated by several states and localities. The Maryland Housing Fund offers up to 100 percent coverage of single-family loans issued on Baltimore properties. The Wisconsin Insurance Indemnity Fund is authorized to reinsure insurance companies that guarantee loans to finance the construction of multiple-unit housing in congested urban areas and in other areas designated for construction intended to replace substandard and deteriorated housing. A number of local insurance programs, such as the Fresno, California effort and more recently the Real Estate Mortgage Insurance Program (REMIC) in New York City, have been developed. These programs differ in detail; REMIC is an insurance approach, while the Wisconsin program offers reinsurance. Other differences concern the percentage of loss covered, the properties eligible for insurance, the premiums to be paid, and the level of capitalization. One benefit of these programs is that lenders are more amenable to granting urban mortgages if their liability is reduced. Additionally, considerable leverage results from the amount of insurance generated from a relatively small public investment. REMIC, for example, was capitalized with a $7.5 million reserve, and this reserve is deemed sufficient to sustain $150 million in insurance coverage, a leverage ratio of 1 to 20. Insurance programs require a comparatively small staff to operate, and most of the paperwork is done by mortgagees who are reinsured. New Jersey is considering a $100 million coinsurance plan to direct mortgages and home improvement loans into redlined areas.

The major drawback to the insurance program is that, since loan interest rates are not subsidized, those urban residents who cannot afford market interest costs are not assisted. Additionally, most of the newly formed programs insure only one-fifth or one-third rather than the entire loan, a coverage lenders consider inadequate for high-risk urban mortgages (New Jersey Department of Community Affairs, 1975).

Expanding the range of insurance to cover most of the loan amount evokes several questions: Should FHA be reinvented? If so, should it resume its former policy of creaming its coverage to minimize its losses? Or should it continue its more recent policy of stressing social need at the expense of actuarial prudence? These questions do not invalidate the insurance approach; some level of coverage is needed to address the urban mortgage crunch. Rather, they emphasize that hard decisions must be made on the structuring and emphasis of any new insurance efforts.

Neighborhood Deterioration and Preservation

Most of the strategies discussed so far are narrow, short-term responses to the urban financing problem. Civil-rights enforcement litigation addresses the alleged discriminatory aspects of the urban mortgage crunch, but it is doubtful that racial-social bias accounts for much of the credit problem. The financial approaches are also palliatives. For example, a public insurance program for high-risk urban mortgages reduces the risk for lenders but transfers the risk and losses to the public insuring body.

Resolving the urban credit problem requires confronting the larger underlying difficulty: how to reverse urban neighborhood deterioration and promote stabilization and preservation. Neighborhood decline is only in part due to the mortgage crunch, which actually comes late in the process. A host of other factors influence the health of an area. A partial listing includes:

Macro changes; such as a decline in regional economic health and desirability. The falling fortunes of the Northeast and the rising star of the "Sunbelt" negatively impacts on northeastern urban areas while having a positive effect on southern cities.

Micro changes; such as the shifting job patterns and communication-transportation networks within a metropolitan area. These changes can hasten decline in some communities and neighborhoods while acting as a growth-stabilization catalyst in other locations.

Submicro changes; a series of factors that include the age and composition of a neighborhood's housing stock, its location (e.g., proximity to parks, transportation, etc.), the decision by local government whether to maintain or improve public facilities and services, and the performance of investors and real estate brokers. Contiguous areas can also play a major role in influencing the health of a particular neighborhood.

Neighborhood Housing Services

Another cooperative approach, characterized by participation of community residents and risk-sharing by lenders, is the neighborhood housing services (NHS) program, which encourages neighborhood conservation by bringing private capital into a declining area. NHS programs have been incorporated into approximately thirty localities and are under development in additional cities. They are modeled after the Pittsburgh pilot program, which since 1968 has made 300 loans, two-thirds of them concentrated on the central north side.

An outgrowth of NHS is the Urban Reinvestment Task Force, established in 1974 and supported through an interagency agreement between HUD and the Federal Home Loan Bank Board. During fiscal year 1976, the task force operated under a $2.5 million demonstration grant. In addition, the task force provides developmental funds in nine selected demonstration projects called Neighborhood Preservation Projects. In December 1975 the FHLBB established an Office of Neighborhood Reinvestment to administer NHS.

NHS, which emphasizes homeownership for existing residents who rent, relies on a partnership among neighborhood groups, local lending institutions, and the municipality. The latter, through its code enforcement program, identifies structures that require upgrading. The NHS program assists the residents in obtaining financing through conventional sources or a special high-risk fund. The heart of the NHS is this High Risk Revolving Loan Fund, which is established through grants from foundations, financial institutions, businesses and corporations, and more recently from the Urban Reinvestment Task Force.

Individuals in the target communities who are denied conventional financing and considered unacceptable for loans by traditional lending institutions make an application to NHS. A loan committee, usually consisting of community residents as well as lenders, reviews the applications. If approved, the applicant is granted a loan from the High Risk Loan Fund at interest rates ranging from zero to the prevailing market rate, depending on the particular financial circumstances. Bankable loans are referred to cooperating lenders, who are expected to be more sympathetic to granting financing as a result of the NHS's supportive activities.

Local governments participate through programs designed to prevent neighborhood deterioration such as code enforcement and improvements in public facilities and services. Some state governments have also aided the program; the New Jersey Department of Community Affairs, for example, has given a grant to help establish NHS in Plainfield.

NHS offers advantages over past voluntary loan programs. Considerable cooperation exists between lenders and urban residents and this interaction fosters much-needed mutual trust. Additionally, the financial institutions are joined by foundations and others in capitalizing and sharing the exposure of the High Risk Loan Fund.

The limitations of this program must also be noted. NHS is most applicable in "gray areas" where lenders can be expected to increase their loan portfolios, where the High Risk Loan Fund can be expected to revolve with reasonable success, and where the local government code enforcement and related activities will have a positive impact. NHS is *not* likely to have an impact in higher risk areas, and the program will have little appeal to the conservative lender who generally fears the risk of urban loans. NHS acts only indirectly to reduce such dangers, and additional programs discussed above should be considered as complementary.

CONCLUSION

Resolution of the urban mortgage crunch will ultimately require dealing with the larger issue of urban decay. This, in turn, mandates implementation of a comprehensive neighborhood preservation strategy that includes the many programs and approaches discussed here. The preservation strategy has been examined elsewhere (Phillips and Agelasto, 1975), so we shall discuss it only briefly. Also necessary will be consideration of the many elements of national housing policy (monetary policy, financial institutions regulation, tax policy, income and housing subsidies, and secondary market operations) that can assist in neighborhood preservation.

The housing elements of a preservation strategy might also include urban homesteading, public land assemblage, municipal rehabilitation loan funds, and historic preservation (Agelasto, 1976). While techniques can be dealt with separately for convenience, it should be noted that they mutually benefit one another. A rehabilitation program, for example, may have only short-term success unless abandoned buildings in the area where renovation is effected are demolished. New construction may encourage rehabilitation and vice versa. Land banking, by helping to control and manage growth, can aid historic preservation. These interactions should be considered in developing neighborhood preservation programs to address local needs. Social elements might include counseling for tenants and homeowners and the encouragement of block and civic organizations. Economic strategies might include manpower development and community economic development.

Preservation is a *comprehensive* strategy that includes rehabilitation, new construction and selective demolition, as well as economic and social supportive efforts such as job-training and family counseling. Preservation is a flexible strategy that recognizes the existence of a continuum of urban neighborhoods ranging from "healthy" to "abandoned." Different responses are suitable for different areas. Basically stable areas may require code enforcement and the maintenance of public facilities and services, while neighborhoods with severe abandonment may need a more comprehensive input of demolition, new construction, land banking, and extensive economic and social support. Preservation is a long-term strategy, for it recognizes the dynamics of neighborhood change and, unlike past categorical programs, forsees an ongoing application of housing, social, and economic support. Some areas may be too devastated for anything short of total redevelopment or total neglect.

Unfortunately, as the different approaches are being debated they are sometimes misunderstood or placed in opposition to one another. An example is the Urban Reinvestment Coinsurance Act, introduced by Chicago Congressman Frank Annunzio. The bill called for establishment of a FHLBB fund to coinsure 80 percent of each loan made by lenders on properties in specific central city neighborhoods and homes built over twenty-five years ago. Lenders would carry the risk of the top 20 percent. The bill was opposed by antiredlining groups, who argued that it would in fact legalize redlining.

The disclosure of data relating to the lending patterns of financial institutions is only one small part of an over-all preservation strategy. Insofar as the redlining/disinvestment debate has helped start a dialogue between federal and local officials, community groups and lending institutions, especially in making the latter more responsive to neighborhood mortgage needs, it has served as an important step in the preservation process (*Washington Post,* 1976). More positive actions need to follow.

REFERENCES

Abrams, C. (1955) *Forbidden Neighbors: A Study in Prejudice in Housing.* New York: Harper and Brothers.

Agelasto, M. (1976) "Neighborhood Conservation Through Housing Preservation." Washington, D.C.: Congressional Research Service (76–154G). U.S. Library of Congress (August).

———, and D. Listokin (1975) "The Urban Financing Dilemma: Disinvestment-Redlining." Monticello, Ill.: Council of Planning Librarians, CPL Bibliography 890 (October).

Ahlbrandt, R. (1975) "Redlining: An Economic Phenomenon." Pittsburgh: Action Housing, Inc.

——— (1976) "Credit Allocation Legislation No Answer to Redlining Controversy." *Mortgage Banker* 36 (March): 6.

American Banker (1975) "Facts, Not Emotion, on Redlining." 140 (May 28): 4.

American Council on Banking (1968) "Urban Financing Guide."

Bill Moyer's Journal (1976) "The People Against Redlining." New York: Public Broadcasting Service.

Boyer, B. (1973) *Cities Destroyed for Cash*. Chicago: Follett.

Bradford, C., and L. Rubinowitz (1975) "The Urban-Suburban Investment-Disinvestment Process: Consequences for Older Neighborhoods." *Annals of American Academy of Political and Social Science* 442 (November): 77–86.

Brophy, D. (1970) "The Usury Law: A Barrier to Home Financing." *Michigan Business Review* 22 (January): 25–31.

Case, F. (1972) *Inner-City Housing and Private Enterprise*. New York: Praeger.

Center for New Corporate Priorities (1975) "Where the Money Is—Mortgage Lending Los Angeles County, 1975." Los Angeles: National Task Force on Credit Policy.

Chicago Mayor's Commission on Human Relations (1962) "Selling and Buying Real Estate in a Racially Changing Neighborhood: A Survey" (mimeographed).

City of Seattle (1976) "Summary and Comparison of Recommendations Made by Mayor's Reinvestment Task Force." Seattle: Office of Policy Planning (June 18).

Clearinghouse on Corporate Social Responsibility (1973) "A Report on the $2 Billion Urban Investment Program of the Life Insurance Business." New York: Clearinghouse on Corporate Social Responsibility.

Contract Buyers League of Chicago (1968) "The Contract Buyers League Demands Justice." Chicago: Contract Buyers League, mimeographed (December).

Devine, R. (1973) "Where the Lender Looks First: A Case Study of Mortgage Disinvestment in Bronx County, 1960–1970." New York: National Urban League.

Dorfman, R. (1975) "Greenlining Chicago: The Citizen's Action Program." *Working Papers for a New Society* 3 (Summer): 32–36.

Duncan, M., E. Hood, and J. Neet (1975) "Redlining Practices, Racial Resegregation and Urban Decay: Neighborhood Housing Services as a Viable Alternative." *Urban Lawyer* 7 (Summer): 510–39.

Federal Home Loan Bank Board (1972) "1971 Survey on Lending Practices." Washington: FHLBB.

Federal Home Loan Bank of Chicago (1974) "Description of Savings/Lending Survey Computer Data Processing." Chicago: Federal Home Loan Bank, February 21 news dispatch.

Federal National Mortgage Association (1976) "Redlining." Washington, D.C.

Fried, J. (1971) *Housing Crisis U.S.A.* New York: Praeger.

Governor's Commission on Mortgage Practices (1975) "Homeownership in Illinois: The Elusive Dream." Springfield, Ill.: State of Illinois.

Governor's Task Force on Redlining (1976) "Interim Report." Lansing, Mich. (August).

Illinois Legislative Investigating Commission (1975) "Redlining-Discrimination in Residential Mortgage Loans." Springfield, Ill.: State of Illinois.

Jaffee, D. (1973) "Credit for Financing Housing Investment: Risk Factors and Capital Markets." Report submitted to the Department of Housing and Urban Development. Springfield, Va.: National Technical Information Service, Document PB-229-980.

Kansas City Star (1975) "Loan Denials Trap Old Neighborhoods." (20 July): 1.

Leadership Council for Metropolitan Open Communities (1976) "Interim Report on Illinois Housing Development Authority Loan to Lender Program. Phase I." Report prepared for Illinois Housing Development Authority (unpublished).

Levin, C. (1976) "Homeowners' Insurance in Detroit: A Study of Redlining Practices and Discriminatory Rates." Detroit: Detroit City Council.

Marshall, R. (1974) "The Flight of the Thrift Institution: One More Invitation to Inner City Disaster." *Rutgers Law Review* 28 (Fall): 113–25.

Maryland Advisory Committee to the U.S. Commission on Civil Rights (1975) "Hearings on Mortgage Lending and Employment Opportunity in Baltimore Savings and Loan Institutions as They Effect Minorities, Ethnics and Women." (unpublished).

McElhone, J., and R. Cramer (1975) "The Costs of Mortgage Loan Foreclosure: Some Recent Findings." *Federal Home Loan Bank Board Journal* 8 (June): 7–12.

McEntire, D. (1960) *Residence and Race*. Berkeley, Calif.: University of California Press.

Movement for Economic Justice (1975) "Organizer Notebook—Redlining Volume 2." Washington, D.C.: Movement for Economic Justice.

National Commission on Urban Problems (1969) *Building the American City*. Washington, D.C.: U.S. Government Printing Office.

National Committee Against Discrimination in Housing (1967) "How the Federal Government Builds Ghettos." New York: National Committee Against Discrimination in Housing.

——— (1972) "Patterns and Practices of Discrimination in Lending in Oakland, California." New York: National Committee Against Discrimination in Housing (mimeograph).

National Urban League (1971) *National Survey of Housing Abandonment*. New York: Center for Community Change.

Naparstek, A., and G. Cincotta (1975) "Urban Disinvestment: New Implications for Community Organization, Research and Public Policy." Washington, D.C.: National Center for Urban Ethnic Affairs.

New Jersey Department of Community Affairs (1975) "Urban Financing Dilemma." Report prepared by D. Listokin.

Northwest Community Housing Association, Inc. (1973) "Mortgage Disinvestment in Northwest Philadelphia" (mimeograph).

Nourse, H., and D. Phares (1975) "Socioeconomic Transition and Housing Values: A Comparative Analysis of Urban Neighborhoods." In Gappert and Rose (eds.) *The Social Economy of Cities*. Beverly Hills, Calif.: Sage.

Orren, K. (1974) *Corporate Power and Social Change*. Baltimore: Johns Hopkins University Press.

Phillips, K., and M. Agelasto (1975) "Housing and Central Cities: The Conservation Approach." *Ecology Law Review* 4: 797.

Phoenix Fund (1975) "Savings and Loan Lending Activity in the City of St. Louis." St. Louis: Phoenix Fund.

Rafter, G. (ed.) (1975) "Crisis in Urban Lending: Myth or Reality." Chicago: Institute of Financial Education.

Rapkin, C. (1959) "The Real Estate Market in an Urban Renewal Area." New York: New York City Planning Commision.

Redlining Rag (various issues). Los Angeles: Coalition Against Redlining.

Smith, W. (1970) "Housing the Underhoused—Oakland, California." Study prepared for Case (1972), unpublished manuscript.

Spidell, F. (1972) "Discrimination in Lending and Employment." *Federal Home Loan Bank Board Journal* 7 (September): 10.

Stegman, M. (1972) *Housing Investment in the Inner City.* Cambridge, Mass.: MIT Press.

Sternlieb, G. (1966) *The Tenement Landlord.* New Brunswick, N.J.: Center for Urban Policy Research, Rutgers.

—— (1971) "The Urban Housing Dilemma." New York: Housing and Redevelopment Administration.

——, and R. Burchell (1973) *Residential Abandonment: The Tenement Landlord Revisited.* New Brunswick, N.J.: Center for Urban Policy Research, Rutgers.

Swan, H.S. (1944) *Housing Market in New York City.* New York: Reinhold.

Taggart, T. (1974) "Redlining—How the Bankers Starve the Cities to Feed the Suburbs." *Planning* 40 (December): 14–16.

U.S. Commission on Civil Rights (1962) Hearings on Housing in Washington. Washington, D.C.: Government Printing Office.

—— (1973) "The Federal Civil Rights Enforcement Effort: A Reassessment." Washington, D.C.: Government Printing Office.

U.S. Department of Housing and Urban Development (1972) Office of Equal Opportunity, "Private Lending Institutions Questionnaire—Initial Report on Returns." In U.S. House of Representatives (1972) Hearings on Federal Government's Role in the Achievement of Equal Opportunity in Housing Before the Civil Rights Subcommittee of the Judiciary Committee. 91st Cong., 1st Sess. (June).

—— (1976). Administrative Meeting on Redlining/Disinvestment. Philadelphia, Pa. (July 14–16).

U.S. General Accounting Office (1972) "Opportunities to Reduce Costs in Acquiring Properties Resulting from Defaults on Home Loans." Washington, D.C.: U.S.G.A.O.

U.S. House of Representatives (1975) Hearings on Bank Failures, Regulatory Reform, Financial Privacy Before the Subcommittee on Financial Institutions Supervision, Regulation and Insurance of Committee on Banking, Currency and Housing. 94th Cong., 1st Sess. (June–July).

Urban Land Institute (1976) "New Opportunities for Residential Development in Central Cities." Washington, D.C.: Urban Land Institute, Research Report #25.

Urban-Suburban Investment Group (1974) "Regulation of Federally Chartered Savings and Loan Associations: Chartering, Branching, Relocation, Redesignation of Home Offices." Evanston, Ill.: Northwestern University.

U.S. Senate (1971) Hearings on Competition in Real Estate and Mortgage Lending Before the Subcommittee on Antitrust and Monopoly of the Committee on Judiciary. 92nd Cong., 2nd Sess.

—— (1973) Central City Problem and Urban Renewal Policy. 93rd Cong., 1st Sess., Committee print.

—— (1975a) Hearings on the Home Mortgage Disclosure Act of 1975 Before the Committee on Banking, Housing and Urban Affairs. 94th Cong., 1st Sess., (May).

—— (1975b) Home Mortgage Disclosure Act, Conference Report. 94th Cong., 1st Sess., report 94-553 (December 12).

—— (1975c) Report on Home Mortgage Disclosure Act of 1975. 94th Cong., 1st Sess., report 94-187 (June 6).

—— (1976) Report on Fair Lending Enforcement by the Four Federal Financial Regulatory Agencies. 94th Cong., 2nd Sess., report 94-930 (June 3).

Vandell, K., B.S. Hodas and R. Bratt (1974) "Financial Institutions and Neighborhood Decline: A Review of the Literature." Report submitted to the Federal Home Loan Bank Board (November).

Vitarello, J., W. Balko, and C. Washington (1975) "Redlining: Mortgage Disinvestment in the District of Columbia." Washington, D.C.: Public Interest Research Group.

Von Furstenberg, G. (1971) "Technical Studies of Mortgage Default Risk." Ithaca, N.Y.: Center for Urban Development Research, Cornell University.

——, and R.J. Green (1974a) "Estimation of Delinquency Risk for Home Mortgage Portfolios." *Journal of American Real Estate and Urban Economics Association* 2 (Spring): 62.

—— (1974b) "The Effect of Income and Race on the Quality of Home Mortgages: A Case for Pittsburgh." In Von Furstenberg, et al. (eds.), *Patterns of Racial Discrimination*, Vol. I: *Housing*. Lexington, Mass.: Lexington Books.

Walton, C. (1967) *Corporate Social Responsibility*. Belmont, Calif.: Wadsworth Publishing Company.

Washington Post (1976) "D.C. Mortgage Funds Up." (3 October).

Williams, A.O., W. Beranek, and J. Kenkel (1974) "Default Risk in Urban Mortgages: A Pitsburgh Prototype Analysis." *Journal of American Real Estate and Urban Economics Association* 2 (Fall): 101–12.

✳ *Part III*

Public Policy: Past, Present, and Future

✳ *Chapter 5*

"A Decent Home": An Assessment of Progress Toward the National Housing Goal and Policies Adopted to Achieve It

John C. Weicher[a]

This paper is written from an unusual vantage point. For the past year, I have been serving as chief economist for the Department of Housing and Urban Development (HUD). Part of my responsibility in that position is to monitor progress toward meeting the national housing goal. Each year since the 1968 National Housing Act was adopted, HUD has prepared the *Annual Report* on the National Housing Goal that the president is required to submit to the Congress; my office has prepared that report for the department and the president. The report is partly a statement of policy and partly a document of record on housing production, mortgage market developments, the quality of the existing housing stock, and program achievements of HUD and other government agencies responsible for housing. In recent years, the report has consisted of sixty pages of text and two hundred pages of appendices; it is a major publication of the department.

This paper draws on my experience in preparing the *Annual Housing Goal Report* to discuss the improvements in housing quality which have occurred since the national housing goal was first established. It then discusses the policies Congress has adopted to achieve that goal, tracing their evolution and discussing their theoretical foundations and the empirical evidence available to support them.

---

[a] The author was deputy assistant secretary for economic affairs, U.S. Department of Housing and Urban Development, when this paper was written. The opinions expressed are his own, and not necessarily those of the Department of Housing and Urban Development.

CHANGES IN HOUSING QUALITY

The national housing goal is "a decent home in a suitable living environment." Congress established this goal in 1949 in the National Housing Act of that year, and reiterated it in 1968 and 1974. In 1968, Congress went further and required the president to report annually on progress toward meeting the national housing goal.

However, Congress has never defined what it meant by "decent" or "suitable." In fact, Congress has never specified what it meant by "living environment"—the physical characteristics of structures in a neighborhood, the quality of public services, access to jobs, all of them combined, or something entirely different. With the goal undefined, in practical terms, it has been difficult to measure progress toward it.

The problem is compounded by the lack of data on housing quality. Until very recently, the only available national data on housing has been the decennial *Census of Housing,* which not only appears infrequently but contains relatively little actual material on housing quality. It is, of course, difficult to report on housing conditions annually when the only information is available decennially. However, since 1973, this problen has been greatly alleviated by the *Annual Housing Survey,* which the Census Bureau has begun to conduct for the Department of Housing and Urban Development. This survey samples about one in every thousand housing units in the United States. The same units are visited each year, making it possible to track, for the first time, changing conditions in a given unit, including improvements and deterioration. The *Annual Housing Survey* differs from the decennial census in that it contains much less information on the characteristics of the people living in the unit and much more on the unit itself. For example, in addition to counting the number of units without complete plumbing facilities, it also counts the number in which the plumbing has malfunctioned significantly.

Data from the *Annual Housing Survey,* when combined with earlier census data, permit a much more precise analysis of changes in housing quality than has previously been possible. Based on these data, it can be said that housing quality has been improving steadily, dramatically so since the end of World War II, and that by every available measure of quality our housing is better than ever. Indeed, it now appears that, insofar as it can be measured, we are very close to achieving the national housing goal of "a decent home" for every American household, as it was conceived in 1949. At present rates of improvement, we will probably achieve it before 1980.

This may sound paradoxical since Congress has never defined "decent" explicitly, but the congressional hearings, reports, and speeches of the immediate postwar period give a strong indication as to the kinds of living conditions that were of particular concern at that time. While many different aspects of housing attracted at least some public attention in the late 1940s, the primary focus was on three major attributes: plumbing facilities, the general state of repair, and the relationship between the size of the housing unit and the number of people living in it.[b] Along these dimensions, we have very nearly achieved the housing goal articulated in 1949.

Table 5-1 shows the proportion of the United States housing stock which has been deficient in each of these three characteristics over the

Table 5-1. Measures of Housing Inadequacy: 1940-75

Characteristic	1940	1950	1960	1970	1975
Percent lacking some or all plumbing	45.2	35.4	16.8	6.5	3.5
Percent dilapidated or needing major repairs	17.8	9.8	6.9	4.6	NA
Percent substandard: dilapidated or lacking plumbing	49.2	36.9	18.2	9.0	NA
Percent with 1.51 or more persons per room	9.0	6.2	3.6	2.0	1.0
Percent of "doubling up" (two families in same unit)	6.8	5.6	2.4	1.4	1.2[a]

[a] Data as of March 1, 1976.
NA=not available.
Sources: U.S. Department of Commerce, Bureau of the Census, Decennial *Census of Housing;* U.S. Department of Commerce, Bureau of the Census and U.S. Department of Housing and Urban Development, Office of Policy Development and Research, *Annual Housing Survey*; and U.S. Department of Commerce, Bureau of the Census, *Current Population Survey.*

postwar period, according to the standards of 1949. As the figures reveal, very few remaining units fail to meet these standards, to the extent that consistent measurement is possible over time.

[b] Examples of congressional evaluation of housing quality include *Housing Study and Investigation,* the Final Majority Report of the Joint Committee on Housing, 80th Cong. 2nd Sess. (March 15, 1948), Part 2, Statistics of Housing, pp. 8–9. See also the statement of Senator Richard B. Russell, *Congressional Record*—Senate, April 22, 1948, pp. 4733–34. The congressional standards were consistent with public opinion, as reflected at hearings. A succinct definition of minimum housing standards was given at public congressional hearings in a report submitted by Mr. Power Higginbotham, mayor of Baton Rouge, Louisiana, "The Master City-Parish Plan for Metropolitan Baton Rouge," a preliminary report prepared for the City-Parish Planning Committee by Harland Bartholomew & Associates of St. Louis; *Study and Investigation of Housing,* Hearings Before the Joint Committee on Housing, 80th Cong. 1st Sess. (October 31, 1947), p. 1670; similar definitions were given by many other witnesses.

Judging from the amount of testimony and supporting documentation presented to congress at the time, the absence of plumbing facilities was the single most important housing deficiency in the country in 1949. Dozens of pages of congressional hearings describe the extent to which homes lacked running water, indoor toilets, or other plumbing.[c] The source of this concern is evident from table 5–1: at the time of the National Housing Act, over one-third of all U.S. housing did not have complete plumbing facilities. The problem was particularly acute in rural areas and in the South. Since 1949, the rate of progress has been impressive, to the point at which so few units lack complete plumbing that the concept has lost most of its significance as a measure of housing inadequacy, and has been omitted from the congressional formula to distribute federal housing assistance.[d]

The second most important characteristic of housing quality was the general condition of the structure, that is, whether it was "sound" or "dilapidated." The Census Bureau offered several criteria in 1950 and 1960 for determining whether a unit was dilapidated: substantial sagging of floors, walls or roof; or holes or open cracks over a large area of the foundation, walls, roof, floors, or ceilings. It even provided sample pictures to enumerators.[e] Data from 1950 and 1960 show a substantial decline in the incidence of dilapidated units over the decade. However, the Census Bureau became dissatisfied with this measure of quality, particularly in 1960, feeling that the concept of a dilapidated unit was too difficult for enumerators to quantify. This dissatisfaction, combined with the decision to conduct a mail census in 1970, caused the bureau to drop this category of housing quality. After significant public expressions of concern, particularly from city governments, the bureau did provide estimates of "dilapidated" units for 1970, using small samples and correlating housing quality with other characteristics for these samples in order to infer the number of dilapidated units from the incidence of the correlated characteristics. The resulting numbers are probably more inaccurate than the figures for 1950 and 1960. They seem somewhat implausible; for example, the number of dilapidated units is reported to have declined in only one of fifteen central cities, and that one is Detroit.[f] Despite these reservations, the data suggest a significant and steady decline in the number of dilapidated units. Further progress since 1970 has probably occurred, given other improvements in housing quality reported in the *Annual Housing Survey*. (Some of these have been shown in table 5–1; others are discussed below.)

[c] For example, *Study and Investigation of Housing*, pp. 1315–16.
[d] Housing and Community Development Act of 1974, Section 213(d).
[e] U.S. Bureau of the Census (1962: 1–246). Pages 1-248 to 1-258 contain the pictures.
[f] U.S. Bureau of the Census (1972).

The third most frequently cited measure of inadequate housing is the extent of overcrowding. However, overcrowding differs conceptually from dilapidated condition or plumbing facilities as a measure of housing condition. An overcrowded unit can be physically sound, unlike the other categories, but has too many people living in it. There is a mismatch between the unit and its occupants, but nothing is necessarily wrong with the unit itself. The distinction is important for housing policy. Overcrowding may be alleviated by physical changes in the unit, such as adding a room, but it can also be alleviated if the large family moves out and is replaced by a smaller one, or if one or two members move (such as an adult son or daughter). As in the case of physically inadequate units, the number of overcrowded units has been dropping sharply since the national housing goal was first enunciated.

The reduction in the number of crowded units is partly a result of growth in the number of single-person households, and there has been some tendency therefore to discount the decline; by definition a single-person household cannot be overcrowded since there cannot be more than one person per room. This matter of definition generates some anomalies, such as the much lower incidence of overcrowding among the elderly, despite their generally lower incomes. These phenomena highlight the limitations of the concept as a measure of housing conditions, but they do not vitiate its usefulness. An increasing number of single-person households is surely, to a substantial extent, a reflection of freely made choices by the individuals themselves; choices that they must believe have improved their well-being. Moreover, there has been a decline in overcrowding even among households with two or more persons; only 1.22 percent of these households had more than 1.5 persons per room in 1975.

Another measure of housing space is the extent of "doubling up" within housing units. "Doubling up" occurs when two families share the same housing unit, regardless of the number of rooms. This type of crowding is now so uncommon that it is difficult to remember how important a problem it was for returning veterans and other families right after World War II. It has been declining steadily since then; the March 1976 figure was the lowest recorded.

These three measures of housing quality were not the only criteria cited in 1949, but they were the most frequent and are probably the most useful. Other quality indices suggested at the time included the presence of electricity and cooking facilities, but 90 percent or more of American homes had these in 1949, so these criteria were already ceasing to be relevant.[g] Central heating was another characteristic that received atten-

---

[g] *Housing Study and Investigation,* part 2, p. 8.

tion.[h] Again, the data show a sharp decline in the incidence of occupied units lacking central heating, from 51 percent in 1950 to 23.6 percent in 1975. However, central heating is a less reliable guide to quality from a national standpoint, since it is much less important in regions with mild climates, such as the South, Southwest, or southern California (regions that have been gaining population during the postwar period). Also, some types of heating systems classified by the Census Bureau as "non-central" are generally regarded as adequate, such as electric baseboard heating.

The fact that we have nearly eliminated the major housing inadequacies that existed in 1949 does not imply that we need no further improvements in housing quality, or that there are no remaining inadequacies to be eliminated. As our housing quality improves, we are able to raise our standards, to reach for levels of amenities unrealizable or unrealistic in earlier years. To some extent, this process has been occurring. For example, the generally cited measure of crowding is now 1.01 or more persons per room, rather than the earlier figure of 1.51 or more. Even by this standard, the incidence of crowded housing units has been declining sharply, from 15.8 percent in 1950 to 11.5 percent in 1960, 8.0 percent in 1970, and 5.0 percent in 1975. In a few years, it is likely that this measure of crowding will become obsolete and another standard will be adopted, perhaps one or more persons per room. This change would mean that an "uncrowded" unit would have more rooms than people; currently a unit is not crowded if it has as many rooms as people.

In the case of crowding, it is relatively easy to define new standards over time as housing conditions improve; the concept can be quantified and easily measured. For other characteristics of housing, however, more subtle and sophisticated refinements on current standards, or altogether new concepts, will clearly be needed.

The *Annual Housing Survey* is beginning to provide measures of the quality of the housing stock which can be used to develop more appropriate standards of adequacy. The survey collects data on some thirty types of housing deficiency in more detail than has previously been available. Ultimately, it may be possible to develop a single measure of housing quality from these deficiences to serve as a replacement for the "dilapidated" concept no longer compiled by the Census Bureau. But this is not yet possible. In the meantime, data are available on individual deficiencies. Table 5–2 contains information on five of the most significant, in terms of dangers to the health and safety of the occupants: (1) lacking complete plumbing; (2) the presence of exposed electrical wiring; (3) fuses that blow at least three times in three months; (4) heating systems

[h] Ibid.

Table 5–2. Incidence of Selected Housing Deficiencies: 1973–75

Characteristic[a]	1973	1974	1975
Lacking Complete Plumbing	3.65%	3.22%	2.86%
Exposed Electrical Wiring	3.97	3.35	1.84
Blowing Fuses[b]	3.70	3.40	3.43
Heating Breakdown[c]	0.71	0.72	0.72
Toilet Breakdown[d]	0.32	0.26	0.26

[a] For housing occupied year-round.

[b] Blowing fuses three or more times in ninety days.

[c] Four or more breakdowns in ninety days in units with same occupant as the previous winter.

[d] Four or more breakdowns in ninety days in one-toilet units.

Source: U.S. Bureau of the Census and HUD, *Annual Housing Survey.*

that break down four or more times in a winter; and (5) toilets that break down four or more times in ninety days. Since the data on these characteristics are only available since 1973, there is little information on trends over time. Nonetheless it is interesting, and perhaps significant, that four of the five show measurable declines from year to year. In this, they parallel the decline in the number of units lacking complete plumbing, also shown in table 5–2. The fifth, heating breakdowns, remains stable.

To some extent, these five housing deficiencies may be encountered in the same unit. However, we lack as yet a full cross-classification of deficiencies. What data are available (several two-way classifications) suggest that the deficiencies typically do not coexist in the same unit. These data are reported in table 5–3 for 1974, the latest year available. Generally, they show that units lacking complete plumbing typically do

Table 5–3. Joint Incidence of Housing Deficiencies: 1974

Percent of all units with the deficiency at the right which also have the deficiency below:	Deficiency				
	Lacking Complete Plumbing	Exposed Electrical Wiring	Blowing Fuses[a]	Heating Breakdown[a]	Toilet Breakdown[a]
Lacking Complete Plumbing	100.0	15.0	2.8	3.5	—
Exposed Electrical Wiring	16.8	100.0	6.2	4.2	NA
Blowing Fuses[a]	2.7	5.4	100.0	6.1	NA
Heating Breakdown[a]	0.6	0.7	1.3	100.0	3.4
Toilet Breakdown[a]	—	NA	NA	0.9	100.0

[a] Same definitions as Table 5–2.

— = no data.

NA = not available.

Source: U.S. Bureau of the Census and HUD, *Annual Housing Survey* (1974).

not have other deficiencies; similarly, units with exposed electrical wiring rarely have other defects. Only limited inferences can be drawn from these data, but they do indicate that deficiencies tend not to be concentrated in the same units; instead, most units with one deficiency have only that one. This pattern suggests that most units with deficiencies can be classed as "high substandard," meaning that they have only one defect. That few units have a concentration of deficiencies is another indication of the improvements in housing quality that have taken place since 1949.

In very recent years, another measure of inadequacy has begun to find currency: the ability of the family to afford decent housing, as measured by the number who are paying above some specified fraction of income for rent. Usually, the fraction is 25 percent; sometimes an additional measure of 35 percent is used for elderly and single-person households. This concept has limitations: it applies only to renters, not to owners. There is little data on the monthly or annual expenditure/income relationships for owners, other than for those currently buying houses. Thus, the number of households with high housing cost is automatically restricted to a subset—and a diminishing subset—of all households.

Even with these limitations, it is still instructive to examine the history of the number of households with high rent-income ratios. Unlike the measures of physical condition and crowding, both the number and the proportion have tended to rise since the housing goal was established in 1949. As of 1975, according to the *Annual Housing Survey,* about 45 percent of renters paid at least 25 percent of their income for rent, up from 41 percent in 1973, 39 percent in 1970, and 31 percent in 1950. There are several reasons for this, such as the growing number of single-person households, particularly among the elderly, for whom current income is especially likely to be a poor measure of ability to pay for housing. Still, the difference in the movement of the rent-income measure and the physical measures of housing quality is striking. While every measure of physical quality shows improvement for as long as we can measure it, the number paying a high proportion of their income for rent has grown.

These data suggest several conclusions. There are relatively few physically inadequate units, and their number is diminishing rapidly. Increasingly, the standard measures of physical quality are obsolete for policy purposes; the number lacking complete plumbing apparently is dropping significantly from year to year, and the number in the highest category of crowding (1.51 or more persons per room) is vanishingly small. We are apparently very close to achieving the national housing goal of a "decent home," as it was originally envisioned in 1949. We will probably meet it, for all practical purposes, by 1980. By that time, however, we will have new goals; indeed, we are beginning to form them now. New goals will be desirable as we meet the old ones. As George Stigler (1952: 2) has noted:

"From an Olympian peak, one may say that the economic system has as its purpose forcing people to find new scarcities." As we find new goals, however, we should not overlook the progress that has already been made.

One likely new goal is the reduction of housing costs, for low-income families in particular. The simplest measure of inadequate housing will probably become the rent-income ratio; a single physical standard of inadequacy is unlikely to be developed that will have the intuitive appeal of the percent-of-income criterion. The shift from physical to economic measures of adequacy is itself an important phenomenon, indicating that we have passed a significant milestone in housing quality.

HOUSING GOALS: THE RELATIONSHIP
BETWEEN MEANS AND ENDS

Much of this chapter thus far has been devoted to a discussion of the data on the quality of the existing housing stock, in part because very little public or political attention is given to it, either as a measure of progress toward meeting the housing goal or as a useful guide to developing policies. For example, in public discussions of the president's annual report on the housing goal, there are few if any comments on the quality of the stock which measures progress toward the goal. Instead, attention is given to the measurement of means to move toward the goal, with the relationship between means and ends almost entirely ignored. The remainder of this chapter discusses the means, and the relationship between means and ends, in light of the current state of the housing stock.

Broadly speaking, three strategies have been adopted for achieving our national housing goal. The first, embraced in the 1949 act that established the goal, was the demolition of substandard housing. This policy was gradually modified during succeeding revisions of the National Housing Act and was explicitly eliminated in 1968, when the numerical target of 26 million units in ten years heralded the adoption of a production strategy. Scandals and other problems associated with the particular programs developed to implement the production strategy led in 1974 to the acceptance by Congress of conservation of the existing stock as at least an alternative means of achieving the goal.

This chronology is admittedly oversimplified; there were elements of the conservation approach as early as the 1954 National Housing Act, in which the Federal Housing Administration (FHA) was permitted to insure mortgages that provided funds for rehabilitation of existing housing in urban renewal projects (under Section 220). Also, as one who must prepare an annual report to Congress on progress toward meeting the national housing goal is acutely aware, there is still a major emphasis on numerical production targets. As in most historical processes, the change from demolition to production to conservation has been gradual; but 1968 and 1974 do appear to be major turning points.

From an economic standpoint, the three policies can be categorized in terms of their assumptions about the supply of housing. Demolition is most efficient when the elasticity of supply of substandard housing is low, and when the cross-elasticity of supply between standard and substandard housing is also low. Under these conditions, the net effect of demolition is almost the same as the gross effect: the number of substandard units is reduced by demolition; few if any new substandard units are constructed; and few if any standard units are downgraded. The higher these elasticities, the less the improvement in over-all housing quality.

A housing production strategy is more efficient if the elasticity of supply of standard housing is low, as well as the cross-elasticity. The new units constructed will all or almost all be net additions to the housing stock; the price of standard quality housing will decline, but few or no units will be downgraded.

With a perfectly elastic supply of standard housing, neither demolition nor production will have any impact on housing quality. New units will simply substitute for units that would otherwise have been built. If the cross-elasticity between the two markets is also high, then some standard units will be downgraded to substandard. With high elasticities, conservation of the existing stock is likely to be the most effective policy to improve housing. It will require subsidies to induce owners to maintain or upgrade their units. As the demand for standard quality housing increases, the improvement in quality will be greater the higher the elasticity of supply of standard housing. With an inelastic supply, such subsidies only raise rents.

The demolition approach advanced in 1949 grew out of the experience with the public housing program in prior years. The underlying rationale appears to have been the then prevalent belief that the quality of housing exerted a large independent effect on the incidence of social pathology, disease, and other undesirable phenomena. This view, expressed most succinctly by then federal public housing commissioner Dillon S. Myer during the hearings leading up to the act (U.S. Senate, 1947: 118), now has few advocates among scholars who have studied either housing, public health, or social pathology. In several surveys of the relevant literature commissioned for the National Housing Policy Review in 1973, the strongest argument offered for the view that housing could affect social pathology or health was that it could at best be treated as one among several potentially important and interacting causal factors (Rothenberg, 1973). Other scholars found little or no evidence for any impact (Nourse, 1973; Kasl, 1973). But in 1949, better housing was apparently widely believed, in Congress and in the country, to generate better health and better citizens. Perhaps the clearest manifestation of the demolition methodology was the requirement for urban renewal projects that new housing could be built only if old substandard housing was torn down. If the housing was torn down, and the former residents had to move to better housing either in the project or somewhere else, then a step toward the national housing goal was taken.

In the process of taking that step, severe costs were imposed on the low-income families directly affected by the program. Most studies show that they generally moved into better housing, but in order to do so paid much higher rents (Hartman, 1964; Reynolds, 1961; U.S. Housing and Home Finance Agency, 1962). They also had to undergo the trauma of moving against their wishes (Fried, 1963).

It is not clear how demolition could have been expected to improve housing for the poor. Unlike public housing, the urban renewal program did not subsidize the housing it provided to an extent sufficient to bring it within the financial reach of low-income households. Simple supply and demand analysis of the interactions between the markets for standard and substandard housing establish the qualitative conclusions that the price would rise to the low-income household and the quantity of substandard housing available would decline, while the price of standard housing would fall and the quantity available would rise. Some low-income households would be forced to move from substandard to standard housing, which would make them better off, given the relative change in prices. Whether they would have been better off in their original situation, absent the change in prices, is another, more difficult question. Given any elasticity to the long-run supply curves, fewer households would move to standard housing than were displaced; therefore, something more than the number of low-income households who were *not* displaced would encounter rising prices and be made worse off.

The underlying economic model would therefore have apparently been one of zero elasticity of supply in each market and zero cross-elasticity. That is, if all the existing slums were torn down, all low-income families would have to live in adequate housing. Even with a zero or low elasticity, of course, the impact of a demolition policy depends on the elasticity of supply of standard quality housing. If that elasticity is low, then a government program to increase the supply of standard units—such as urban renewal or public housing—is likely to be more appropriate than reliance on market forces, from the standpoint of enabling the displaced low-income families to find standard housing they can afford. If the elasticity of supply of standard housing is very high, then no particular program is likely to be needed or effective.

Increasing public dissatisfaction and sheer outrage among those directly affected brought a progressive movement toward emphasis on rehabilitation within urban renewal projects and housing programs generally (Weicher, 1972: 7–10). By 1969, in fact, the original requirement was reversed: an old housing unit could be torn down only if a new one was built.[1] Demolition now has virtually no advocates; instead, the loss of existing units is treated as a matter of national concern.

By 1968, concern with housing for low-income families established production as the preferred methodology. The 1968 Housing Act explicitly stated: "The Congress . . . determines that [the national housing goal] can be substantially achieved within the next decade by the construction or rehabilitation of 26 million housing units, six million of these for low- and moderate-income families." Despite that explicit statement, however, the process by which these targets were to meet the national housing goal remains unclear. By any estimate, there were substantially more than six million substandard units in 1968. The Kaiser Committee, whose work supposedly provided the basis for the 26 million unit target, estimated the number of substandard units at 8.7 million.

The 1968 act also envisioned some relationship between the production of twenty million units for middle-income and upper-income families and the elimination of substandard housing for lower-income households. The linkage was never defined, and some analysts have concluded that the 1968 target represented an apples-and-oranges combination of a new housing demand forecast for those who could afford it, and an estimate of the number of substandard units that would need replacements to meet the goal. However, it seems likely that Congress expected the construction of new units for higher-income families to enable lower-income families to improve their housing through a filtering process.

FILTERING AS A MEANS TO ACHIEVE THE HOUSING GOAL

Filtering is probably the most confused concept in housing economics—the most frequently mentioned, ill-defined, uninvestigated notion in the literature. Its existence or nonexistence—even its impossibility—has been invoked in support of a wide range of policies. Since filtering is such an important concept, serving as the logical basis for a production strategy, it is worthy of an extended discussion.

This chapter assumes that the filtering process occurs if the price of the housing services provided by existing housing falls when new housing is built, and if it remains below its previous level for a significant period of

[1] Housing and Urban Development Act of 1969, section 210.
[j] Housing and Urban Development Act of 1968, section 1601.

time. Stated slightly more formally, filtering occurs if the long-term supply of housing services from existing housing is less than perfectly elastic at points to the left of the initial equilibrium position.

The importance of filtering from a policy standpoint is obvious. The Tandem Plan, urban renewal, and even Sections 235 and 236, must rely on filtering to help those at the bottom of the income distribution. Thus, filtering is important to the demolition strategy as well as the production approach.

The intellectual history of filtering is interesting. Since the concept first gained currency about twenty-five years ago, it has gone through a cycle of popularity. During the 1950s, it was extensively discussed, but was usually assumed to be valid. In 1960, however, Lowry strongly criticized the concept on purely theoretical grounds, arguing that it could not occur. Lowry's view dominated for about a decade, but some recent studies have utilized the concept, assuming it to hold true.

The theoretical discussion is confusing because the participants, especially the proponents, have not been very clear in defining the concept. Ratcliff (1949) focused on housing turnover as a key element. Fisher and Winnick (1951) described it in terms of housing units filtering down relatively in the quality distribution of the housing stock. Since nearly every unit is among the best units when it is built and among the worst when it is taken out of the stock, this definition is almost tautological. It is much more useful to define filtering in terms of the price per unit of housing services; in Grigsby's terms, a unit filters when its value falls more rapidly than its quality (1963).

Lowry does define filtering in terms of changing prices of housing services. His main criticism of this concept is that it ignores the response of landlords and other owners to a fall in the value of their property. Lowry argues that landlords will reduce maintenance expenditures in this situation and will thus let the quality level deteriorate until it is once again in line with the rent they can charge. When this happens, the price per unit of services will be back to its initial level. This same point has been made in somewhat different contexts by Olsen (1969) and Brueggeman (1973), who start from the premise that the housing market is competitive and the price per unit of service will tend to the minimum long-run average cost of producing services.

This entire discussion is both purely theoretical and purely literary. None of these authors has presented any real empirical evidence for his view, and none has written out his underlying assumptions or developed a formal model of the process. Olsen bases his work on an article by Muth (1960) which concludes that the housing market is competitive and that the process of adjustment is nearly complete in about six or seven years. However, Muth is concerned primarily with the demand for housing and presents very sketchy evidence that the supply is infinitely elastic, so that filtering could not occur. Also, Muth's work covers the period from 1915 to 1941. While the demand analysis has been extended by others to more recent years, his work on the supply side has not yet been carried further.

In contrast to this literature, there have been a few purely empirical studies of filtering. Probably the most thorough was conducted by Lansing, Clifton, and Morgan (1969). They traced the sequence of moves generated when a new house was built and a family moved into it. They found out where the family used to live, went to that house to talk to the new resident, found out where he used to live, went to that house, etc. The interviews continued until some natural end to the chain of moves was reached, such as the house being demolished after the family moved out of it or the people moving into some unit that didn't occupy a housing unit formerly (such as newlyweds who lived with their parents before marriage or college graduates who used to live in a dormitory).

This empirical literature tends to focus on the characteristics of the individuals involved as much as on their housing. Generally, it appears that people move to better housing and pay more in rent or purchase price for it. These studies contain a good deal of information about the dynamics of the housing market but do not really come to grips with the filtering question. They do not attempt to calculate the price per unit of housing services in both the new and old unit for any family, or for the new and old tenant of any unit. Moreover, they are very short run, focusing on characteristics just before and after moving rather than on longer-term behavior. Thus, they cannot establish whether filtering occurs in any long-run sense, nor whether it occurs in the very short run.

Several recent theoretical papers have assumed that some sort of filtering occurs. Articles by Muth (1974), Sweeney, (1974), and Ohls (1975) focus on submarket relationships on the supply side of the housing market. Muth assumes that housing units deteriorate at a fixed rate over time and investigates the filtering of these units to lower income groups. His concept of filtering in this paper focuses on the lower level of housing services provided by the unit over time and does not allow for changes in price per unit of service. Both Sweeney and Ohls, on the other hand, permit the price per unit of housing services to vary with quality, so that price changes can occur as a unit deteriorates. However, both papers are purely theoretical and do not attempt to provide empirical evidence for or against the possibility of filtering, as it has been defined in this paper. At this point, there appears to be no significant empirical evidence on the extent of filtering.

There are good reasons, unfortunately, why empirical studies have not been more fruitful. They concern the nature of the filtering process and the available data. For example, consider Lowry's argument that land-lords will reduce maintenance expenditures when the value of their property falls. Undoubtedly this could occur and a lower level of housing services would result. But it is important to consider the way in which the service reduction becomes manifest. Lower maintenance expenditures generate a reduction in the quality of the unit, not a change in its physical dimensions. A six-room, two-bath apartment will continue to have six rooms and two baths. A unit with gas heat and central air conditioning will still have gas heat and central air conditioning. Instead, the level of services will be reduced by not repairing peeling plaster or by not responding to minor plumbing or heating problems. Or, even more subtly, decorating allowances may be reduced or eliminated.

The reason, of course, is that it is very expensive to reduce the level of services by changing the physical dimensions of a unit. A large unit can be subdivided into smaller ones, but only at some cost for the carpentry and further cost for the additional kitchen and other facilities.

This obvious point has important implications for the empirical investigation of filtering. It is always easier to collect information on the physical dimensions and facilities of a dwelling than it is to collect more qualitative information. *the Census of Housing* is a good example of this. There is much detail on the number of rooms and bathrooms, heating system, kitchen facilities, etc., but there is virtually no information on the quality of the unit. The history of the one attempt by the census to measure quality—the "sound, deteriorating, dilapidated" classification—has already been discussed. Unfortunately, this is exactly where any impact of reduced maintenance is likely to show. This means that census data—and most other generally available housing data, such as assessment records—are not very useful for investigating filtering.

CONSERVATION AND UPGRADING

By 1973, serious public concern had developed with regard to the effects of the production strategy. At the same time that record numbers of subsidized units were being built, other neighborhoods, particularly within the central cities, were losing units at alarming rates. While it was not possible to establish a causal relationship, or even a clearly measurable empirical one, the juxtaposition of the two phenomena seemed to many policy-makers and students of housing to be more than coincidental. The costs of the production approach began to seem unacceptably high. Accordingly, the 1974 Housing and Community Development Act relied on the existing housing stock to provide shelter for low-income families. This was accomplished through a program of direct financial assistance for such families which was intended to enable them to acquire adequate housing on their own initiative.

Analytically, the strategy is opposite to filtering; it might perhaps be termed "percolating." The ability of lower-income households to afford better housing is expected to increase the stock of standard housing, through upgrading of the existing stock. Whereas filtering depends on the less than infinite elasticity of supply at points to the left of the current level of services, percolating, or upgrading, depends on a highly elastic supply at points to the right of the current level.

The process of upgrading has not been subjected to the same intensive analysis in the literature as has filtering. There is much casual empiricism, however, based primarily on the "Components of Inventory Change" and similar census data, which suggests that a large number of housing units do in fact percolate upward in quality. Muth in particular has stressed the importance of upgrading in explaining the general improvement in housing during the 1950s (Muth, 1969). More recently, the *Annual Housing Survey* data suggest the importance of the process of upgrading.

However, there has not been to my knowledge any sophisticated formal analysis of the process of upgrading, nor any empirical work to suggest how much upgrading can be expected in response to the increased income of the assisted families. There is a vast literature on the income-elasticity of demand for housing, much of it concluding that the elasticity is substantial. This literature has provided one basis for the widespread professional support for housing allowances. There is no corresponding literature on the elasticity of the supply of services, particularly from the existing stock.

IMPLICATIONS FROM THE DATA FOR ALTERNATIVE POLICIES

While there is not enough rigorous analysis for policy purposes, some inferences can be drawn from data on the quality of the stock. First, there have been steady declines in the most severe physical defects. Second, relatively few units have combinations of less severe defects. Both these facts suggest that the existing substandard housing stock is in the "high substandard" category, which suggests in turn that it could be raised to the level of standard quality by a relatively small expenditure—given an appropriately elastic supply curve.

Third, the most prevalent problem among the "housing poor" is their income, not their housing. Families in the high rent-income ratio category can be helped most directly by raising their incomes. A production approach is a tortuously indirect route, whose efficacy is at least open to serious question. Paradoxically, however, the rent-income ratio may be difficult to reduce, given the empirical evidence that the income elasticity of demand is high.

While the data are never as conclusive as would be desirable, they do not support a strategy of production and filtering to aid low-income families.

THE RELATIONSHIP BETWEEN MEANS AND GOALS

It was mentioned earlier that there is a strong tendency on the part of Congress, and many private analysts of housing, to focus on the extent to which means are being used rather than the extent to which goals are being met. HUD is required (under the 1968 act, which established the production approach) to report on how many new units are being produced each year. Earlier, HUD and its predecessor agencies kept detailed data on the number of substandard units being demolished under urban renewal, but very little data on how many new units would replace them. Currently, the department is continually being asked how many families are being assisted under the conservation approach as well as how many new units are being built. Part of the concern is based on a desire for an accounting of the public funds being spent to implement programs, which is understandable and proper. Part, however, seems to confuse the means with the goals.

On the other hand, while it is easy to criticize policy-makers for focusing on means rather than goals, it is not so easy either to provide adequate information about goals or to infer progress toward goals from data concerning means. Housing economists and housing specialists from other disciplines have not provided a widely accepted framework for analysis, or a base of empirical relationships that illuminate the *process* of attaining the housing goal. How does production improve housing quality for the poor? and how much does it do so? How hard is it to upgrade the existing stock? and how costly? At this point, these questions remain inadequately answered.

HUD is starting to gather the detailed data that will enable us to measure progress toward goals. So far, the data suggest that substantial progress has been made and is likely to continue. I hazarded the opinion earlier that we may well substantially achieve the national goal of a decent home, as originally defined, by 1980. Given the rate of progress in the social sciences, I will hazard with at least as much assurance the opinion that we will not have a well-developed body of analysis of housing sub-markets by that time. Thus, by 1980, we may well be in the position of having met the national housing goal of 1949 without knowing how we got there.

REFERENCES

Brueggeman, W.B. (1973) "An Analysis of the Filtering Process with Special Reference to Housing Subsidies." Washington, D.C.: U.S. Department of Housing and Urban Development.

Fisher, E. M., and L. Winnick (1951) "A Reformulation of the 'Filtering' Concept." *Journal of Social Issues* 7, nos. 1 & 2: 47–58.

Fried, M. (1963) "Grieving for a Lost Home: Psychological Costs of Relocation." In L. J. Duth (ed.) *The Urban Condition*. New York: Basic Books, Inc.

Grigsby, W.G. (1963) *Housing Markets and Public Policy*. Philadelphia: University of Pennsylvania Press.

Hartman, C. (1964) "The Housing of Relocation Families." *Journal of the American Institute of Planners* 30 (November): 266–86.

Kasl, S.V. (1973) "Effects of Housing on Mental and Physical Health." Washington, D.C.: U.S. Department of Housing and Urban Development.

Lansing, J.B., C.W. Clifton, and J.O. Morgan (1969) *New Homes and Poor People: A Study of Chains of Moves*. Ann Arbor, Mich.: Institute for Social Research.

Lowry, I.S. (1960) "Filtering and Housing Standards: A Conceptual Analysis." *Land Economics* 36 (November): 362–70.

Muth, R.F. (1960) "The Demand for Non-Farm Housing." In A.G. Harberger (ed.) *The Demand for Durable Goods*. Chicago: University of Chicago Press.

——— (1969) *Cities and Housing*. Chicago: University of Chicago Press.

——— (1974) "Moving Costs ad Housing Expenditures." *Journal of Urban Economics* 1 (January): 108–25.

Nourse, H.O. (1973) "The Rationale for Government Intervention in Housing: The External Benefit of Good Housing, Particularly with Respect to Neighborhood Property Values." Washington, D.C.: U.S. Department of Housing and Urban Development.

Ohls, J.C. (1975) "Public Policy Toward Low-Income Housing and Filtering in Housing Markets." *Journal of Urban Economics* 2 (April): 144–71.

Olsen, E.O. (1969) "A Competitive Theory of the Housing Market." *American Economic Review* 54 (September): 612–21.

Ratcliff, R.U. (1949) *Urban Land Economics*. New York: McGraw-Hill.

Reynolds, H.W. (1961) "What Do We Know About Our Experiences with Relocation?" *Journal of Intergroup Relations* 2 (Autumn): 342–54.

Rothenberg, J. (1973) "A Rationale for Government Intervention in Housing: The Externalities Generated by Good Housing." Washington, D.C.: U.S. Department of Housing and Urban Development.

Stigler, G.J. (1952) *The Theory of Price* (revised edition). New York: Macmillan.

Sweeney, J. L. (1974) "A Commodity Hierarchy Model of the Rental Housing Market." *Journal of Urban Economics* 1 (July): 288–323.

U.S. Bureau of the Census (1962) *1960 Census of Housing,* Final Report HC (1)-1. Washington, D.C.: U.S. Government Printing Office.

——— (1972) *1970 Census of Housing,* Vol. IV, *Components of Inventory Change.* Washington, D.C.: U.S. Government Printing Office.

——— and U.S. Department of Housing and Urban Development (various years) *Annual Housing Survey.* Washington, D.C.: U.S. Government Printing Office.

U.S. Congress, Joint Committee on Housing (1947) Study and Investigation of Housing: Hearings. Washington, D.C.: U.S. Government Printing Office.

——— (1948) Housing Study and Investigation, Final Majority Report. Washington, D.C.: U.S. Governnent Printing Office.

U.S. Congress, Senate Committee on Banking and Currency (1947) Housing Hearings. Washington, D.C.: U.S. Government Printing Office.

U.S. Housing and Home Finance Agency (1962) Relocation from Urban Renewal Project Areas. Washington, D.C.: U.S. Government Printing Office.

Weicher, J.C. (1972) *Urban Renewal: National Program for Local Problems.* Washington, D.C.: American Enterprise Institute for Public Policy Research.

 *Chapter 6*

Emerging Issues in
American Housing Policy

Roger Montgomery and Martin Gellen

FORCES AFFECTING HOUSING POLICY

In some sense every era is an age of transition. This is especially so in public policy because of the long lags that separate the appearance of new social forces and economic trends from their emergence as issues of policy. We are in the midst today of a transition between old policies shaped by past conditions and a new set of housing policies arising out of current forces in U.S. society. In this sense this chapter is not an exercise in crystal ball gazing. The shape of the transition is somewhat clear, and what follows examines some of its demensions.

The Politics of Housing

In American academic circles housing policy typically denotes a style of rational, microeconomic analysis of alternative courses of government action (Aaron, 1972; Solomon, 1974; U.S. Dept. of HUD, 1974). This tendency should not obscure the fact that in most areas of public policy, ideology and interest politics often have a far greater impact on specific policy moves. Legislators holding critical positions in the distribution of power, the bureaucracy, and the regulatory agencies have become more or less the captives of the giant corporate suppliers. Housing, in this regard, offers a somewhat curious picture because the key lobbies do not represent highly concentrated industries. Rather, the fragmentation among housing suppliers supports a continuous debate over policy directions which in other sectors have already largely been determined. Housing policy often gives the appearance of an ongoing social dialogue. For example, production policy assumes a continuing contest between those who favor an active role for government in setting targets, rationalizing supply factors (especially money), and using broad subsidies to bring the product within reach of mass demand, and those on the other side who favor a hands-off, minimum public intervention stance. The first group seeks to achieve high levels of production and believes the trickle-down and multiplier effects will take care of equity. The latter wants the best possible approximation of the classical marketplace; they tend to accept as inevitable certain market failures and seek to aid the unfortunate victims through a direct income strategy. The recent changes within the National Association of Home Builders (NAHB), a major lobby with extensive influence, illustrates perfectly this dichotomy in housing policy. When Nathaniel Rogg resigned as NAHB executive vice-president and took early retirement, a leading trade journal headlined the move "Staff Pilot Nat Rogg Leaving as Good Ship NAHB Swings to the Right" (*House and Home,* 1976a: 3). The balance of power in the NAHB now lies with conservative President Hart and his associates who are, according to *House and Home*: "little inclined to favor government programs as a way of life for the housing industry" (1976a:16).

Our two major political parties tend to reflect these positions. The Democrats generally advocate an activist role for government, while the Republicans seek to minimize regulation and omit direct financial aid. As the two parties alternate control of the presidency, the thrust of national housing policy fluctuates accordingly. Johnson's Great Society program set staggeringly high production targets and enacted a broad set of supply-side subsidies in order to attain them. The program was a brief success after a lag of several years. Ironically, success came only toward the end of Nixon's first term and lasted into the first year of his second term. That year marked a traumatic policy shift as Nixon extinguished overnight all the Great Society production subsidy programs in the "moratorium" of January 1973. Thereafter, the Republicans experimented with income supplements. In a small way, the Housing Act of 1974 contains the first steps toward this market approach to housing demand subsidies. Recent scholarly analyses have supported this shift in the orientation of national housing policy. Academics have argued that welfare economics generally confirms the demand-subsidy perspective and raises serious questions about the spillovers and unanticipated effects of the Keynesian Great Society production strategies.

In the next decade, however, housing policy will face a quite different range of difficulties. Primary among these are changes in the demographic structure of demand and housing price inflation. Judging from its previous policy preferences, the new national Democratic administration probably will be less wedded to a conservative microeconomic view of housing policy. It is not clear, however, that the Carter administration and the Democratic majority in Congress will press for a return to the Great Society housing programs and the massive production subsidies that seemed so effective at an aggregate level in the early 1970s. Nor is it apparent what will become of the small beginnings of demand subsides. In general, if inflation and this unique decade of housing-demand problems absorb the attention of policy-makers, we shall in all likelihood see the emergence of much broader ranging policies targeted at a much larger number of American households.

Demographic Changes Affecting Demand

Housing demand in the years to come will be shaped by two mutually reinforcing demographic factors. First, individuals born during the baby boom of the mid-1950s to mid-1960s, during which the birth rate averaged about 10 percent higher than during the immediate postwar period—are now arriving at the age of household formation. More of this new generation will choose to marry late, live alone, divorce early, and otherwise feed a sharp rise in the relative number of housing units the population will want to consume. Second, the number of elderly people, widows, widowers, and couples is growing both proportionately and in absolute numbers. Many of these older consumers will opt to live alone and thus add further to total housing demand relative to population.

These swelling extremities in the age pyramid are generating an effective demand because of increases in personal disposable income available to the young and elderly. As a result, per capita housing consumption among these age groups has increased relative to that of the rest of the population. Traditionally, at the beginning of the housing consumption life cycle, youth lived at home with their parents until marriage, perhaps even until the first children were born. Thus, prior to World War II, space consumption per capita was half of what it is now. Today young adults leave home and establish households much younger. The elderly and retired, instead of living with their children, live alone or in couples, supported by pensions, often occupying large family-size dwelling units.

At the same time, the increased labor force participation of women combined with a rising divorce rate produces an additional source of increase in per capita housing consumption. For example, during the past ten years women have entered the full-time labor force at unprecedented rates. As a consequence, the number of two-earner families in which both husband and wife work rose by 35 percent between 1966 and 1974. Even if the economy does not grow at a rapid pace in the future, there is little indication that these trends will be reversed (U.S. Dept. of HUD, 1976).

The behavior of local housing markets in recent years splendidly typifies these developments. In favored areas like San Francisco, the total number of dwelling units has increased and vacancies declined while total population continues to drop or remain stagnant. At the national level, these trends in housing demand are reflected in U.S. Census projections of 1,550,000 new households annually between now and 1985. This represents a continuation of the present annual rate of 1,543,000 over the period 1970–75 and more than a 50 percent increase over an average annual rate of 937,000 during the 1960s. Combining the number of new households with locational shifts in demand due to migration to the Sunbelt, the traditional need to maintain a sufficient vacancy rate to lubricate markets, plus replacements for losses due to catastrophe, public works, conversions, and abandonment, several independent forecasts have estimated new housing demand at about 2.25 million units a year through the mid-1980s (Birch, 1973; Frieden, 1977; Schechter, 1976). Only briefly during the early 1970s have suppliers been able to produce new units at such a rate. It seems unlikely that these production records will be matched at any time in the near future. Price and resource constraints on money, land, and energy promise to prevent a substantial fraction of this demand from becoming realized. It seems reasonable to expect that effective demand will remain well below 2 million units annually.

The Impact of Housing Inflation

The era of the suburban housing bargain has passed. Gone is the decent, affordable, single-family, detached, suburban villa for the stably employed working and middle class. Beginning in the middle 1960s, housing prices relative to income began a steady rise. Nothing suggests that this trend has yet run its course. In fact, prices can be expected to continue to rise faster than income. In a recent discussion of the performance of dwelling prices relative to income, Urban Institute housing researcher deLeeuw and colleagues conclude that "nearly a decade of increasingly burdensome housing costs is in prospect" (1976: 139).

This price escalation has many sources. Direct construction costs have increased somewhat faster than the consumer price index since 1968, partly because of the rising cost of lumber and oil. Financing costs have escalated because of higher interest rates. Maintenance, energy, and other utility prices, as well as property taxes, have all climbed sharply as well. Of all the cost factors, however, land has exhibited the most meteoric rise. The most recent Federal Housing Administration (FHA) data show that land prices doubled between 1969 and 1972, a period when the consumer price index increased by about 25 percent.

While the mid-1970s slowdown in construction may have tempered the inflation of housing cost, three convergent institutional forces have pushed hard on urban-fringe land prices. First, for almost fifty years officials in suburban communities have been forcing developers to internalize in the sale price some of the social costs of urbanization such as streets, utilities, parks, schools, etc. The recent fiscal problems of cities is lending added momentum to this trend. Municipal cost-revenue studies have shown that many of the conventional forms of residential development aggravate the fiscal crisis. Local governments have used such studies to coerce developers into absorbing even more infrastructure costs, especially school construction. Second, the environmental movement in its desperate quest for amenity rights has succeeded in halting development in many suburban communities, notably in Florida and California. This trend also shows no sign of abating. The third of these convergent pressures—exclusionary zoning—may, however, weaken substantially as a result of legal action by civil-rights groups and developers and requirements for community development funding set by Congress. Yet even if suburban zoning barriers are lowered, increases in permitted development densities will not necessarily result in lower land prices; rising demand and tightness in the land market would probably keep land prices up and shift to landowners much of the productivity benefits of increased density.

The Demand-Price Crunch
Taken together, these broad currents on the supply and demand sides of the American housing market promise to trap middle-class consumers and the industry in a terrific crunch. With potential demand at unprecedented high levels, income rising only modestly, additions to supply constrained and costly, these ripple effects will intensify inflationary pressures, reduce vacancy rates to minimal levels, contribute to instability in financial markets, and lead to new low dwelling production rates. Barring improbable changes in exogenous factors such as startling increases in productivity or GNP and thereby real income, millions of people, particularly the old and the young, will experience great difficulty in obtaining housing. Either they will be forced to pay a burdensome price or to cut back in their expectations. These people will not be poor in terms of their access to other consumer goods. Rather, they will be in the mainstream of society and thus quite different from ghetto residents whose unfulfilled demand represented such a serious social problem in the 1950s and 1960s. These newcomers to the ranks of the housing-deprived will better fit the mold of the ''submerged middle class'' of the Great Depression and the immediate post World War II period (Friedman, 1968: 20–21).

Over the next decade, the problem of ensuring adequate housing for middle-income Americans suffering from the demand-price crunch will loom as the central issue of U.S. housing policy. The government will undoubtedly attempt to subsidize demand and production, reduce housing costs through regulation, or some combination of these. Unfortunately, years of effort at cost reduction have offered little promise. The Kaiser Committee study of production efficiency in housing concluded that, at most, monthly costs of a single family house could be reduced by 12 percent through a variety of reforms, including the introduction of more efficient methods and technology. However, the authors added the reservation that for each 1 percent increase in interest rates, monthly costs would go up by 5.3 percent; so that if interest rates rose from 6 to 9 percent (as they have since 1968), most of the cost savings due to these efficiency measures would be eaten up by higher financing charges (Burns and Mittlebach, 1968).

Inflation in combination with the demand factors mentioned earlier will, however, lead U.S. housing policy in three directions. First, both financial institutions and the government will attempt to restructure the mortgage contract and to alter the institutional arrangements in mortgage markets. Second, consumers and government will adopt a more positive attitude toward the existing housing stock as the demand-price crunch continues; for as the reproduction cost of housing increases, the stock of existing dwellings will become a more highly valued resource. Finally, at the local level, the mismatch between demand and supply promises to release strong drives for broader regulatory power such as rent control and institutional changes in landlord-tenant relations.

THE ELEMENTS OF HOUSING POLICY

The four most important variables in our national housing policy are the demand for housing, the supply of housing (in terms of both services and stock), the supply of credit (purchasing power), and taxation. The first two are largely exogenous variables. The U.S. government does not produce much housing nor does it directly generate much demand aside from the military. It does, however, regulate money and collect taxes, and these have been the key variables for national housing policy ever since the 1930s. Through monetary policy, credit regulation, and tax deductions the federal government attempts to manage aggregate housing demand and supply. It is unlikely that this general framework of policy will change in the near future.

Housing Finance

The supply-demand problem in housing credit policy has traditionally been viewed as a problem of stabilization, that is, managing interest rates and expansion of the money supply so as to provide adequate finance for housing purchase and construction. Since 1966 the federal government has relied on restrictive monetary policies to reduce the rate of inflation in the economy as a whole. This approach to controlling inflation has destabilized the housing sector. Housing has borne the brunt of anti-inflation policies not simply because credit plays such a large role in housing purchase and construction, but also because the bulk of funds used to finance housing have come from short-term, highly liquid deposits of savings associations and banks. During periods of monetary restraint, upward swings in short-term rates interact with interest-rate ceilings (Regulation Q) to induce depositors to withdraw savings deposits for the purpose of investing directly in treasury notes, treasury bills, commercial paper, etc. Twice in the past seven years these wild fluctuations in the supply of credit have forced mortgage-lenders to ration credit, thereby reducing both the level of housing purchases and construction starts.

At the same time, lenders tied into fixed interest rates and expecting the purchasing power of their money to decline in the future because of inflation have added sizable inflation premiums to the interest rates they attach to new mortgages. These premiums interact with the rising sale price of both new and existing houses to generate extraordinarily large increases in monthly mortgage payments. This practice has produced distortions in the payment stream of the traditional fixed-level payment, fully amortizing mortgage. Inflation premiums tilt the time profile of monthly payments expressed in constant dollars upward in the early years and downward in the later years. Borrowers are thus forced to make considerably higher monthly payments in relation to income in the early years of the mortgage (Poole, 1972). The most severe impact falls first on owners, particularly young families who because of their growing numbers in the adult population constitute a growing proportion of today's mortgage demand (McElhone and Cassidy, 1974). Unable to meet high monthly costs, these borrowers have reduced their demand for housing in terms of quantity and quality or have simply foregone purchase until they accumulate enough savings to cover a larger down payment and thereby achieve a lower monthly payment. Both consumers and lenders believe some type of structural reform of the mortgage credit system is necessary in order to ensure an adequate supply of credit at suitable prices and to stabilize the supply of and the demand for housing at a level commensurate with the current rate of household formation.

One avenue of reform lies in the direction of altering the structure and regulatory environment of financial markets themselves. Conservatives, for example, believe that the removal of Regulation Q interest-rate ceilings on time deposits and savings accounts would solve the supply problem. In their opinion, Regulation Q represents an unnecessary bit of tampering with the market. Were interest rates allowed to find their "natural" level, adequate supplies of credit for housing would be forthcoming (Meltzer, 1970). The savings and loan associations, however, have opposed this type of measure for fear that in an unregulated savings market commercial banks would easily outcompete them and reduce their market share. In order not to run the risk of further disrupting mortgage markets, Congress has supported the savings and loan's and refused to remove Regulation Q.

In terms of reforming financial markets, the most logical approach might be the development of a mortgage system based on the matching of the maturities of a lender's assets and liabilities. Under this approach, the vast bulk of housing credit would come from long-term liabilities such as mortgage bonds and pension funds. The Canadian mortgage system, for example, operates with such a matched maturities system and maximizes the supply of credit by utilizing roll-over mortgages. The latter have been widely used in Canada since the 1930s. In 1973 virtually all single-family residential mortgages were of the roll-over type. They were written with a twenty-, thirty-, or forty-year amortization rate but with a fixed interest rate for only a five-year term. When the term is renewed the interest and amortization rates can be renegotiated. The bulk of savings deposits in Canadian institutions are five-year certificates. Although inflation has affected housing costs in Canada over the past decade, the Canadian mortgage market, because of its matched maturity system, did not suffer the effects of credit rationing in 1970 and during 1973–74 which were so widespread in the U.S. (Lessard, 1975). Since it would require a vast institutional restructuring of financial markets with all sorts of unanticipated distributive effects, this approach has received little attention in the United States except as a means for expanding the financial base of the secondary mortgage markets (Ganis, 1974).

Both Congress and the mortgage-lending industry broadly support some type of reform of the mortgage contract as the main way to overcome inflationary distortions in mortgage markets. The fixed-level payment, fully amortizing mortgage was designed for an era subject to periodic declines in property values and income. If over the long term both income and property values are going to rise, however, and if the federal government is firmly committed to preventing the onset of a deflationary cycle, then the fixed-level payment, fully amortizing mortgage is clearly obsolete as a financial instrument for homeownership. A mortgage instrument adapted to an inflationary environment would require a mechanism for adjusting cash flow to fluctuations in money market rates so as to allow institutions to continue to depend on short-term liabilities. At the same time, it would have to adjust the payment burden in the early years of a mortgage so as to accommodate first-owners (Lessard and Modigliani, 1975).

The revised mortgage design favored by financial institutions is the variable rate mortgage (VRM). Under a VRM, the interest rate on the outstanding balance is allowed to move up or down in accordance with some agreed upon "reference rate." This may be a deposit rate or a short-term money market rate. VRMs are being used extensively today in both New England and California. Approximately half of all new originations in California are VRMs (*Business Week*, 1976). The VRM, however, does not really alleviate the demand effects falling upon first-owners. California lenders, for example, charge a rather large inflation premium on VRMs so that they carry an interest rate at origination only .25 percent below that on fixed-rate mortgages.

Congress, on the other hand, favors the graduated payment mortgage (GPM). Under this design, the monthly payment is set initially at a low level with an imputed interest rate presumably below the market rate. The monthly payment is then adjusted upwards as the borrower's income rises over time. The rate of upward adjustment can be tailored to whatever rate at which the borrower's income can reasonably be expected to grow. Sweden has experimented with such a plan under a system called government parity mortgages. Despite implementation problems, it was relatively successful. Lending institutions in the United States object to GPMs because they reduce cash flow in the early years of the mortgage and probably exacerbate some of the supply-side effects mentioned above (Cohen and Lessard, 1975).

Given the shortcomings of both VRMs and GPMs, Congress and the mortgage-lending industry have come up with a compromise in the Young Families Housing Act (S 3692) sponsored by Senator Edward Brooke of Massachusetts. The bill proposed an equity adjusted mortgage (EAM) which combines a fixed interest rate for the borrower with a variable rate for the lender. The fixed rate would be set at 7 percent. The difference between that and the variable market rate would be covered by a loan from the Government National Mortgage Association (GNMA) for each year of the mortgage term that market rates exceed the contract rate. When the house is sold, the borrower would pay off the accumulated borrowings from GNMA out of the proceeds from the sale (U.S. Senate, 1976).

While this design is well suited to the needs of young middle-income borrowers as well as institutional lenders, it may bode ill for buyers of older central city housing. Under the EAM, the total indebtedness does not drop below the original loan amount until after some nine to ten years. The EAM design assumes that property values will increase at a rate equal to, or greater than, the difference between the borrower's subsidized interest rate and the lender's market rate—or at a minimum of about 3 percent per year. If property appreciates at a lower rate, the homeowner will be unable to pay off the GNMA loan with the proceeds of the sale. Since property values in large portions of the older central cities of the North Central and Northeast sections of the United States are rising slower than the national average (and even declining in some instances), an EAM system may give lenders an added incentive to practice redlining in these cities.

Nevertheless, something like the EAM with increased use of mortgage insurance is probably in the cards for most homeowners over the next decade. Despite its previous resistance to VRMs, Congress recently gave the Federal Home Loan Bank Board (FHLBB) and the Alternative Mortgage Instruments Study Committee approval to evaluate all the above proposed mortgage designs and to determine which would work best. If the FHLBB can come up with a plan that satisfies both consumers and mortgage-lenders, Congress will probably pass legislation in 1978 directing FHA, VA, and all federally chartered financial institutions to adopt the new mortgage design.

Taxation Subsidies

Despite criticism that reformers have directed at "loopholes" in the federal income tax system during the past few years (Stern, 1972), the tax expenditure approach to subsidizing housing will probably endure and perhaps be expanded in several directions. The Tax Reform Act of 1976, for example, appears on the surface to be an attempt to pare down the widespread use of tax shelters. However, real estate has emerged relatively unscathed and as a result may well attract the bulk of funds that have been going into tax-sheltered investments over the past six years. This means a high demand by investors for residential income properties.

In addition, residential investment property will be favored over commercial and industrial real estate by the gradual phase out of the practice of reducing the recapture rate after a seven-year holding period. For low-income and moderate-income housing the phase out will not begin until 1982. This will give subsidized rental housing a slight edge over conventional rental projects for the next five years. Also, the five-year write-off for rehabilitation investment in low-income rental housing has been extended and refined (U.S. Congress, 1976).

The future will probably bring expanded income tax benefits for homeowners, especially if President Carter's upcoming tax reform program receives congressional approval. Proposed deductions will cover rehabilitation, improvements contributing to energy conservation, and special tax credits for first homeowners. State governments have themselves been moving in this direction through programs of property tax relief for the elderly and tax abatement for rehabilitation. The idea is not new. New York City has used the property tax system to subsidize housing for years. Today all fifty states have established some form of relief, and twenty-six provide special abatement programs (Aaron, 1973).

Generally speaking, property tax subsidy and relief schemes are designed to aid the middle class more than lower-income groups. In addition, the strong emphasis by state governments on relief for homeowners means that only a small proportion of these subsidies will find their way to renters. The use of the property tax system for subsidizing homeowner operating costs and rehabilitation will increase significantly over the next five or six years. Many states, especially in the Midwest, Far West, and South, periodically accumulate large surpluses in their treasuries, much of which can be used to finance tax relief. Because state governments cannot run deficits without engendering a legal and political crisis, this type of subsidy approach has distinct and relatively fixed limits as an escape valve for the high pressure of inflation unless property tax relief is federally financed.

Neighborhood Preservation
The contradiction between strong demand among middle-income households and the spiraling inflation that afflicts new construction has turned popular attention to preserving the existing stock of housing. Ever since the Eisenhower administration began to aim some of its housing efforts in that direction some twenty years ago, rehabilitation, code enforcement, and neighborhood betterment have played a minor but noticeable role in housing policy. Recently, under Nixon and Ford, a new rhetorical emphasis and locally determined portions of block-grant revenue sharing programs have added to these efforts. Now the market has joined in. Led by adventurous and youthful sectors of the middle class, buyers have begun searching in older areas for the housing bargains of the 1970s and 1980s. As a result, prices have risen swiftly in these areas. This illustrates the tight linkage between new construction and existing dwellings. The high price of new construction has rippled through the entire stock. Even in some of the most depressed inner city markets, islands of old houses located in defended neighborhoods have experienced substantial appreciation in value.

As middle-income demand shifts to housing bargains in older areas, a process begins for which the British have coined the work "gentrification": units filter up from lower to higher income occupants. Price increases reinforce the upward filtering of the stock. In terms of the model developed by Leven and his colleagues (1976), a *reverse* arbitrage takes place. From the standpoint of the physical condition of the stock, the shift produces a highly beneficial result. Increased income triggers a sequence that includes catching up on deferred maintenance, investment for rehabilitation and modernization, and upgrading of neighborhood facilities and services. Conversions occur, not to maintain rents in the face of poorer classes of tenants, but to respond to the demand of small middle-income households. Gentrification makes it possible to preserve neighborhoods that a few years ago would have been "urban renewed" or abandoned. The irony of this is underscored in strong inner city markets like San Francisco, where a massively destructive urban renewal program limps along in the face of a buoyant market for old houses, particularly the "Victorians" that renewal action targeted.

Associated with gentrification is a powerful demand for antiredlining policies. Blessed for years by the FHA and regulatory authorities, banks, savings and loan associations, and other mortgage-lenders practiced red-lining as a systematic way to avoid the high risk associated with low-income and changing neighborhoods. Attacks on this practice have become a popular cause in the mid-1970s. As the market picks up in older areas, these traditional discrimination practices come under fire. At the state and federal level disclosure legislation has forced certain classes of lenders to reveal the geographic patterns of their activities. This applies moral suasion directly to the lender and arms consumer activists with hard data on their practices. As more middle-income people join this consumer movement, pressure for change will build. Antiredlining activity will have the effect of bringing to the older standing stock and its new owners more of the package of housing finance aids that traditionally have supported middle-class demand in suburbia. This nicely illustrates another of the ironies of the present and near future: as trickle-down becomes trickle-up, downward filtration—the cornerstone of America's traditional low-income housing policy—comes to a halt.

Federal aid seems certain to flow toward neighborhood preservation in increasing amounts. Already localities have directed a significant portion of their Community Development Block Grant (CDBG) money (some 62 percent in fiscal year 1975) to housing and neighborhood preservation. Using CDBG funds, hundreds of cities and counties have gone into the housing finance business. Many more will follow, for the movement has just begun. Typically, a city forms a partnership arrangement with one or more local banks or savings and loan associations. The city deposits a substantial sum with the institution and this is leveraged into a much larger revolving loan pool. The deposit, and the interest it generates according to some locally agreed formula, is used to offset risk to the lender, reduce the effective interest rate to the borrower, provide for loan servicing and program administration, or some combination of these. Though the start-up has been slow and money scarce, these local programs look very promising in their broad outlines. In addition to CDBG dollars, some localities have financed their rehab programs from local taxes or general revenue sharing while others have floated tax-exempt revenue bonds for this purpose.

Neighborhood preservation has stimulated neighborhood organization. Today this is an active movement centered around the defense and development of older urban areas and particularly focused on issues like redlining. In addition to relatively traditional activities such as lobbying city hall for improved services and putting the heat on recalcitrant neighbors about unmowed grass, the new generation of local organizations demands some real decentralization of power (Perlman, 1976). A few wield an effective veto over new development. Some seek historic district status with its attendant local control over practically every physical detail—and through such control exercise considerable influence over social and economic matters. Although formal public policies in the next decade may not actively encourage neighborhood organization among the middle class in a way that parallels the encouragement given the poor to organize in the 1960s, events promise to nurture them, and public policy must perforce take them into account.

Perhaps the most interesting aspect of all this activity, and the one that holds the greatest meaning for the future, is the degree to which it puts local government firmly in the business of housing and housing finance. General purpose governments and special districts have traditionally held entrepreneurial responsibility for important pieces of community development and neighborhood preservation, but not for housing. Basic services and facilities, parks and schools, main streets and trunk drainage, recreation, education, and public safety typically came from local government in neighborhood-sized chunks. What is new, and what promises to burgeon in the years to come, is direct intervention in housing finance and in relations among owners, tenants, landlords, and financial institutions.

Perhaps the best model of this new type of intervention appears in the quasi-public Neighborhood Housing Services (NHS) program that originated in Pittsburgh and spread experimentally to some twenty other cities under the aegis of the Federal Home Loan Bank Board (Ahlbrandt and Brophy, 1975). NHS offers an attractive interlocking of flexibility in finance, direct counseling to residents, and coordination of public services. Their experiments with rehab loan arrangements—especially nonamortizing, often zero interest rate, open-period loans that run as a lien on the property until paid off at sale—suggest the range of these approaches. Suppose all housing debt was carried this way: transferred at purchase to the new owner, with a nonmarket, income-related, monthly charge levied by the public-private housing "credit" institution. It is safe to say that this will not happen in the foreseeable future. But as the next decade unfolds, cities and counties may find themselves offering neighborhood housing and preservation services that could become as complex and fundamental to modern urban life as the services embodied in public education or public safety.

Local Housing Institutions

The recent growth of neighborhood preservation programs suggests that much of consequence in future housing policy will emerge in government and regulatory law at the local level. Traditionally speaking, most regulation in housing markets comes from state and local law. With the exception of zoning, local regulation has by and large remained passive. In the future, however, local and state governments are going to intervene more actively in housing markets through special finance agencies, strong efforts to preserve the standing stock, rent control, and eventually perhaps a restructuring of landlord-tenant relations. The design of such intervention raises critical policy issues.

Since the mid-1960s, state governments in different parts of the country have subsidized the financing, and in some cases actually sponsored the development of multiunit housing. This has been particularly true in highly urbanized states with large tenant populations and strong trade union movements where not only low-income but also middle-income rental housing is required in such large quantities that its provision must be specially encouraged and organized by government. New Jersey, New York, and Massachusetts are prime examples and Massachusetts, New Jersey, and Minnesota have developed Fair Share plans for the allocation of low-income subsidized housing which are supported by state housing finance agency (HFA) programs. In other places, HFAs are instrumental in financing rehabilitation of both rental and owner-occupied housing. In all, about thirty-two states now operate HFAs, although only fifteen have active development programs (Stegman, 1974; Betnun, et al., 1974). Many states are planning to expand these programs over the next decade.

Working at the same time, inflation in operating costs of rental housing and the spread of community organizing techniques have been responsible for growing interest in rent control and tenant unions: rent control movements have developed in California, Massachusetts, and New Jersey. Working from bases in university towns with tight housing markets, activists in California and Massachusetts have fought for rent control in local communities and made it an issue at the state legislative level. Massachusetts has passed enabling legislation empowering localities to control rents. The California legislature, on the other hand, approved law last year reserving these powers for the state, thus prohibiting localities from controlling rents. This legislation was initiated by powerful real estate lobbies in response to rent control initiatives in Berkeley and Davis. In a last-minute switch, Governor Brown vetoed the act. Should the law pass a second time, a veto may be politically impossible. In New Jersey the situation is more dramatic. Nearly 150 localities, primarily middle-income suburban communities, have instituted rent controls, and the state supreme court has repeatedly upheld their right to do so. Washington, D.C., Bangor, Maine, and a number of Connecticut localities also have rent regulation laws.

These developments on both coasts illustrate the remarkable degree to which the current crunch in housing costs has opened the possibility of local public regulation of the rental market on a scale never before seen in peacetime United States outside of New York City. Especially as middle-income tenants experience sizable annual rent increases, this type of market regulation gains enormously in political appeal. Unlike the rent controls of the World War II era, this "second generation" of rent control has received little federal encouragement. In fact, the Department of Housing and Urban Development has overridden local regulations covering federally subsidized projects and projects financed with federally guaranteed mortgages.

Other more daring forms of local regulation may also be in the offing. Tenant unions, for instance, have appeared only fitfully in the past. Now they may become more prevalent as the crunch deepens. If they proliferate, local or state governments may seek to establish and supervise—either formally or informally—collective bargaining relations between tenant and landlord. In the past, tenant unions were commonly found among lower-class renters, particularly where effective community organizers had been at work. In the years ahead, we may see instead the growth of coalitions of lower-class and middle-class tenants. Already intimations of this have appeared in the amazing neighborhood-based, multiclass tenant movement in Dallas, Texas. In a city with 60 percent of its population renters, the Dallas Tenants' Union has as its goal the establishment of a collective bargaining system for the Dallas rental housing market (Bois d'arc Patriots, 1977). The flowering of a large tenant movement may prove to be a long and slow process because of enormous political resistance to the idea on the part of landlords and banks; but the objective basis for it may develop swiftly if rents continue to rise faster than income and community organizing continues to spread throughout big cities in the United States.

These various trends in local housing market regulation will undoubtedly reinforce one another and may eventually lead to an elaboration of large organizations by the different factors in the market. We may, in fact, be witnessing the "cartelization" of the housing market as tenants, landlords, and lenders operate more and more through organized interest groups and associations. Perhaps the recent saga of the Coop City rent strike in New York foreshadows this type of evolution. Coop City's 50,000 residents live in 15,000 units laid out in an isolated, comprehensively planned development with nearly all urban services provided on the site. Many of the tenants are retired trade unionists with long experience in collective action. The strike was in effect a conflict between occupants and lenders over the pass-through of large-risk and inflation premiums on a refinanced mortgage and of unanticipated increases in operating costs charged by suppliers of services. The state government, which had guaranteed the mortgage, finally stepped in to mediate the conflict after thirteen months and brought it to a resolution by refinancing the mortgage on terms more favorable to the tenants. This case illustrates how state or local government activities in subsidizing or encouraging the supply of certain types of housing or housing services can lay the groundwork for direct intervention in managing the housing stock.

Some observers have envisioned an even more futuristic restructuring of market organization. Gallagher (1976), for example, predicts that by the year 2000 individual homeowners, small landlords, and savings associations will have given way to huge management corporations, special corporations administering pension-fund investments in housing, and large government regulatory agencies set up to ensure the smooth operation of the local housing sector. The management corporations would act in concert with local government to provide profits to lenders (the pension funds) and service suppliers; stability, legitimacy, and power to government; and an affordable bundle of acceptable housing services to occupants. This scenario is no doubt a bit extreme. However, it does typify the degree to which the housing sector institutions in the United States are coming to resemble less and less those of the "free market" and more and more those of a highly cartelized and regulated industry.

STRATEGIES TO MEET HOUSING NEEDS

The overriding importance of the conflict between rising middle-income demand and price inflation has begun to redirect attention away from several other housing policy issues that were of much concern in the recent past. These issues, many of them key components of Great Society programs, include production targets, deep subsidies to the poor (as distinguished from shallower subsidies to middle-income households), technological solutions to high unit costs, new towns and the related idea of new towns in-town, and the concept of geographic dispersion of racial and lower-class minorities in order to achieve the ideal of a balanced community. Discussion continues to revolve around these issues, but with less sense of national urgency.

Production Policy
Since the 1930s Americans have shown enthusiasm for housing policies that emphasize high rates of new unit construction. Behind this lies the firm conviction that trickle-down is good and works. This means that new homes and new urban or suburban environments are, in Downs' word,

"inserted" at the top of the income spectrum. This, in turn, opens up a chain of vacancies permitting the rest of us to march through the housing stock, or "filter," in carefully ordered class and income-defined cohorts. Great Society housing policy adhered to this tradition. A series of well-known studies (U.S. National Advisory Commission, 1968; U.S. National Commission, 1969; U.S. President's Committee, 1969) has defined the policy problem as a shortage of standard quality units and, secondarily, as the inability of a poor minority to afford such standard units. Put another way, the problem was a supply that was inadequate to keep filtering going at a rate sufficiently high to satisfy all of the *needs* for shelter. Once quantified, the need figures became production targets: 26 million new or substantially rehabilitated units in ten years, 6 million of which would be subsidized so that they could be inserted at lower levels in the income spectrum (U.S. President's Committee, 1968).

The production targets were based on determinations of housing need. They combined generous projections of new household formation with estimates of the units needed to replace demolitions, conversion to other uses, catastrophic losses, and other diminutions in the housing stock. To arrive at the final need figure, the calculation added in arbitrary quantities representing a substantial increase in vacancies plus a sufficient number to replace *all* existing and projected-to-exist substandard and dilapidated units. Presumably these added quantities would allow new subsidized units—combined with the vigorous filtering triggered by massive, new, market-rate construction and lubricated by high vacancy rates—to re-house all Americans in decent homes within the decade.

Congress embodied the targets in the Housing Act of 1968 and enacted a new set of supply-side subsidies to support new construction through the real estate and home building industries. Under these subsidy programs the federal government paid the difference between debt service at FHA market rates and a below-market rate that could go as low as 1 percent; the saving was passed on to the consumer. Over the next five years production rose dramatically, thanks in large part to these programs, and to the sharply increased delivery of mobile homes, a type of housing heretofore not included in national accounts. Though production in the five years between 1969 and 1973 fell short of the targets, it came close, 12 versus 13 million units.

Democrats and Great Society supporters have interpreted the target shortfalls as an exacerbation of the housing problem. Not so, in fact. High production policies had worked so well that even before these programs had begun to take effect, substandardness and overcrowding had ceased to be the dominant housing problems they once were. Perversely, instead of solving a no longer critical old problem, the high production policy helped create new problems of neighborhood decline and price inflation.

By stimulating new home production at a rate substantially above the rate of household formation, the policy intensified filtering and suburbanization, thus destabilizing old neighborhoods and hastening their abandonment. By adding to the stock at the high end of the price continuum, and destroying units at the low end, it tended to shift upward prices of the standing stock. By maintaining market pressure on land and money resources the Great Society programs helped power inflation.

Policy analysts have defined a number of other flaws in what Solomon calls our "obsession with new construction" (1974: 7). Among these are the inherent problems of using new production to aid poor people. Efficiency considerations would suggest that such aid draw largely on the less expensive standing stock. Solomon's cost-effectiveness figures developed from data on Boston show that standard quality housing leased from the existing stock costs but 64 percent as much as newly constructed public housing units (1974: 184). At a constant level of expenditure the lease program would house nearly 60 percent more households. This last figure illustrates a strong equity argument against a high-production policy. Of course, American production policy has never intended to aid many poor people directly; it meant to help them indirectly through filtering. The perversities of this approach were dealt with above. Neither new low-rent construction nor trickle-down puts enough sound housing within reach of enough low-income households in stable neighborhoods with affordable maintenance and services.

Despite these counterarguments, the building industry and its allies will continue to advocate high production. Now, however, formal targets have all but disappeared in the split between the pro- and anti-federal interventionists. The new national policy emphasis on supporting middle-income demand will place an effective floor under production and thus deflect the conflict. In the years to come, demand changes coupled with the revived interest in old houses, a strengthening market in many metropolitan areas, and the two decades or more of heavy demolition behind us suggest that high production will have less destabilizing, abandonment-provoking effects than it has had in the recent past. In a perfect demonstration of the lag phenomenon so characteristic of public policy, now discredited production targets as such may reappear later in this decade. If that happens they will be resurrected ironically in close synchrony with a precipitous drop in household formation that can be predicted for the late 1980s from present declining birthrates.

Subsidies to House the Poor

Almost as a by-product of policies directed at maintaining high levels of economic activity and employment, the federal government has since the 1930s provided a small quantity of deep and expensive subsidies aimed at housing the urban poor. The great bulk of this effort has gone into constructing low-rent public housing projects. After more than forty years of program activity, these units sheltered about 4 percent of the population with 1970 and 1972 incomes below $6000 (Aaron, 1972: 115; U.S. Dept. of HUD, 1974: 128). Little has changed since. This program has been under almost continuous attack since its birth in the New Deal. During the intervening years it has been closed down repeatedly due to Supreme Court action, lapsed enabling legislation, congressional failure to appropriate authorized funds, and hostile policies like the Article 34 referendum requirement in the California State Constitution. Only a die-hard public housing management lobby with occasional help from big labor and big city mayors has kept it alive at all. Now even they seem to have failed the cause of low-rent public housing. In recent years the final blows have come from the same scholarly program evaluations that questioned production policy, the moratorium of 1973, and the dynamiting of the infamous Pruitt-Igoe project in St. Louis which provided the coup de grâce.

With low-rent public housing thoroughly discredited, and with the overshadowing policy issues generated by the effects of inflation on middle-income demand, perhaps the less said the better about the future of deep subsidies. Despite the fact that during his campaign President Carter took pains to inform the housing policy community that he once lived in a Plains, Georgia public housing project, there is little to suggest that the program will rise again. To some extent this embodies another of those familiar lag-generated ironies. In response to problems and criticisms, the Great Society programs included a critical and effective modification of public housing practice. Under the so-called Section 23 program, instead of constructing new projects, public housing funds could be used to lease units in the existing stock, paying market rents, but renting them to poor households at a deeply subsidized rate. In operation, Section 23 seems to have been as nearly perfect as a low-income housing program could be. Among its many demonstrated virtues were use of lower-cost existing units, impetus to rehabilitation, strengthening of weak markets, flexibility in time and location, invisibility and lack of stigma, public acceptance, and outreach to the old or infirm or other low-income people who need housing counseling and assistance. Whether it would continue to work so well in the tightening markets that lie ahead is open to question. In any case, its modest success lies buried under the wreckage of the conventional public housing program.

Out of this disenchantment a strong thrust has emerged to shift deep subsidies to the demand side of the market. Among the early advocates of this shift, sociologist Rainwater (1970), who studied daily life in Pruitt-Igoe, came to believe that only an income redistribution strategy could cope with the defects of the projects. Soon economists joined in. With the arrival of the 1973 moratorium, it seems fair to say that a preponderance of analysts supported housing allowances or other demand-side policies. Based on this HUD undertook a number of social experiments designed to reveal the efficacy of the approach (RAND, 1977; Solomon and Fenton, 1974). So far, reported results are inconclusive. While people do use earmarked aid to improve their housing and to reduce its economic burden, the experiments indicate a substantial fraction of the aid can end up as inflated rent. As markets get tighter, it is safe to predict that rents will increase faster. Demand subsidies may not look as promising from the vantage point of the late 1970s as they did five or ten years ago. Also, from a political point of view, it is unlikely that an expensive, new program of income supplements or housing allowances for the poor will be enacted in a period when the middle class is experiencing such a crunch. Perhaps the decade to come will not see major efforts directed at housing the poor.

Technological Innovation

Most considerations of technological advances in housing have centered around new construction techniques that reduce costs. For years the vision of industrialized housing production captured the imagination of architects, materials suppliers, aerospace companies, and appliance manufacturers, who felt that with the aid of government-financed research and development programs such a new era of low-cost mass housing production might be within reach. Unfortunately, Operation Breakthrough became a breakdown. This experiment in technology-transfer exemplified what unions have always claimed: the high cost of new construction is the result of high land and financing charges. Labor costs and site construction methods themselves account for only a relatively small part of the inflation that has ravaged the housing sector over the past ten years.

However, technological innovation in housing has not become a dead issue. Its orientation will shift radically over the next decade. As utility costs continue to escalate, architects and engineers will introduce innovation in structural design and mechanical systems to make houses more efficient in their use of resources. In the case of heating, for example, estimates by the Federal Reserve Bank of San Francisco (1976) show that the cost of natural gas will rise from $1.05 per cubic foot in 1975 to $3.45 by 1985. California's situation is by no means atypical. Even now the extreme winter of 1977 has generated a great ground swell of support for deregulating interstate natural gas prices and letting them float upwards as an incentive for producers to develop new supplies. Solar heating and vastly improved insulation methods will mark the introduction of conservation-oriented technologies in housing.

A similar wave of innovation will also alter the design of plumbing systems if the water shortages predicted for the end of the century are realized. Although today it may appear bizarre to some, chemical toilets and water recycling systems may be standard on new housing a quarter century from now. If constraints on the availability of natural resources are intensifying, as ecologists claim, so will the incentives for technological innovations which reduce household consumption of energy and water.

New Towns

No housing policy has been more tenaciously advocated by city planners and architects than new towns; many continue in their enthusiasm. Yet, after the fiasco of the Great Society era programs directed at stimulating construction of new towns, any early return to such a policy seems out of the question. At last report only three of the fifteen federally approved projects remained on the list; the others, having gone bankrupt, are now being liquidated by HUD. Of the three, only Woodland near Houston has shown any real economic vitality; HUD has kept the other two afloat for what appear to be primarily political reasons (*House and Home,* 1976b).

The much vaunted "new town in-town" program variant has met with even less success. On the surface it seems unlikely to revive. However, one rather remote constellation of factors may lead to a few cities flirting once again with the new town in-town idea. In those areas where enormous abandonment has occurred, where inner city property values have in fact depreciated to nearly zero, and where the city holds title to vast amounts of land, a modest, incrementally planned, comprehensive development could orchestrate a gradual awakening of market interest or public initiative. In more active markets the experience with Fort Lincoln, Cedar-Riverside, and Yerba Buena indicate that front-end costs are as prohibitive as those in true new towns. These same cases demonstrate that energetic resident defense of their home turf has also made the idea unworkable in inhabited neighborhoods (Derthick, 1972; Hartman, 1977).

In contrast, truly depressed areas like inner city St. Louis, Detroit, and Cleveland may possibly host large, comprehensively planned projects meriting the label "new town in-town." Such projects, perhaps on the order of New York's Coop City, may become feasible if the demand for central city locations revives—by no means an unrealistic prospect. In fact, it becomes more and more likely given the shift in cities to publicly supported corporate entrepreneurship, the effects of inflation on the middle-class, energy problems, the availability of vast areas well served by urban infrastructure, and the burning out of the abandonment process. Architects and planners may yet get another chance.

Dispersion

Housing policy, the balanced-community concept, and a concern with racism have had a long-standing association. Among the earliest federal policies related to these themes were FHA regulations designed to insure homogeneous neighborhoods in race and class terms. Only recently have these objectives changed, at least in terms of official action. The principal thrust of these newer policies has been directed at dispersing housing opportunities for low-income and nonwhite people on a metropolitan-wide "fair-share" basis. Beginning with the Dayton Plan in 1970, recent successes of dispersion in the Minneapolis-St. Paul metropolitan area and in a few other places support modest hopes. However weak the federal administration of the dispersion provisions of the 1974 Housing and Community Development Act, the cumulative effect of it, the A-95 review, and the subsidization of metropolitan planning have generated quite a bit of momentum behind this thrust.

Much policy in this area is now being made in the court system as legislatures have evidently found race too tough a question for open action. This trend is likely to continue. It will grind painfully slow, especially since the U.S. Supreme Court has taken a hard line, acting only against overt racial discrimination and not admitting litigation on class and income discrimination. State courts, however, show much variation in outlook, and one, New Jersey, stands out for its activist position on class and race dispersion policy. Other state courts are likely to follow New Jersey's lead in mandating fair share allocations of low- and moderate-income housing to all comers. In California, for instance, groups seeking a Mt. Laurel type judgment have formed, and one has already scored a small initial success. The next decade should be an active one, though courts and litigating parties will make more policy than will legislatures and lobbies (Falk and Franklin, 1976; *House and Home,* 1977a).

The legal campaign for dispersion has already had a relatively significant impact in several states. In Massachusetts, for example, where an antisnob zoning law has been on the books for a number of years, the number of communities with 10 percent or more of their housing stock devoted to low-income subsidized units has doubled since 1973 (Altman, 1976). Yet it is not clear what the eventual social impact will be. Without redistribution, dispersion may only create minighettos scattered through broad suburban expanses of metropolitan America. As Harrison (1974) has argued, dispersion by itself does not improve minority welfare, but only redistributes low-income minority households geographically.

CONCLUSION

In the decade to come, more and more Americans, especially those just starting households, will find themselves unable to afford what they have come to define as a decent home and a suitable living environment. To some extent they will react individually and psychologically by redefining downward their own subjectively ordered housing standards. They will also modify their preferences in the opposite direction in terms of their ideas about what is affordable. New Yorkers, for instance, have been conspicuously successful in doing both of these things for years. Some people will find traditional housing standards inappropriate as they opt for single, nonfamily life-styles or adopt resource-conserving ethics. For most people, however, the decade will witness a real contradiction between rising costs and restricted supply on one hand, and less swiftly rising incomes and competition for housing because of high household formation rates on the other.

To a great extent, the central questions for policy-makers will revolve around maintaining the effective demand of the great middle-class mass. These problems may prove to be so intractable that the traditional policy issues—substandard housing and provision for the poor—will fade into relative insignificance. From this vantage point, it looks as though the response of public policy to these new conditions will lead to a changed housing economy which looks less and less like the classical market and more and more like the state-managed housing economies of Western Europe.

While such a shift in policy orientation may emerge simply through drift, it is more likely that political clashes over extending government intervention in our housing market system may become almost as heated as those of the 1930s and the immediate postwar years. During the previous decade we have witnessed a continuing debate over the rationale for, and the forms of intervention in, housing, health care, and other services. In the housing policy area these debates are bound to intensify as the costs of housing market disequilibrium grow at a compound rate and the demands for intervention multiply. Ideological differences will also intensify, especially if property relations are altered by interventions such as rent control. Indeed, as local governments become more active in regulating housing markets, we may find that debates over policy which to date have been confined to small groups of academics, bureaucrats, and politicians that cluster around federal and state agencies will be extended to countless citizens who have an enduring stake in these issues.

REFERENCES

Aaron, Henry J. (1972) *Shelter and Subsidies: Who Benefits from Federal Housing Policies.* Washington, D.C.: The Brookings Institution.
——— (1973) "What Do Circuit-Breaker Laws Accomplish?" In George E. Peterson (ed.) *Property Tax Reform.* Washington, D.C.: The Urban Institute.
Ahlbrandt, Roger S., Jr., and Pam C. Brophy (1975) *Neighborhood Revitalization.* Lexington, Mass.: Lexington Books.

Altman, Dorothy (1976) "Anti-Snob Law Produces Low Income Housing." *Practicing Planner* 6 (December): 31–33.
Bois d'arc Patriots (1977) "Organizing in Dallas." *Green Mountain Quarterly* 5 (February): 9–35.
Betnun et al. (1974) *A Place to Live: Housing Policy in the States.* Washington, D.C.: Council of State Governments.
Birch, David L. (1973) *America's Housing Needs: 1970–1980.* Cambridge, Mass.: Joint Center for Urban Studies of MIT and Harvard Universities (also update comment Research Report No. 12, Joint Center).
Burns, Leland, and Mittlebach, Frank (1968) "Efficiency in the Housing Industry," in *Report of the President's Committee on Urban Housing,* vol. 2. Washington, D.C.: U.S. Government Printing Office.
Business Week (1976) "Mortgages to Beat Inflation." 27 (September): 80.
Cohen, David L., and Donald R. Lessard (1975) "Mortgage Innovation to Facilitate Investment in Housing: The Case in Sweden." In Franco Modigliani and Donald R. Lessard (eds.) *New Mortgage Designs for Stable Housing in an Inflationary Environment.* Boston, Mass.: Federal Reserve Bank of Boston.
de Leeuw, Frank, Ann B. Schnare, and Raymond Struyk (1976) "Housing." In W. Gorham and N. Glazer (eds.) *The Urban Predicament.* Washington, D.C.: The Urban Institute.
Derthick, Martha (1972) *New Towns In-Town: Why a Federal Program Failed.* Washington, D.C.: The Urban Institute.
Falk, David, and Herbert M. Franklin (1976) *Equal Housing Opportunity: The Unfinished Agenda.* Washington, D.C.: The Potomac Institute.
Federal Reserve Bank of San Francisco (1976) *California Energy: The Economic Factors.* San Francisco: Federal Reserve Bank of San Francisco.
Frieden, Bernard J. (1977) "Housing." In *Encylopedia of Social Work.* Washington, D.C.: National Association of Social Work.
Friedman, Lawrence (1968) *Government and Slum Housing.* Chicago: Rand McNally.
Gallagher, Thomas P. (1976) "Who Will Own Our Homes in 2000 A.D.?" *Real Estate Review* 6 (Summer): 108–11.
Ganis, David R. (1974) "All About the GNMA Mortgage-Backed Securities Market." *Real Estate Review* 4 (Summer): 55–65.
Harrison, Bennett (1974) *Urban Economic Development.* Washington, D.C.: The Urban Institute.
Hartman, Chester (forthcoming, 1977) "Housing Struggles and Housing Form." In Sam Davis (ed.) *The Form of Housing.* New York: Van Nostrand-Reinhold.
House and Home (1976a) "Nat Rogg to Retire as Conservatives Gain Strength." 50 (September): 3-16.
——— (1976b) "HUD's New-Town Program Shakes Down into Multi-Million Dollar Mess." 50 (October): 4–5.
——— (1977a) "California Growth Curbs Upheld." 51 (March): 28.
——— (1977b) "How New Towns Borrowed Selves Broke." 51 (March): 40.
Lessard, Donald R. (1975) "Roll-Over Mortgages in Canada." In Franco

Modigliani and Donald R. Lessard (eds.) *New Mortgage Designs for Stable Housing in an Inflationary Environment.* Boston, Mass.: Federal Reserve Bank of Boston.

————, and Franco Modigliani (1975) "Inflation and the Housing Market." In Franco Modigliani and Donald R. Lessard (eds.) *New Mortgage Designs for Stable Housing in an Inflationary Environment.* Boston, Mass.: Federal Reserve Bank of Boston.

Leven, Charles, James T. Little, Hugh O. Nourse, and R. B. Read (1976) *Neighborhood Change: Lessons in the Dynamics of Urban Decay.* New York: Praeger.

McElhone, Josephine, and Henry J. Cassidy (1974) "Mortgage Lending: Its Changing Economic and Demographic Environment." *Federal Home Loan Bank Board Journal* 7 (July 1974): 7–15.

Meltzer, Allan H. (1970) "Regulation Q: The Money Markets and Housing." In *Housing and Monitary Policy.* Boston, Mass.: Federal Reserve Bank of Boston.

Perlman, Janice (1976) "Grass Rooting the System." *Social Policy* 7 (September/October): 4–20.

Poole, William (1972) "Housing Finance Under Inflationary Conditions." In U.S. Federal Reserve Staff Study, *Ways to Moderate Fluctuations in Housing Construction.* Washington, D.C.: Board of Governors of the Federal Reserve System.

Rainwater, Lee (1970) *Behind Ghetto Walls.* Chicago: Aldine.

RAND (1977) *Third Annual Report of Housing Assistance Supply Experiment.* Santa Monica, Calif.: RAND Corporation, R-2151-HUD.

Schechter, Henry B. (1976) "The Depth of the Housing Crisis." *AFL-CIO Federationist* 83 (January): 8–11.

Solomon, Arthur P. (1974) *Housing the Urban Poor: A Critical Evaluation of Federal Housing Policy.* Cambridge, Mass.: MIT Press.

————, and Chester G. Fenton (1974) "The Nation's First Experience with Housing Allowances: Kansas City Demonstration." *Land Economics* 50 (August): 213–23.

Stegman, Michael A. (1974) "Housing Finance Agencies: Are They Crucial Instruments of State Government?" *Journal of American Institute of Planners* 40 (September): 307–20.

Stern, Philip M. (1972) *The Rape of the Taxpayer.* New York: Random House.

U.S. Congress, Joint Committee on Taxation (1976) *General Explanation of the Tax Reform Act of 1976,* 94th Congress, Public Law 94–455. Washington, D.C.: U.S. Government Printing Office.

U.S. Department of Housing and Urban Development (1974) *Housing in the Seventies.* Washington, D.C.: Government Printing Office.

———— (1976) *Women in the Mortgage Market.* Washington D.C.: U.S. Government Printing Office.

U.S. National Advisory Commission on Civil Disorders (1968) *Report.* Washington, D.C.: Government Printing Office.

U.S. National Commission on Urban Problems (1969) *Building the American City.* Washington, D.C.: Government Printing Office.

U.S. President's Committee on Urban Housing (1969) *A Decent Home*. Washington, D.C.: Government Printing Office.

U.S. Senate Committee on Banking, Housing and Urban Affairs, Subcommittee on Housing and Urban Affairs (1969). *Hearings: Development of New Types of Mortgage Market Instruments,* 94th Congress, 2nd Session. Washington, D.C.: U.S. Government Printing Office.

Index

abandonment, 71, 81
accelerated depreciation, 37-38
ADMATCH, 109
administrative costs, on loans, 88
Agelasto, Michael, 86n
American Bankers Association, 92, 110
American Institute of Real Estate Appraisers, 83
American Real Estate and Urban Economics Association, xv
A-95 review, 178
Annual Housing Goal Report, 137
Annual Housing Survey, 138, 140, 142, 144, 152
Annunzio, Congressman Frank, 129
appraisal, property, 82
arbitrage, 167
arbitrage model, 64, 67, 68, 71, 75-77

Bailey, Martin, 68
Balko, W., 86n
Baltimore, 81, 83
Beasman, William, 98
blockbusting, 84
Boston, 174; Urban Renewal Group, 124
boundary market, 68-70, 75
boundary price, 68
Bronx, 87, 89
Brooke Amendments, 13, 39
Brooke, Senator, Edward, 165
Brown, Governor, 170
Brueggeman, W.B., 149

building codes, 48, 54
building industry, management, 58
Burchell, R., 84

California, California Savings Association Mortgage Co., Inc., 124
Carter, administration, 159; President, 166, 175
Case, F., 81, 89, 93
Center for National Policy Review, 91, 122
Center for New Corporate Priorities, 86n, 87, 92
Center for Urban Ethnic Affairs, 92
Chicago, 81, 87, 91-92, 98; Citizen Action Program, 133; First Federal Savings and Loan Association, 110; Metropolitan Area Housing Alliance, 113; National People's Action on Housing, 91, 113; National Training and Information Center, 91; West Side Coalition, 91
Cincinnati, Coalition of Neighborhoods, 91
Civil Rights Act: of 1866, 120; of 1964, 119; of 1968, 96, 122
civil rights enforcement, 119-122
Clark v. Universal Builders, 120
Clifton, C.W., 150
Committee for Economic Development, 57
Community Development Block Grant, 168
Comptroller of the Currency, 96-97, 115, 119
conservation, to upgrade housing stock, 151-152
Coop City, 177

credit allocation, 122-123
cyclical activity, in housing market, 46, 49-50

Dallas Tenants' Union, 171
Dayton Plan, 178
decay, of housing stock, 71
"decent home," 63, 138-139, 144
decentralization, of housing administration, 30
deLeeuw, Frank, 160
demand/price crunch, 161-162
demographic changes, affecting housing, 159-160
demolition, as a housing goal, 146-147
Department of Housing & Urban Development (HUD), 10, 15, 23, 26-28, 32, 35-36, 86n, 87, 102, 127, 137, 153, 171, 176
deposit-loan ratio, 95
Depression, the, 161
Detroit, 140
Devine, Richard, 86n, 87
dilapidated, as a housing deficiency, 140
disclosure: California, 112-113; Chicago, 117; Cleveland, 118; costs, 110; Illinois, 113-114, 122; Massachusetts, 114-115; Michigan, 117, 122; New Jersey, 116; New York, 115-116; Pennsylvania, 116; Wisconsin, 116
discrimination, in housing, 86-88, 119-120
disinvestment, defined, 80
dispersion, of housing, 177-178
"doubling up," as a housing deficiency, 141
Downs, Anthony, 172-173

economic policy, federal impact on housing, 51, 54-55
Eisenhower, administration, 18, 167
elderly housing, 22, 26, 32, 39, 144
equilibrium, in housing market, 65n, 68
equity adjusted mortgage, *see* mortgage
"equity syndication," 37-38
eviction, 33, 35
Executive Order 11603, 119-120
expectations, 70, 77-78
externalities, in housing market, 63

Fair Access to Insurance Requirement (FAIR), 89
Fair Housing Act of 1968, 120
Fair Housing Lending Practices Pilot Project, 96, 115

"fair market rental," 32
Federal Deposit Insurance Corporation (FDIC), 57, 96-97
federal government, role in housing, 58
Federal Home Loan Bank Board (FHLBB), xv, 57, 110, 120-121, 127, 166, 169; survey of lenders, 96
Federal Home Loan Mortgage Corporation (FHLMC), 56
Federal Housing Administration (FHA), 82, 86, 91, 102, 145, 160, 168, 173, 177-178
federalism, new, 102
Federal National Mortgage Corporation (FNMC), 56
Federal Reserve Board, 51, 96, 103, 110
Federal Reserve System, 57, 80
filtering, 67, 168, 173; defined, 148-149; as a means to achieve housing goal, 148-152; *see* "percolating" and "gentrification"
financial institutions, role in succession, 70
fiscal policies, of housing developments, 14
Fisher, E.M., 149
Ford, President, 79, 99, 167
foreclosure, 90
Freedman, Leonard, 17n

Gallagher, Thomas P., 172
"gentrification," as upward filtering, 167-168
George-Healey Act of 1936, 3
Government National Mortgage Corporation (GNMC), 56, 165
graduated payment mortgage, *see* mortgage
Great Society, 102, 158-159, 172-173, 177
"greenlining," 111
Grigsby, W.G., 149

Harlem Savings Bank, 89
Harrison, Bennett, 178
Hartford, 81
Hart, John C., 45, 51
heating facilities, as a housing deficiency, 141-142
Higginbotham, Power, 139n
High Risk Loan Fund, 127-128
Home Mortgage Disclosure Act of 1975, 79, 98-103
home ownership, costs of, 45
homesteading, 85
House and Home, 158
household formation, 160
household preferences, 66

housing: age of stock, role in neighborhood succession, 76; attributes, 64, 66; bundle, 65; code and neighborhood deterioration, 75; cost reduction strategies, 45, 57-58; definition, 43-44; deficiencies (table), 143; deficienceis, multiple incidence (table), 143; inadequacy (table), 139; goals, means vs. ends, 145-148; median price trend, 44; politics of, 157-159; starts, 48-50; state finance agencies, 170

housing acts; 1934, 3; 1937, 3, 5-9, 12, 31; 1949, xvii, 3, 6, 8, 12; 1954, 145; 1961, 22; 1965, 3, 13, 24, 30-31, 35; 1968, 23, 27, 137-138, 145, 173; 1969, 23, 27, 33; 1974, 3, 12, 24, 27-29, 31, 33-35, 102, 151-152, 158, 178; 1976, 29

human ecologists, 67

income, impact on neighborhood, 66-68, 77, 84-85, 87-88

incrementalism, in housing policy, 17

Independent Bankers Association of America, 92

Indianapolis, Coalition to End Neighborhood Deterioration, 91

industrialization, of housing, 47, 52

inflation, 49, 51, 54; impact on housing, 160-163; related to mortgage system, 164-165

interest costs, 45

interest rate, 162; variable, 56-57; ceilings, 57

Internal Revenue Service (IRS), 37

Investors Mortgage Insurance Co., 44

Illinois: Fairness in Lending Act, 114; Financial Institutions Disclosure Act, 113-114; Housing Development Authority, 124; Savings & Loan Act of 1974, 113

Jackson, Philip, 51

Johnson, President, 158

Jones v. Alfred H. Mayer Co., 120

Kaiser Committee, 55, 148, 162

Kennedy, President, 119

land installment contracts (LIC), 83

Lansing, J.B., 150

Laufman v. Oakley Building and Loan Co., 121-122

leased housing, 29; new construction, 35-38; existing stock, 31-32

lending institutions, movement to suburbs, 84

Leven, Charles, 63n, 64, 167

Listokin, David, 86n

Little, James, 64n, 66

loan repayment, delinquency, 88-89

loan security, 89

local government, expanded role in housing, 169-172

local housing authority (LHA), 7, 9, 14, 21, 25, 31-32, 34; diminution of authority, 37

local public sector, 66

Los Angeles, 87, 112, 118

Love v. DeCarlo Homes, Inc., 120

Lowry, Ira, 149-151

Lozano, Edwardo, 45-46, 58

maintenance and repair expenditures, 46

Martin, Preston, 56

Memphis, 89

Michigan, Governor Milliken, 117

Milwaukee, 81; Alliance of Concerned Citizens, 91

Moakley, Joe, 99

moratorium, of 1/73, 158, 175

Morgan, J.O., 150

Mortgage Bankers Association, 83

mortgage, 80, 95; equity adjusted, 165-166; funds, 49-51, 56; graduated payments, 165; variable rate (VRM), 57, 164-165; voluntary loan pools, 123-125

mortgage credit system: Canadian, 164; reform, 163-164; Sweden, 165

Mt. Laurel, 178

Muth, R.F., 149-150, 152

Myer, Dillon S., 146

NAACP, 91

National Association of Home Builders, 45, 158

National Association of Mutual Savings Banks, 98

National Association of Real Estate Boards, 30

National Association of Realtors, 44

National Commission on Urban Problems, 48

National Committee Against Discrimination in Housing, 86, 91

National Housing Policy Review, 146

National Recovery Act of 1933, 3

National Savings & Loan League, 92

National Urban League, 91

neighborhood, 63
Neighborhood Housing Service Program
   (NHS), 127-128, 169
neighborhood preservation, 126, 128-129,
   167-169
Neighborhood Preservation Projects, 127
Newark, New Jersey, 81
New Deal, 3, 7, 175
New Jersey, state Senator Joseph Merlino,
   116
new towns, 177
New York City, 80, 166, 171; Real Estate
   Mortgage Insurance Program, 125
Nixon, President, 158, 167; administration,
   23
Nourse, Hugh, 63n, 64, 72, 76-77, 85

Oakland, California, 86
Oak Park, Illinois, Oak Park Community
   Organization, 91
Ohls, J.C., 150
Olsen, E.O., 149
Operation Breakthrough, 52, 176
Orren, Karen, 86n, 87
overcrowding, as a housing deficiency, 141-
   142

Peat, Marwick, Mitchell & Co., 110
"percolating," as upward filtering, 152
Phares, Donald, 63n, 72, 75n, 76-77, 85
Philadelphia, Northwest Community Housing
   Association, 86
Pittsburgh, 169
Plains, Georgia, 175
plumbing facilities, as a housing deficiency,
   140
PMI Corporation, 56
poor, housing subsidies, 174-176
President's Committee on Urban Housing,
   16n
privatization, of public housing, 24-26
production, as a housing goal, 146, 172-174
Professional Builder, 47
property taxes, 46
Providence, R.I., People Acting Through
   Community Effort, 91
Proxmire, Senator, 98-99
Pruitt-Igoe, 6, 29, 175
public housing, 146; capital costs, 15; conventional, 3, 5, 29; development policies, 8;
   economic stimulus, 5; financial reserves,

15; management, 27; rent, 16, 33-34; subsidies, 21-24; tenancy, conditions for, 11, 33;
   tenant management, 24, 27-28

racial composition, impact on neighborhood,
   66-67, 77, 85
Rainwater, Lee, 175
Ratcliff, R.U., 149
Read, R.B., 64n
real estate investment trusts, 56
redlining, 70, 79, 86, 94; data problems,
   95, 97, 103-111, 118-119; defined, 80;
   limitations of citizens' studies, 92-96;
   loan data, census tract versus zip coade,
   109-110; local hearings, 118
refinancing, to recapture equity, 81
Regulation Q, 163-164
rent control, 170; New York City, 80, 89
rent/income ratio, as a measure of housing
   inadequacy, 144-145, 152-153
rent strike, 13; Coop City, 171-172
reservation price, 65
residential location, 64
residential sites, 65
risk, reducing urban lending risk, 125-126
Rogg, Nathaniel, 158

St. Germain, Fernand, 99
St. Louis, 9-11, 16, 22, 24-26, 28, 66, 76;
   rent strike of 1969, 12
San Francisco, 159-160, 168
scattered housing, 26
Seattle Reinvestment Task Force, 82
Section 23, 30-32, 175
Section 23 Leased Housing Association, 31
Section 235, 149
Section 236, 149
Section 236 housing, 31, 37-38
segregation, in housing, 13, 21
Shapley, L.S., 65n
"shopping incentive credit," 34
Shubik, M., 65n
Singer Housing Company, 47
single-family home, 47, 53
Smith, Adam, 5
Society of Real Estate Appraisers, 83
socioeconomic status, 65, 67, 71, 76, 78,
   93-95; measurement of, 72
Soloman, Arthur P., 174
speculators, 84-85
sprawl, suburban, 54

Sternlieb, George, 80, 84
Stigler, George, 144-145
submarkets, 68-69, 77
succession, neighborhood, 64, 67-71
"suitable living environment," 63
Sunbelt, 90
Sweeney, J.L., 150

Tandem Plan, 149
Target Projects Program, 24
tax exemption, for public housing, 9, 14-15, 32
tax expenditures, for housing, 45, 166-167
tax incentives, for public housing, 37
Tax Reform Act of 1976, 166
Taylor, Louise, 63n
technological innovation, in housing, 176-177
tenant unions, 171
Thompson, J. Neils, 45-46, 58
Toledo, Ohio, Toledoans Against Redlining, 91
transport costs, 71
turnkey housing, 3, 24-25
"20-percent gap," for admission, 12, 33
26 million unit goal, 145, 148, 173

uncertainty, role in succession, 71
union work rules, 48
U.S. Chamber of Commerce, 30
U.S. Civil Rights Commission, 94

U.S. Home Corporation, 47
U.S. League of Savings Associations, 83, 92
U.S. Supreme Court, 13, 178
University City, Missouri, as an example of the arbitrage model, 72-78
urban credit crunch, 80, 86
Urban Institute, 23, 160
Urban Investment Program, 89
Urban Reinvestment Task Force, 127
usury laws, state, 57, 90
utility costs, 46, 176; impact of, 14

variable rate mortgage (VRM), *see* mortgage
Vitarello, J., 86n
Voluntary Home Mortgage Credit Program, 123-124

Washington, D.C., 86n, 87; Public Interest Group, 87
Wells Fargo Bank of San Francisco, 57
Wellston, Missouri, 75-76
Winnick, L., 149
Wisconsin Center for Public Representation, 117
World War II, impact on housing, 18-19

Young Families Housing Act, 165

zoning, 54; antisnob, 178; exclusionary, 161

ABOUT THE EDITOR

DONALD PHARES is associate professor of economics and a fellow in the Center for Metropolitan Studies at the University of Missouri-St. Louis. He is author of the book *State-Local Tax Equity: An Empirical Analysis of the Fifty States*, coauthor of *Municipal Output and Performance in New York City*, articles in *Social Science Quarterly, Proceedings of the National Tax Association, Annals of Regional Science. Journal of Regional Science, Economic Geography, Journal of Drug Issues, Journal of Psychedelic Drugs*, sections in several books and government reports. His research deals primarily with housing and neighborhood change, state-local finance and governmental structure, and drug abuse. He holds a B.A. from Northeastern University in Boston, Massachusetts, and an M.A. and a Ph.D from Syracuse University, Syracuse, New York.

ABOUT THE CONTRIBUTORS

MICHAEL AGELASTO is an analyst in American national government with the Government Division of the Congressional Research Service, U.S. Library of Congress. His articles and reports on community development block grants, urban conservation, the location of federal facilities, and inner city housing have appeared in *Ecology Law Quarterly, Evaluation, Planning Comment, Equilibrium, Parametro, Management and Control of Growth* and congressional hearings. He holds the B.A. from Columbia University and an M.C.P. from the University of California, Berkeley. He has worked as a VISTA volunteer, director of a housing development corporation, and as a policy analyst for the U.S. Department of Housing and Urban Development.

JOSEPH DAVIS is assistant professor of real estate at Arizona State University. He is a contributor to the book *Forecasting Transportation Impacts Upon Land Use* and author of articles in *Arizona Business, Real Estate Today, Real Estate Life,* and several monographs. He is a consultant to the Arizona Department of Real Estate on licensing and education and a research consultant to the Texas Real Estate Research Center. Dr. Davis holds a B.S. from the University of South Carolina, an M.B.A. from Texas A & I University, and a Ph.D from the University of Georgia.

MARTIN GELLEN has been associated with the National Housing and Economic Development Law Project in Berkeley and the Bay Area Institute in San Francisco. He is currently a doctoral candidate in City and Regional Planning at the University of California, Berkeley.

DAVID LISTOKIN is a research associate at the Rutgers University Center for Urban Policy Research. He is the author of numerous monographs including *Housing Rehabilitation; Funding Education: Problems, Patterns, Solutions;*

Environmental Impact Handbook; and *Fair Share Housing Allocation* and his articles have appeared in *The Urban Law Annual* and *Real Estate Review.* He holds a B.A. from Brooklyn College and will be receiving a Ph.D. in urban planning from Rutgers University.

JAMES T. LITTLE is assistant professor of economics and associate director of the Institute for Urban and Regional Studies at Washington University. He is a coauthor of *Neighborhood Change: Lessons in the Dynamics of Urban Decay* and has published articles in *The Journal of Urban Economics, The Review of Economic Studies,* and *The Journal of Economic Theory.* He has also served as a consultant to the Department of Housing and Urban Development, the RAND Corporation, and the United States Army Corps of Engineers.

EUGENE J. MEEHAN is professor of political science and staff urban planner in the Center for Metropolitan Studies at the University of Missouri-St. Louis. He has published extensively in the field of political theory and methodology. His major works include: *Theory and Method of Political Analysis, Contemporary Political Thought, Explanation in Social Science, Value Judgment and Social Science, Foundations of Political Analysis: Empirical and Normative, Public Housing Policy: Myth Versus Reality,* and numerous articles. Professor Meehan holds a B.A. and M.A. in political science from Ohio State University and a Ph.D. from the London School of Economics.

ROGER MONTGOMERY is professor in the departments of City and Regional Planning and Architecture at the University of California, Berkeley. With Daniel Mandelker he edited *Housing in America.* His articles on housing and related themes appear in a number of journals and edited collections. Recently his research has dealt with the Community Development Block Grant Program, housing finance in the inner city, and tax increment funded redevelopment. Montgomery also writes widely on architectural and urban design history.

JOHN C. WEICHER is associate professor of economics at Ohio State University. From 1975 to 1977 he was deputy assistant secretary for economic affairs at the U.S. Department of Housing and Urban Development. He has written in the areas of urban economics, housing, and public finance. He is the author of the book *Urban Renewal: National Program for Local Problems,* articles in several scholarly journals, including the *Journal of Political Economy, National Tax Journal, Journal of Regional Science, Urban Studies, Journal of Urban Economics,* and the *American Economic Review,* papers in several books, and government reports. He holds a B.A. degree from the University of Michigan and a Ph.D. from the University of Chicago.